AF531625

PROBLEMS OF EDUCATION

PROBLEMS OF EDUCATION

By

Veeramachaneni Venkateswara Rao

M.A.

Secretary & Correspondent

Ravindra Bharathi Public School

Satyanarayanapuram

Vijayawada–520 001

Andhra Pradesh

General Editor

Dr. Digumarti Bhaskara Rao

M.Sc., M.A., M.A., M.Ed., Ph.D.

Reader

R.V.R. College of Education

Srinivasa Nagar Colony

Guntur–522 006

Andhra Pradesh

India

DISCOVERY PUBLISHING HOUSE

NEW DELHI-110002

First Published - 2004
Reprinted - 2017

ISBN: 978-81-7141-841-1

Problems of Education

Published by:
DISCOVERY PUBLISHING HOUSE PVT. LTD.
4383/4B, Ansari Road, Darya Ganj
New Delhi-110 002 (India)
Phone: +91-11-23279245, 43596064-65
Fax: +91-11-23253475
E-mail: discoverypublishinghouse@gmail.com
sales@discoverypublishinggroup.com
web: www.discoverypublishinggroup.com

Printed at:
Infinity Imaging Systems
Delhi

Preface

Education, like other areas in practical life and society has its own share of problems and difficulties. However, *Problems of Education* are distinguished and different from those in other walks of life.

Educational problems are manyfold and exist at all levels and in all stages — primary, secondary, higher and research levels. In accordance with the conditions and any particular situation, the academics have to cope with what comes their way and also find the solutions.

Earlier, the educationists used to form policies and plan strategies and teachers were simply concerned with teaching only, but now, with changing times, the responsibilities have expanded and the visions have broadened. The teachers of today are supposed to be well aware of all the happenings in the world of education and the new trends in store. The modern teacher is not merely an instructor, he, in fact is the guide and role model for the students.

In the given situation, the need for a comprehensive book covering all the problems, to be faced by those, engaged in the field of education, including students. Here is an effort in the same direction. This book not only helps the reader study the problems in depth, but also suggests the solutions to improve the state of affairs.

The Author is confident of being recognised and acknowledged by all concerned.

Author

Contents

1 Introduction

Donald K. Adams had written well about the modernisation process. We produce below some extracts from his paper.

There are a number of interpretations of the character of modernisation, for it is filtered by the distinctive lenses of the observers. In this complex and still, somewhat mysterious process, however, there is perhaps a fairly general consensus that the following changes take place.

Technology will change towards the increased application of scientific knowledge; agriculture will move from subsistence farming to cash crops to commercial production, in Industry the trend is away from muscle power to the use of machines which derives power from other forms of energy, in religion there becomes a secularization of belief pattern; in ecological arrangements movement of urban concentration in familiar patterns, a reduction in size and number of functions in education, growth in quantity available and variety of curricula offered.

Some scholars, however, do distinguish between the notions of modernization and development Modèrnisation, one argument goes, refers more to the values, attitudes and styles and living of people, while development is more fundamentally an application of technology in processes of production and distribution.

From this interpretation, it follows that modernization may towards dewart development. That is, the effort expended in producing and acquiring modern clothing, entertainment, and services detracts from the accumulation of capital through savings and thereby limits investment in agriculture, industry or infrastructure. While this distinction has merit, we will primarily rely on the term "modernisation" to describe, processes we are discussing.

Perhaps most controversy exists when an attempt is made to describe the political requisites for modernization. James Coleman, for example, gives the following definitions of political development.

The acquisition by a political system of consciously sought and qualitatively new and enhanced political capacity as manifested in the successful institutionalization of:

(1) New patterns of integration regulating and containing the tensions and conflicts produced by increased differentiation, and (2) New patterns of participation and resource distribution adequately responsible for the demands generated by the imperatives of equality.

The emphasis on 'New pattern of integration' and 'new patterns of participation' is perhaps quite standard in the definition of most political scientists. Coleman, in describing the modern participatory state' identifies to possible models, the totalitarian and the democratic.

His preference for the latter is obvious and the finds the democratic model viable for a modern society; that is, he believes that a democratic polity is better vehicle for bringing about and sustaining development and social change.

Some political scientists such as Word and Rustow are more cautious, whereas they emphasize that developed politics is characterized by interest and involvement, they do not argue that political development necessarily implies democratic decision making.

Indeed, in commenting on the communist belief that all societies move along a single path toward one preordained goal, these authors conclude that of this artless and simplistic notion society does not gain invalidity as we change the sign on the finish line from 'communism' to 'Democracy'.

What political scientists call Participant Political System, that is, nations with elected public officials, multiple political parties and the like, are often associated with higher incomes. However, successful economic performance has been associated with authoritarian Government as well as the democratic ones.

There appears then, to be little direct evidence to suggest that the more participant forms of democracy ensure rapid economic growth. More likely there are common social individual elements underlying transformation of political and economic institution.

While democracy may neither be a prerequisite to, nor a necessary outcome of modernization, several scholars note that the nature of modernization does appear to be supportive of democratic institutions. As the result of empirical inquiry, Adelman and Morris conclude: "It is reasonable to assume that before fully participant nationwide democratic institutions can evolve, certain levels of mass communication, urbanization and literacy, for example, must be achieved and nationalist, positivist attitudes must be sufficiently diffused throughout the society."

This position is in keeping with the finding of a number of empirical studies including those of Daniel Lemer and other social scientists who study the communication process which suggest that modernization consists of a sequence of phases beginning with urbanization, followed in order by increased literacy and the spread of mass media. The latter phase, Lerner has argued, is a requisite for democratic participant political system.

Education fits into this process in a variety of ways. In itself, it has become one measure of modernization and presumably undergrade development of the economy, polity and so forth. By way of example:-

Schools also inculcate pupils with the disciplined attitudes and motivations requisite to the demands of industrialization. Human capital is more valuable than physical and we can give you the differential value in percentage points.

Educated people produce more on the job, adjust more quickly to the demands for new skills and are more committed to their work. An investment in education becomes an investment in the health of the economy.

Schemes and Plans

Not only does education generate economic growth but also accomplishes miracles in other faces of society. Schooling curbs population growth because the better educated are more rational and see the folly of large families. Educated women want few children and have few children than uneducated women.

In terms of migration, even a little schooling makes rural youth seek the city and the scent of higher education makes the city youth look to universities abroad. University training abroad reduces the student from the less developed nation into the abundant carefree life of the rich nation, where he stays and inspite of occasional conscience pangs, lives happily ever after.

Education and social structure modernization means a more equitable spread of the wealth and an open social structure where the main constraint to an individual's upward mobility is lack of talent. The educational system promotes opportunity for the poor, it is the great leveller of society.

Within the schools, universalistic and achievement oriented teachers make regard only on the basis of talent and once the talented are appointed with a diploma they are guaranteed success and respect in the greater society.

Thus, the obvious policy for poor nations is to expand rapidly enrolments and provide a longer period of compulsory education to maximize the school's influence.

This story cannot end without a reference to educational planning. Overwhelmed by the power importance of education and impressed with the growth in our understanding of its complexities, we have succumbed to our own wisdom and advocate formal, elaborate uncompromising planning.

From the classroom to the national level, we tabulate projects and endeavour to mould the system that it may produce to its capability. The stacks of national plans lying in ministries of

education all over the world represent the ultimate, if mute, tribute to our confidence.

This is, of course, but a capsule description of the most romantic tales of the century.

New Prospects

We are living in a fast changing world. Due to advanced science and technology man has acquired such powers as could be helpful in wiping out poverty, ignorance and sickness from the world. Scientists have visualised life future changes that are likely to occur as a result of scientific and technological advancement.

According to Dr. Phillip Handler (1971). We have attained such scientific and technological knowledge as would enable us to stabilise world population and improve conditions of living. In the terms of educational technology, Dr. Handler states-

"In the near future, each individual will have a private, pocket size, two-way television instrument and immediate personal access to a computer serving as his news sources. It will be his personal communicator with the world at large, with his bank, his broker, government agents, shopping services, and so on."

The future impact of science and technology on human society has been visualised by Dr. Handler. According to him, "Less than five percent of the working population will be engaged in primary agriculture with no more than another 20 percent engaged in other primary productive activities such as food processing, mineral extraction, construction or manufacturing."

"The bulk of the labour forces, then, will engage in activities currently classified services, rather than production of goods. The principal pursuits of mankind will be cultural, recreational or devoted to the expansion of knowledge and understanding."

"Most of the diseases which have been man's most ancient enemies will be matters of historic interest only. Each individual may look forward to about four score year of vigorous, healthy painfree life before succumbing to the ravages of old age."

There is an explosion of knowledge in the modern world and

this is also creating problems for education. Whatever we knew in 1901, was doubled in 1950. Our accumulated knowledge in 1950 was doubled in 1960 and in 1970, this was again doubled. Thus, human knowledge due to advanced science and technology has been multiplying itself leading to the explosion of knowledge.

Another important fact to bear in mind is that due to advanced science and technology the modern world has shrunk and its size has become small. We have such means of communication as enable us to know and reach any corner of the world. According to Wilbert E. Moore:

"In these times, scarcely a day passes without the newspaper and the mass media reporting a new or continuing crisis of great international import in some little known part of the world. The technology or communication and travel has, it is said, shrunk the size of the world. The politics of international tension has made that small world a dangerous place for human habitation."

Practical Difficulties

The modern science and technology can be useful if they are utilised properly. But at present man does not possess the wisdom to use this scientific and technological power properly. A number of crises have appeared due to human selfishness, short-sightedness and hunger for power. It has already been noted that with the help of science, span of life has increased and there is also a postulation that if mankind has to survive in the future, efforts must be made to check population growth and to develop such a world understanding as will lead to the development of a world wide government which will be responsible for maintenance of world peace.

Prof. James A. Parking Chairman and Director of the Centre for Education Inquiry, New York has stated that almost all the universities of the world are faced with five crises. These are:

(1) Crisis of number.

(2) Crisis of finance.

(3) Crisis of relevance.

(4) Crisis of priorities.

(5) Crisis of scepticism.

Crisis of Number. The population of India is now about 88 crores. More than half of this population is below the age of 18 years. Thus, in India there is a need for many more educational institutions. According to Kothari Commission (1964-66), "The total number of teachers exceeds 2 million. The total student population, which is now (that is in 1966) about 70 million; will more than double in the next 29 years, and by 1985, it will become about 170 million or about equal to the total population of Europe. The size and complexity of these problems argue the need for rapid action in involving an appropriate educational policy...."

The crisis of numbers in the educational world is a universal phenomenon. According to Dr. James A. Parking. "While experience differ from country to country, on the average the number of students entering higher education had doubled in the decade from 1960 to 1970. If there were no other problems, miss astonishing growth would, by itself, result in almost intolerable strains in most institutions of higher education in most countries."

If education has to be an effective instrument of planned social changes, it must adopt itself to the changing needs of society. The modern age is essentially a technological age. In order to live in this age every man must acquire technological knowledge and skills. The Kothari Commission has rightly emphasized the need for science-based education.

Crisis of Finance. Due to increase in number of pupils more educational institutions are needed and in order to run them more finances are required. Educational institutions all over the world, even in a rich country like U.S.A. require more finances because costs of education have risen tremendously. Previously, universities were receiving financial support mostly from private funds. Now a days they have to look for financial assistance from the government. University autonomy all over the world is being threatened due to governmental interference through its control over academic expenditures. This is not a good sign because education can be an effective instrument of social change only when it is allowed full play and not controlled or interfered by any vested interest

Crisis of Relevance. In a static society, change is very slow and social patterns continue in the same form for a number of generations. Means of production and distribution are simple and social institutions perform their functions mostly undisturbed.

Due to rapid changes brought about by scientific and technological advancement much of knowledge and learning which was considered useful in a traditional and static society has become irrelevant and meaningless in a modern and dynamic society.

In India, the question of relevance has been raised in the form of student unrest. Students all over the world are dissatisfied with the kind of education which is given to them because it does not prepare them for life. Students today want much education as will enable them not only to understand their past but also, equip them for future. Contents of many courses in our universities are meaningless in the present context. We want to build a socialistic society and from this point of view it is necessary that there should be equal educational opportunity for all. Such education will be an effective instrument of planned social changes as will fulfill the needs and aspirations of youth.

Crisis of Priorities. The time has come to think of priorities with a view to bringing about desirable social change. In our educational system again there is a need for such changes as will emphasize first thing first. In other words, whatever was considered good in the past may not be regarded so now because of changes in political, social and economic conditions of life. Today, the need is to provide such education as will enable young men and women to be self employed. The educational system needs to be based on work-experience. In other words, learning by doing and earning while learning is necessary, if education has to be an effective instrument of planned social changes.

Crisis of Scepticism. There are times when doubts are raised in the accepted beliefs, ideals and principles. In a healthy society individuals are permitted to express their view without fear. Unfortunately those in power in our universities and other

educational institutions do not like to hear the voice of dissent. They were only to be denoted by a passive group of teachers and pupils, but this is no more possible. In a fast changing world where ideas flow from one corner to the other easily and quickly, it is not only difficult but rather impossible to exercise control over expression and exchange of ideas.

One of the functions of the university is to encourage new thinking so that new avenues of thought are discovered. Due to lack of courage and initiative, educational leadership in most of the countries of the world is for the status quo. Most of the people, who are responsible for making education an effective instrument of social change lack foresight initiative and boldness to leave the beaten path and lead the new generation to the brave new world.

Due to rapid scientific and technological changes, we are faced with a cultural crisis. In other words, we have come to the point which requires concise formulation of our moral and social values. It has been observed that when a traditional society proceeds towards industrialisation there are three alternatives open before it.

(1) The first is that it may continue to hold its traditionalism and refuse to assimilate the values, ideas and attitudes typical of an industrial society.

(2) The second alternative open to such a society is that it may remain uncertain in regard to its policy matters and permit a kind of drift in all matters. Such a policy is very harmful for it does not help is progress and leave the individuals at the mercy of the prevailing democrats. In many societies of the world we find there are two trends. That is, some societies look behind and receive inspiration from their ancient but without caring for the present or the future. This is typical of some of the societies in the east. In some of the western societies where tradition is weak and there is no deep sense of history, a feeling of uncertainty for the people who refuse to take up a position.

(3) The third alternative, perhaps the most desirable alternative is to resolve the cultural crisis and adopt a world view

which will include "all mankind and emphasize essential unity of all religions. In other words we need a spiritual regeneration in this world today."

Along with this we have to strengthen democratic institution and safeguard political and social freedoms. These are the three alternatives which are before the world today. As it has been pointed out earlier, the first two alternatives have no value. The third alternative of world community should be our good and the task of education is to pave the way for such a society as will be based upon the concept of the good of all and a glorious future.

Role of Masses

Education of the future must take into account the rapid industrialisation in the world to bring about the supremacy of the masses specially in industrial society. As a matter of the fact industrial society has become a mass society characterised by mass production and mass communication. It seems that the masses have a lot of comforts for things are produced on a mass scale and there are such media of communication as to enable the masses to know about a thing quickly and conveniently. What is missing in this set up to the human factor.

Modern man finds himself lonely in the crowed while a large number of people are engaged in large scale productions, the totality of life in society is lost. Individuals have become more or less mechanical and the masses are working towards an end which appears to be meaningless for them. In such a mass society the main problem is to rehabilitate the individual in terms of his potentialities, his need for novelty of experience.

The problems of the masses today are being solved at the economic and political level by various social techniques and mechanisms. Nonetheless, the individual is losing his freedom to think and to act as he desires. The means of mass production are mostly in the hands of a few people who manipulate the economic system and try to have the largest amount of profit leaving only a little for workers in the fields and factories.

So long as we fail to plan for prosperity on a mass scale as the

modern man remains ignorant. In spite of all the means of mass communication, the problem for education will remain.

Thus, on the one hand we get that supremacy of the masses as emerging and on the other hand we observe that masses are losing their human touch on account of mechanisation is the fields of production and distribution as well as in their lives for, as stated above, he feels himself lonely in the crowd.

Due to industrialisation 'we find that groups of people engaged in various industries are getting organised. There are workers' unions, labour organisations, professional guilds etc. This has become necessary, for without an organisation the interest of a group cannot be safeguarded and its difficulties removed. These organised groups exercise pressure on political parties and legislatures to serve their interests.

Organised groups are active and influential not only in the social and economic fields but also in political spheres. In western societies where industrialisation has reached to a high level, we find a two party political system. The party in power has a strong opposition. But in such societies as are gradually getting industrialised, the two party system has not emerged in a satisfactory manner.

In India, the party in power is very strong and the opposition is rather weak. Such a state of affair is not desirable in a democratic society. It is imperative that organised groups not only safeguard their own interest but also see that there is a healthy opposition to the government in state Legislatures. The education of the future should facilitate it

The impact of industrialisation, science and technology on society has also brought a new class in existence. In pre-industrial era the elite belonged to a feudal aristocracy and states depended upon the landed property of the high caste of an individual. Now-a-days, the basis of social status is the capacity to earn.

We find that people who do not have high status traditionally are becoming influential in their groups on account of their high rate of profits and economic prosperity. In other words, the emergence of a new class on the basis of industrialisation has upset the traditional class and caste status and created new categories for social significance.

In this connection, it may be mentioned that industrialisation has not only created a new class of people who are rich and powerful in spite of their lack of status, it has also created a high degree of mobility, we find people moving from region to region in search of lucrative jobs and prosperity. Thus, it is not uncommon to find that in a new industrial society people from far and wide come and settle down.

They build their new traditions, breaking almost completely from their social past. It is desirable to examine the implications of these new relationships in an industrial society and devise such a system of education as will bring about integration and develop healthy social relationships.

In an industrial society, where we have mass production the problem of leisure is acute, for people work less and produce more. In those countries where population is on increase mass production has led to unemployment. But in some Western countries where population is under control the problem of unemployment has not been so acutely felt. Nonetheless, workers today have more leisure, for there are machines which require less number of people to produce more. That is why, a modern worker is comparatively paid more and given enough leisure.

The problem of leisure become serious when the worker does not know what to do in his spare time. Since he has been working in a large mechanical set-up, his approach to life also becomes somewhat mechanical and he gradually loses human touch. It is extremely necessary to see that the right type of education is provided for the proper use of leisure. The mass media of communication like cinema, radio and television are there not only for information but also for recreation. It is desirable that the mass media of communication are not be exploited and misused by vested interests and thereby empoverish the masses culturally.

As a matter of fact, the problem of leisure is related to the problem of culture for millions. Previously, culture was considered to be the sphere of new and the rest of the people were left to their footways. Now a days, mass media of communication have assumed great importance in view of the large scale publicity and propaganda carried out by business organisations, political parties and other organised groups. The masses are bewildered and they fail to recognise the subtle nature of propaganda. Therefore, a worker at leisure is constantly bombarded with all kinds of propaganda material and he is culturally deprived of or displaced.

It is extremely important that there should be a well organised scheme of education for leisure and informal agencies of education should devote some time to the spread of culture in the masses.

It is a sad commentary on the state of affairs today that while we have all the means to wipe out hunger, ignorance and disease from the world, we lack the necessary ideals and moral value to organise our efforts to apply modern means of production and communication for public welfare purposes.

One of the strong agencies in the modern, world is that of democracy. People at large are gradually realising that there cannot be any real peace or progress without democracy. It is rightly said that the world of today is gradually becoming democratic. The forces at work are numerous, some of them are helping the democratic forces and some are against democratization. As a matter of fact, in every society positive and negative forces are at work all the time. It is the task of education to help the positive social forces and weaken the negative forces.

Purpose of Democracy. It may be noted here that the concept of democracy has also been undergoing gradual change. Now a days, while it is accepted that all people are equal, they are also different in some sense. In other words, the concept of equality does not mean that individual differences should be wiped out and all individuals in spite of their mental abilities should be given the same kind of education.

Today, it is realised that the purpose of democracy would be better fulfilled if there are opportunities for self-growth to the maximum. For example, if a child has superior intelligence he should be provided with such type of education as will be challenging enough as well as interesting for him.

Thus, in a democracy while the principle of equality is accepted, it is at the same time realised that individuals with superior abilities should be provided with special opportunities for self- growth. This requires a kind of planning in education which will meet the requirement of all sections of people.

Fundamental Freedoms. While we accept the principle of planning in the context of democracy, it has to be emphasised that there are certain fundamental freedoms which must be assured for all. In a democracy, freedom of worship, speech, opinion and to hold meetings for social and political purposes are generally recognised and granted.

But these freedoms are not enough. While people may have political freedom they may not have social and economic freedoms. It is, therefore, necessary that freedom in a democracy should mean freedom from want, ignorance, disease and unemployment. This is the welfare aspect of a democratic society.

Social Responsibilities. In the context of freedom and planning, another important factor is the consent of people and sharing of social responsibilities. It is one of the features of a democratic society that people agree to planning and collective action so that social and political freedoms can be safeguarded.

People surrender their certain rights to the State in order to provide for such mechanisms as will ensure proper distribution as well as production of goods and other requirements of life.

In a democratic society, the, State cannot perform its duties without willing co-operation of the people. That is why, democratic societies plan for such educational system as ensures democratic attitudes among the people.

One of the important democratic attitudes is that of co-operation and participation. People co-operate and participate in the democratic process of society when they feel a sense of responsibility for the actions of the Government.

The famous definition of democracy which emphasises the government for the people, by the people and of the people invariably underlines the fact that no democracy can function without a sense of identification on the part of the people with the State and democratic government.

Karl Mannheim has rightly pointed out that society is moving from lassies fair state to a planned one. But in a planned society, according to him, there can be two tendencies in regard to power and control.

One tendency could be that of democratization and the other that of authoritarianism. As we know, in a democratic set-up there is so much of freedom that sometimes certain people misuse it. In an authoritarian set-up power and control resides in the hands of a few. Thus, both the tendencies in a planned society cannot fulfil the aims and objectives of a real democratic society.

In order to meet their needs, Mannheim suggests a Third Way. The essential features of this Third Way are that the planning is not for conformity but for the variety. According to Mannheim, we can plan in such a manner as will produce harmony.

The second important feature of this Third Way, according to Mannheim, is that the planning done in such a manner as provides enough scope for individual enterprises and avoids control for the sake of it.

We have seen that sometimes when the government has got this power to control, bureaucracy introduces control without any regard for the place given for free enterprise. In democratic planning public and private sector work in harmony and contribute jointly to social welfare.

Mannheim also emphasises the element of social justice in democratic planning. Without this element, it is likely that certain sections of the society will take advantage of planning and drive extra benefits. In a militant democracy, planning of social justice is a must.

The third way of militant democracy as emphasised by Mannheim also requires the control of those people who misuse democratic freedom and try to destroy the democratic institutions of the society. It is evident that people have not only to be taught to be democratic but they must also learn to safeguard their democratic institutions of society. Their democratic rights from those who want to exploit them.

Mannheim would also like the people of democratic society to be clear in their minds in regard to the basic values governing social life. When the goals, objectives and values are quite clear to the people there is little possibility of difference in the fundamental approach to freedom and planning. Thus education in a democratic society will teach people not only how to behave as democratic nation but also translate into feelings, thoughts and action the basic value of a militant democracy.

Significance of Education

While discussing the crux of an industrial society planning, freedom and control we have also seen at places the role of education in a democratic society. Nonetheless, it is desirable that we focus our attention on the role of education in times to come.

From this point of view, the first requirement is that the scientific and technological potentialities of a people have to be developed by education. If it is desired that a society should have industrialisation in order to banish poverty and unemployment, it must try to educate its people in scientific and industrial fields.

It is not only enough that the core of curriculum becomes scientific and industrial but also there should be emphasis on the education of the talented and gifted. While the duty of the State is to spread education as widely as possible, there is also a compelling need to educate, to the highest level, the talented and the gifted.

Role of education in future society will be dynamic and not limited to one field of study or only one aspect of life. Educators have visualised inter-disciplinary approach in the field of education. Peter Wilby, while discussing further education, pointed out that if education of the future has to be meaningful it must make efforts to adopt inter-disciplinary courses that integrate several subjects. This will require dropping of the single subject degrees which are taken without paying any regard to the inter-disciplinary relation among the different subjects of study.

Education of the future can play its role effectively, if it confines itself only to material aspect of life and ignores self knowledge, it cannot play its role according to the needs to time.

Professional Education

In an industrial society, skilled workers and technicians are in great demand. Modern machines are quit complicated and they can be well manipulated by educated workers. Thus, we need something like a technical high school to spread technical and industrial education in a society. But along with technical and industrial education we have to provide for individual differences and interests.

It is a well-known fact that all individuals are not equally interested in technical or scientific subjects. Keeping in view this fact, it is necessary that in a job-oriented education, there should be a provision for humanistic and liberal studies so that an industrial worker does not receive only one-sided education.

We know the purpose of education is the all round development of the individual. Education must enable the individual to realise his individuality first and later on it can prepare him for any vocation or profession. But to emphasise only vocational aspect of education or job-oriented education will defeat its purpose.

Education for All

Traditionally, liberal education has been given to children. The pre-industrial society cared more for traditional and cultural view of life. Therefore, there was great emphasis on the teaching of liberal and humanistic subjects. But due to industrialisation, there has been a great demand for scientific, technical and industrial education. In view of this, a conflict has arisen between liberal student and technical education. How to resolve this conflict is a problem before educationists of the world.

Recently, there has been a move for a plan of general education.

In this plan, a provision has been made for essential elements of liberal and humanistic studies. In other words, all children in an industrial society will have to study some such subjects as will provide them with liberal outlook on life.

The teaching of social subjects is to be done with a view to make children responsible citizens. It is, for example, suggested that social responsibility should be developed through teaching of social studies in a historical frame-work and against a universal back-ground. Thus, it is evident that children in an industrial society should be educated in a manner as will enable them to have a fairly good idea about philosophy, literature, history and other humanistic and social studies.

In this connection, it has to be pointed out that in a democratic society every citizen has to feel responsible for the decision made by the government. It has been observed that people and government do not work in a co-operative way. The result is that people at large do not feel responsible for the decisions and actions of their government. This attitude defeats the purpose of democracy. Hence, education of the future has to be of such type as will develop a sense of responsibility among the people towards the state of affairs in the society.

Another important element in general education is that of science and its impact on life. It is generally accepted that modern science has affected thinking and brought about various changes in our outlook. Nonetheless, it is also true that some of the prejudices and superstitions still continue. We know that certain races consider themselves superior to others and scientifically it is proved that there is no racial superiority.

So the plan for general education should try to develop among the people a scientific attitude and provide them with such knowledge as will help them in getting rid of their traditional prejudices and superstitions. It has also been observed that a lot of emphasis on science has led to the development of a narrow outlook. In order to avoid this it has been suggested that there should be a course in the philosophy of science. In other words, scientists should try to understand the philosophical basis of scientific investigation and try to visualise the impact of scientific discoveries on human life.

Modern Man

The problems created by urbanization and industrialization reveal the fact that modern man is dominated by machines. As a matter of fact, human society today is gradually becoming a victim of machines. It is led towards a king of dehumanization. By living and working with machines modern man has become somewhat mechanical in his approach towards life and society. The result is that we are faced with a danger of losing the human touch.

Thus, education of the future has to preserve human values and see that human factor is not neglected. In other words, education should continue to pay proper attention towards the harmonious development of human personality. If individuals have an integrated individuality, if personality of all persons flowers to the full, the danger to human values will be removed and dehumanization will be controlled.

Finally, the task of education of today as well as of tomorrow is to help the individual to know himself as Socrates wanted centuries age. So long as the individual is ignorant of his real self, his potentialities, his limitation and his mission of life, he cannot contribute in a creative manner towards his self growth and development of his society.

Education can help develop a sense of self-respect and esteem among their pupils by respecting them as individuals of unique abilities. As a matter of fact, a real teacher always does so. When a real teacher teaches his pupil he makes him feel his uniqueness and the things that he can do after his full development education of the future is a challenge as well as an opportunity for those who dream of a world community and world government.

2
New Setup

The existing structure of the Indian education is based on the suggestions of wood's Despatch, 1854. In this Despatch there were 4 steps for educational programmes:

(1) Primary, (2) Secondary, or Middle, (3) High School, and (4) University. There have been some changes in the structure proposed by Wood's Despatch, but still it is almost the same. Until the 20th century, the period of school education was 9 years. Later on, the period of 9 Years was extended to the period of 10 years. There was provision for the 4 year's Primary Education, 2 years lower middle education and 2 years High School Education.

The Secondary Education Commission or the Mudaliar Commission proposed this very structure. This Commission was of the opinion that the period of Primary Junior Basic Education should be of 4 or 5 years. The period of Middle or Junior Secondary or Senior Basic Education should be 3 Years while that of Secondary Education be 4 Years. There should be provisions for the 3 Year's Degree Course, and 2 Year's Post-graduate Course. In this way Mudaliar Commission suggested that the period of Secondary Education should be 7 years. Though Mudaliar Commission was entrusted with the job of making recommendations for the secondary Education but the Commission also gave certain valuable suggestions for Degree Education. The Commission was of the opinion that we have to face a lot of difficulties because in some provinces there was the degree course of 3 years while in other it was of 2 years. The Commission proposed that 'there should be uniformity in all the provinces. It was the reason that the Commission proposed that total period of primary and secondary education should be of 11 years. While there should be 3 years Degree Course and a period of 2 years should be allotted for the Post-Graduate Education.

Kothari Commission and the Re-organisation of Education. In 1964, Commission under the Presidentship of Sri D.S Kothari was appointed to give its suggestions regarding the Education System and the changes to be made. The Commission submitted its report in 1966. Kothari Commission was of the opinion that the entire structure of Indian Education should be reorganised. The Commission recommended that educational system should consist of:

A pre-school stage consisting of one to three years:

- a primary stage of seven or eight years divided into substages, a lower primary stage of four or five years and a higher primary stage of three years:
- a lower secondary or high school stage of three or two years in general education or one to three years in vocational education;
- a higher secondary stage of two years of general education or one to three years of vocational education;
- a university stage having a course of three years or more for the first degree and followed by courses for the second or research degree of varying durations.

Kothari Commission also gave valuable suggestions for the 10 years education. The Commission also recommended for the modification of higher secondary pattern course corresponding to Higher Secondary stage. About the transfer to pre-university course, it also recommended for the lengthening of duration of Higher Secondary Course and Re-organisation of education at the University stage.

Here we are giving a number of accounts of its recommendations:

Initial Period

The Commission visualises:

(i) The first ten years of schooling, covering a primary stage of seven or eight years and lower secondary stage of three or two years, will provide a course of general education without any specialisation.

(ii) The primary stage will be preceded, wherever possible by pre-primary education period of one or three years.

(iii) The age of admission to Class Ist should ordinarily be made not less than six years.

(iv) At the end of primary stage, about 20 percent students will step off the school system and enter working life, about 20 percent will step off the stream of general education into different courses whose duration may range from one to three years and the remaining 60 percent may continue their general education.

(v) One external examination will be held after ten years of school education.

(vi) At the end of ten years of school education, about 40 percent students will get into working life, others about 30 percent will go to vocational courses and the remainder will continue further in the stream of general education.

Process of Modification

The Commission attaches great significance to the changes that have to be made in the existing higher secondary pattern in the light of the above proposals and recommends as follows:

(i) The system of general education which now begins in Class IX, should be given up and no attempt of specification should be made till after class X. This will need a considerable reorganisation of the existing curricula of the higher secondary schools.

(ii) The idea of raising every secondary school to the higher secondary status should be abandoned. It is unwise in rural country to try to raise every high school to the higher secondary status. The Commission has, therefore, visualised as a permanent feature of educational system, secondary schools of two types, first, high schools of ten years course and the higher secondary schools of twelve years course of education. An essential requirement for raising the standard should be that the institutions need be large, centrally located and equitably distributed between rural and urban areas. It would also be necessary to review the status of the existing higher secondary schools and those which are uneconomic or are substandard may be reconverted into high schools.

(iii) There should be an integrated course of studies beginning from class IX if we want to provide specialised studies in different subjects at the higher secondary stage.

(iv) There should be an external examination at the end of Class X to mark the termination of the first ten years of general education. A student studying in a ten year high school will thus have to appear for two external examinations at the end of Classes X and XI at the interval of one year. This handicap can be removed by extending higher secondary course to two years.

(v) Existing higher secondary schools with a well organised integrated courses in Classes IX, X and XI may be permitted to carry on if they so desire, with such course until they add Class XII. It will not be obligatory for the students of such schools to appear for an examination at the end of Class X. They may take one final examination at the end of Class XI or take in two parts at the end of Class X and XI.

Vocational courses at the end of primary stages will need that the schools should provide adequate facilities for suitable form of education either part-time or on a full time basis.

New Courses

The name, duration, location and control of courses corresponding to higher secondary stage vary from State to State.

In all the States, where the higher secondary pattern is adopted but all high schools have not been raised to the higher secondary status; the stage is provided as Class XI in the secondary schools and pre-university courses in the colleges.

The main reforms are needed for re-organisation of educational structure at this stage:

(a) The transfer of pre-university course from the universities and the colleges to the schools; and

(b) The lengthening of duration of the courses of general education uniformly to two years.

The programmes may be implemented in successive stages.

Extension in Period

The duration of the higher secondary courses should be lengthened to two years and the whole programme be spread over to 20 years divided into two stages. The first stage of five years should be devoted to secure a better utilisation of existing facilities and to make required preparation for a successful implementation of this important reform. Even during this period selected higher secondary schools should be allowed to add the twelfth year and even some high schools of good quality and possessing the necessary facilities may be allowed to introduce two year higher secondary course as pilot projects. The stage will cover a span of 15 years which will be completed by the end of seventh.

The next popular demand is related to lengthening the total duration of higher education. The duration for the professional degree is not less than sixteen years practically in all the advanced countries. Hence, the demand only refers to the first degree in Art and Science, which is four years after matriculation or equivalent examination. It is generally contended that this duration should be lengthened by a year. This view accords with the thinking of several bodies on the subject. The Calcutta University Commission, the University Education Commission and the Committee on Emotional Integration also support the view. The State Education Ministers' Conference in 1964 proposed twelve year course of schooling before admission to degree course. The Commission agrees with the recommendations in full.

Structure for Education

Besides lengthening of the duration of school education, it is recommended that the re-organisation should be carried out through a phased programme spread over at least twenty years, keeping in view the variety of educational patterns, limited resources and the vastness of the country. The pre cent higher secondary pattern in which specialisation begins from class IX, need be abandoned. Along with this measure, a systematic attempt should be made to transfer the pre-university course to secondary schools. The next step would be to increase the total duration by adding a year to the higher secondary course.

University Education

The Commission observes that the principal criticism of higher education is directed, not so much against the pattern of organisation as against comparatively low standards of the degree awarded by the Indian universities in arts, commerce and science. Several factors are responsible in respect of the structural re-organisation of the university stage:

(1) The duration of the first degree should not be less than three years and second degree may be two or three years.

(2) Some universities should start graduate schools with a three year Master's Degree course in the subject which they purpose themselves.

(3) Three year special courses for the first degree need be started in selected and in selected institutions.

(4) Suitable bridges need to be built between the present courses and the new courses of longer duration.

(5) Those who offer the longer course should be given incentives in the form of scholarships.

(6) In Uttar Pradesh, the degree should be lengthened with the establishment of three years graduate schools in selected subjects and in selected universities. The first

degree colleges should be raised to three years; to other colleges, fifteen or twenty years.

Efforts made by the Natto. A Council or Educational Research and Training for the Reorganisation of Education. The suggestions of Kothari Commission for the reorganisation of Indian Education were very valuable. On the basis of these suggestion National Council of Educational Research and Training proposed a new scheme of Education which is popularly known as 10 + 2 + 3 scheme. Following were the chief suggestions made by the Council.

15 Year's Degree Course. National Council of Educational Research and Training proposed out the Degree Course should be of 15 years instead of 14 years, in India, period of Secondary Education was in various forms from State to State. In Some States, it is of 12 years while in some other States, it is of 11 years. In some States the Degree Course after the Secondary Education is of 2 Years, while in some it is of 3 years.

National Council of Educational Research and Training proposed that there should be general education for 10 years. After that, there should be 2 year's academic and vocational education and the Degree Course should be of 3 years.

10 Year's General Education. According to the Plans of National Council for Educational Research and Training, period of general education was kept as 10 years. The proposals were that the diversi-fication of the curriculum should not be there within the 10 years of education. The Curriculum for Class 1 and 2 should be as follows:

(1) Mother Tongue, (2) Mathematics, (3) Environmental studies, (4) Practical experience, and (5) Health Education.

The curriculum for classes 3 to 5 should be as follows:

(1) First Language, (2) Mathematics, (3) Environmental Studies, which should include Social Studies as well as General Sciences, (4) Practical Experience, and (5) Health Education and Games.

Syllabus of Class 6 to 8 should be- (1) First language (Mother Tongue), (2) Second Language (where the mother tongue is not Hindi, the second Language should be Hindi), (3) Mathematics,

(4) Science, (5) Social Studies (History, Geography, Civics and Economics), (6) Practical experience, and (7) Health Education and Games.

Courses for class 9th and 10th were following :

(1) First Language (mother tongue), (2) Second language, (3) Third language, (4) Mathematics, (5) Scientific subjects (Physics, Chemistry and Biology etc.), (6) Social studies (History, Geography, Civics and Economics), (7) Different Fine Arts, (8) Practical experiences, and (9) Health education.

Abolition of Public Examination System. Under the scheme of National Council of Educational Research and Training, there was no scheme of public examination system. A proposal was, that the existing examination system shall not be useful under the new scheme and so it should be abolished.

No Question of Failures. Under the scheme of National Council of Educational Research and Training, there was no question of any failures. Under these plans there was the system of grades A, B, C, D etc.

Diversification of Curriculum after 10 Years general Education. National Council of Educational Research and Training proposed that there should be diversification of curriculum only after 10 years of general education. Those who have received 10 years general education, 50 per cent should go for the vocational education while the 50 percent should opt for academic education. Those who do not have much interest in the academic education, should opt the vocational and technical education. Those who receive higher grades, should be allowed to proceed for the academic education while those who get inferior grades should be diverted towards the vocational and technical education.

3 Year's Degree Course. Under the Plan of National Council of Educational Research and Training there was provision of 3 Year's Degree Course. In BUS plan 2 year's Degree Course was totally abolished.

Scheme of 8+4 and Reorganisation of Education. In 1977 there was fall of Congress Government at the Centre and under the

Janta Government Dr. P.C. Chunder was entrusted with the job of Education Ministry. At this time, in some States the scheme of 10+2+3 was implemented while it was not implemented in others. Janta Government was of the opinion that the scheme of 10+2+3 was roll of difficulties. It was not practical. Dr. Chunder himself was against 10+2+3 system. He was of the opinion that in this scheme Degree Course shall be of 15 Years. This Period should only be of 4 years. He also criticized the heavy curriculum at the secondary stage under the 10+2+3 years scheme. In July, 1978 there was a conference of Education Ministers of all the States of the country. This Conference proposed for the abolition of 10+2+3 scheme. The period of secondary education was divided into 3 parts-Primary, Secondary and Higher Secondary. The period of Primary and Secondary Education would be 8 +2 or 7+3. It was for the different states to opt for 8+2 or 7+3 according to their needs and resources. Conference also proposed that the period of Higher Secondary Education should be kept as 2 years. The Conference proposed that the Degree Course shall be of 2 years. However, the Honours Course shall be of 3 years. The Conference of Education Ministers held in 1978 gave certain valuable suggestions but they were not properly implemented.

Re-implementation of 10 + 2 + 3 Scheme. After the fall of the Janta government, it was again felt that the 8 + 2 or 7 + 3 scheme was not useful for all-round development of the country and it should be properly implemented. The present situation is that the structure of education is almost the same as it was proposed by the Wood's Despatch. After the implementation of 10 + 2 + 3 scheme in all the states, it is expected that revolutionary changes shall take place in the sphere of education.

3

Educational Administration

School Organisation

The organisation of education in India can ordinarily be divided into the following parts:

(i) Pre-primary education.

(ii) Primary education.

(iii) Secondary education.

(iv) Higher or university education.

(i) ***Pre-primary education.*** Pre-primary education is organised for the children of the age 1 to 2 years to 6 years. There are following types of pre-primary schools in India:

(a) Nursery schools.

(b) Kindergarten schools.

(c) Montessorie schools.

(d) Pre-basic schools.

(e) Schools for the poor,

(f) Schools of unitary education and

(g) Child Centres.

The number of Nursery Schools is very less in India, most of the Kindergarten schools are run by Missionary Institutions and mostly, the children of rich people receive education there. Common people are not able to send their children to such schools. The provision of Montessorie schools has been made by Government and many private agencies. For several years the number of Montessorie Schools is increasing day by day. The number of pre-basic schools is also very less. Some schools have also been opened for the education of poor children. There are very few schools of unitary education and the number of such schools is decreasing day by day, although even today many schools of this type are found in villages. Child centres are also making useful contributions in the field of primary education.

(ii) Primary education. According to Article 35 of the Constitution of India. "The State shall endeavour to provide within a period of 10 Years, from the commencing of this Constitution for the free and compulsory education for all children until they complete the age of 14 years, "According to this Article, this work should have been completed by the State by the year 1960. But this objective could not be achieved until now because of economic and administrative Obstacles. However, an endeavour has been made to expand primary education by opening different types of schools. From the point of view of organisation there are following types of primary schools:

(1) Schools organised by District Boards,

(2) Schools organised by Municipal Boards,

(3) Schools organised by Notified and Town Areas,

(4) Schools organised by Cantonment Boards,

(5) Schools organised by Religious Institutions,

(6) Schools organised by Gaon Sabhas,

(7) Schools organised by Private Individuals,

(8) Schools organised by Collective Organisations,

(9) Schools organised by the Government.

Missionary Institutions have also contributed much in the expansion of primary education. District Boards have also performed praiseworthy work for the expansion of primary education. The Government gives grant-in aid to different types of schools to give impetus to the expansion of primary education.

(iii) Secondary education. According to Mudaliar Commission Secondary Education should be for the boys and girls from 11 years to 17 years of age. The Mudaliar Commission has divided the whole system of secondary education into two parts- (1) 3 years of Junior Secondary Education; and (ii) 4 years of higher Secondary Education. It has also been recommended by the Commission that Intermediate classes should be abolished and 11th class should be joined with the high school and the 12th class should be made a pan of the degree course of the university.

Kothari Commission has also divided the secondary education into two parts (i) Secondary, and Higher Secondly. According to the Commission, the period of secondary Education should be 3 years and the period of higher Secondary education should be for 2 Years.

We will now discuss the organisation of the secondary education under the following headings:

Two Forms of Secondary Eduction. At present two forms of secondary education are found in India. In some provinces classes from 6th to 12th have been included under the secondary education, but in most of the provinces classes from 6 to 11 have been included under the Secondary Education. In the provinces where 12th class has not been included under the secondary education and it has been joined with the degree course, the term of which has been extended to 3 years.

Lower Secondary Education. The lower secondary education starts after the completion of the primary education. In Utter Pradesh its term has been fixed for 3 years. This type of education is imparted in Junior High Schools or Senior Basic Schools. The lower secondary education includes classes from 6th to 8th. The boys and girls of nearly 11 or 12 years receive this type of education which is also called the education of Junior Higher Schools. There are 3 types of schools for imparting lower secondary education. The first type of schools are such which impart primary and lower secondary education. The second type of schools are those which impart only lower secondary education. In other words, such schools made provision of education from classes 6th to 8th. They are called Junior High Schools. The third category of schools are such where secondary education is also imparted along with the lower secondary education.

Secondary Schools are of three types:

(1) Government Schools.

(2) Government Aided Schools.

(3) Schools run by Local Bodies.

At Higher Level

In India, autonomy has been given to the universities. The government do not interfere in their activities and works.

There are following 3 types of universities:

(i) Affiliated Universities.

(ii) Unitary or Residential Universities:

(iii) Federal Universities.

Affiliated Universities. The jurisdiction of these universities is very vast and the colleges affiliated to it are spread far and wide. The are affiliated to it. The universities inspect and supervise the colleges affiliated to it. The affiliated colleges have to follow and observe the rule of the universities and their curriculum is also determined by the universities. The universities possess the power to affiliate or recognise any college within its jurisdiction. The universities of Agra, Meerut, Kanpur, Calcutta, Bihar, Andhra Gorakhpur, Gauhati, Gujarat, Madras, Nagpur, Osmania, Punjab, Rajasthan Poona and Saugor, etc., are affiliated universities.

Residential Unive:sities. The jurisdiction of the Unitary University is limited to only one centre. They are called Residential Universities. This type of universities themselves organize the whole teaching work. They themselves organise teaching, administration, and management. The universities of Lucknow,

Patna, Allahabad, Aligarh, Baroda, Jadavpur, Vishwabharti, etc. are the Unitary or Residential Universities of the country.

Federal Universities. The Federal Universities are those Universities whose jurisdiction is limited to one centre or place but some colleges are also affiliated to them. Each college takes part in the administration of the university and has to surrender some of its freedom and autonomy to the university. All the colleges mutually cooperate with each other under the direction and supervision of the university. Bombay and Jabalpur, etc. are such type of universities.

From the point of view of administration, there are two types of universities. Some universities are central universities and the rest of them are autonomous universities having no control of the Central Government. Aligarh, Banaras, etc., are the universities which are under the control of Central Government

Forms of Affiliated Colleges. The colleges which are affiliated to the universities are of two types: Government and non-Government. The Government colleges are directly administered by the Government; whereas there are Managing Committees for the administration of the Non-Government Colleges. The Government exercise some control over these Managing Committees.

Keeping in view the rapid growth in number of the students in the modern period, some colleges have been affiliated with the unitary or residential universities also. For example many colleges such as Lucknow Christian College, Shia College, Kanyakubja College and Manila Degree College, etc. have been affiliated to the Lucknow University. But the university exercises full control over these affiliated colleges. These affiliated colleges have no freedom in respect of examination, etc. and they have to carry on their whole works in accordance with the direction and instructions of the university.

The affiliated colleges are also two types. In some affiliated colleges, teaching is imparted only for graduation course whereas some universities have certain affiliated colleges which impart teaching of post-graduate courses also.

Problems of Administration

The whole educational administration of India can be studied under the following three headings:

(i) Central Government, (ii) State Government, (iii) Local Bodies.

Central Government Level

The following three units are available for the educational administration at the central or National level:

(A) Ministry for Human-Resources and Development.

(B) University Grants Commission.

(C) Central Educational Council for Research and Training.

Ministry for Human Resources and Development. Now, the education is under the concurrent list Minister for Human Resources and Development is the highest authority at the Centre in the field of education. His main task is to plan the educational policies of the country and put them before the Cabinet. There is an Education Department in the Central Secretariat to help him. There is a Deputy Education Minister and separate advisors for Lok Sabha and Rajya Sabna. Under his Ministry, there is deputy secretary, superintendent and other personnels to assist him. There are many departments for education at the central level.

Under the Minister, there is 'Central Advisory Board', 'Central Education' and a 'Foreign Education Bureau'.

University Grants Commissions. University Grants Commission has a President and other members Amongst them there are three vice-chancellors of universities, four educationalists and two representatives of the Central Government. University Grants Commission has to perform the following chief functions:

1. To advise for the improvement and raising of standard of higher education.
2. To examine the economic needs of the universities and make policies for giving grants to the universities from its own funds.

3. To collect datas regarding the examinations, curricula and research-works of the universities.

4. To have discussion with the educationists, traders, industrialists and representatives of different private agencies on educational matters.

5. To hold discussions with the vice-chancellors of different universities.

The University Grants Commission is doing a commendable job in the field of education.

Central Educational Council for Research and Training. 'Central Educational Institute' performs the functions of this council. Under it, there are eleven departments and four Regional Colleges. The council works on the problems and the research in the field of education. Kothari Commission suggested that it shall be the apex body for improvement of higher education and shall work in co-ordination with the education departments of different states. There is provision for a full time Director and an Assistant Director in the Council. The four Regional Colleges attached to the Council give emphasis to multi-propose education and its different departments are in New Delhi.

State Govts. Level

Education was included under the State List in the Constitution of India but now it is in the Concurrent List. The structure of the administration of education at the state level is almost same in all the provinces. Only a time difference is found in some States. We will here discuss the administration of education at the State Level as is found in Uttar Pradesh:

Education Minister and other Officers. The Education Department of the State is under a Minister, who is called the Minister of Education. He is appointed by the Governor on the advice of the Chief Minister. There are also Minister of State and Deputy Minister. There are also the following officers to work under the Education Minister at the Secretariat level:

(a) Education Secretary,

(b) Special Secretary,

(c) Joint Secretaries,

(d) Deputy Secretaries, and

(e) Under Secretaries.

With the assistance of different officials, Education Minister puts-up the budget for Education in the legislature. There is also a 'Permanent' Council of the members of the legislature to advice the Education Minister.

Directorate of Education. In Uttar Pradesh, there are three Directors viz.. Director of Higher Education, Director of Secondary Education, and Director of Basic Education. All the Directors are responsible for the administration of their Directorates. In the Directorate there are Additional Directors, Joint Directors, and Deputy Directors to help the Director of Education in the administration of the Department In U.P. there are eight Deputy Directors at the Directorate level:

1. Deputy Director, Finance, 2. Deputy Director, Training, 3. Deputy Director, Urdu, 4. Deputy Director, Women, 5. Deputy Director, Sanskrit, 6. Deputy Director, Camp, 7. Deputy Director, Basic, and 8. Deputy Director, Secondary. There are also Assistant Deputy Directors to perform different functions.

For the convenience of administration, the entire state has been divided in thirteen educational zones viz. Paudi, Faizabad, Meerut, Agra, Bareilly, Muradabad, Varanasi, Gorakhpur, Lucknow, Jhansi, Allahabad, Kanpur and Nainital. There are separate Deputy Directors for each zone, having some districts under their educational purview.

District Inspector of State and other Officials. Each province has been divided into many districts and in each district a District Inspector of Schools is appointed to look after the Educational administration of the district. The District Inspector of Schools are the highest officials of the Education Department of the District Under them, there are Assistant District Inspectors of Schools at some places.

Educational System of Autonomous Bodies. For the educational systems of the cities and villages there are some local institutions. City Corporations are established in big cities. In these city Corporations, there is a separate officer for Education Department and all the primary schools of the city work under his control. This education officer works under the control and supervision of the Executive Officer and Chairman of the Municipality. In rural areas, the organisation of the primary education is made by the District Boards. The District Boards have been conferred wide power in the field of educational administration. The President of the District Board and his Education Committee make provision of appointment of the teachers and the maintenance of the Schools. In this connection, the Board has to work in accordance with the advise of the District Inspector of Schools. The main responsibility of the District Board is in the field of primary education. As far as the secondary and higher education are concerned they are under the control and supervision of the State Government.

4
The Infrastructure

The Concept

Our system of education is of such that students seldom get opportunity of learning by doing. They learn very few thing through practical experience. Generally, they are passive listeners in the class. If the opportunity is provided for 'work' in education, the students will be able to learn by their own experience. In such a case they will not be dependent upon others experiences and shall be able to learn many things through works. In education, 'works experience' has been accepted as a technique through which 'work' and 'education' are correlated. Here 'work' means the activity which is productive. Thus, 'work experience' in education is that activity which develops a tendency for productivity.

In India, the old traditional methods of education are still continuing. Even to vocational education we are not using the latest technological and scientific methods. Through work experience we may be able to use modern methods in productive activities. We can also learn to bring out productive activities on modern ones. This will definitely enhance the rate of production in our factories and other places.

It is very essential to keep in view the needs of our people while trying to make our education production-oriented. It is to be noted that modernization does not mean westernization. Our work experience methods should be devised according to our Indian needs. Here, we are giving some of the characteristics of work experience which will be suitable for our Indian conditions:

(1) Work experience should not be related only with productivity and it should rather aim at developing skill in the students for productivity.

(2) It should give self experience to students and should be according to their interests and aptitudes.

(3) The students should employ latest technological and scientific methods in work experience. This will result and pave way for our society for imbibing modern culture.

(4) Work experience should be as such that the students may be self-dependent upto certain extent so that they may earn for their expenses of education.

(5) Work experience makes the educational institution a centre of community development and so it should meet some of the needs of the community.

(6) If the education is imparted through work experience both the students and the schools are benefited. Some products of the daily use can fetch them materially.

The Significance

In India basic education, initiated by Mahatma Gandhi is an example of work experience in education. Kothari Commission also recommended to make work experience as an integral part of education. The Commission was of the view that work experience to education can play a vital role in our social and economic development. Here, we are giving some of the points mentioned by Kothari Commission :

(1) With the introduction of work experience in education, we may be able to the reform our stereotyped educational system. Work experience emphasises at leaning By doing and 10 so education imparted through it becomes a part of life.

(2) It develops a sense of respect for manual labour and so students do not hesitate to take manual jobs in their future

life. It also helps in bridging the gap between the labour and intellectual class.

(3) Work experience in education also develops social and communal unity. Through work experience school imparts education according to the needs of community and society and thus it helps in bringing the class relationship between the school and community. Through work experience in schools an attempt is made to find solutions of some of our social problems and thus school becomes a community centre.

(4) The problem of unemployment can be solved up to a certain extent through the introduction of work experience in education. Students may be able to learn some trade in the school which may help them after completing their education.

(5) Education based on work experience teaches us to utilize our natural resources intelligently. If the education is imparted through work experience, students become more skilful and may be able to contribute more for educational prosperity.

The following points should be kept in view while employing work experience in education:

(1) Work experience can not be treated as an independent subject of study. This should be integrated with other subjects of study.

(2) For the success of work experience we should make total atmosphere of the school favourable to it.

(3) Suitable text books should be prepared and teachers be trained on new lines. The courses of study at our training colleges should be revised.

(4) Work experience method may be freely utilized up to the secondary level of education. Children at the primary stage should be taught through practical activities so that their hands and feet become suitably trained to use certain

implements at the secondary stage. Work experience method can not be used at primary stage but children at this stage may be taught sensory training which may help them at later stage.

The Difficulties

Some problems shall definitely crop of by including work experience in education. Here, we are giving a brief account of them.

Problem of Determination. People assign different aims to work experience. According to some it is a means for creating the trait of productivity. Others regard it as a means to develop the capacity for production. Thus, the aim of work experience in education is controversial.

Solution. The fact is that aim of work experience should be dependent on principles of work experience. Work experience does not make the child an artisan by developing in him a capacity for production. Its aim is to develop the virtue of productivity in the child. If he develops this virtue in himself he shall definitely be successful in due course of time.

Problem of Suitable and Trained Teachers and Guides. In our training colleges teachers are trained to impart theoretical knowledge to the students. They are not suitable for imparting education based on work experience. Our multi-purpose schools have not succeeded to bring fruitful results due to the lack of training to the teachers in work experience and so our work experience based education may not succeed in the absence of suitable teachers.

Solution. In our training colleges, we should make all out efforts to train teachers in work experience. These trained teachers and guides should establish a close relationship between the general education and work experience. Up to the time we are not able to get such teachers. We should seek co-operation of trained workers from the nearby industries. It is essential to establish a close relationship between the teachers and industries for making the work experience more practical and purposeful.

Lack of Interest and Motivation for Work Experience. There is a lack of interest and motivation for work experience in our schools. Education based on work experience means a close relationship between education and practical work. In our schools we find that due to the lack of interest and motivation our students are not interested in education based on work experience.

Solution. The creative tendency in the child keeps him active. We should introduce work experience in education through play-way method. The interest and the capacity of the child should be adequately taken care while introducing work experience in education. Every child should be acquainted with the benefits of work experience in which he is to be engaged. Thus, he shall be motivated and take the task in an interesting manner.

Problem of Incorporation in Work Experience in the Curriculum. The incorporation of work experience in the curriculum is yet another problem. What should be various aspects of work experience and how to plan them and incorporate them into the curriculum are some of the difficult problems in the field. The main purpose of work experience will remain defeated unless these problems are solved.

Solution. First of all we should decide the programmes of work experience according to the mental age interest and aptitudes of the children. Afterwards we should plan and organize them psychologically and scientifically. While incorporating them into the curriculum it should be kept in mind that they should be related with local industries and with the needs of immediate society.

Problem of Instruction and Method of Work. Work experience can be obtained only through doing. The problem of instructions and method of work is one of the chief problems of work experience in education.

Solution. It is suggested that 'correlation' and 'free methods' are useful in this connection. In correlation method, instructions in different subjects are given around the work experience as a nucleus. In the 'free' method, students are left free for obtaining experience in the workshop. Those subjects which can not be taught through the correlation can be left for the 'free' method.

Problem of Teaching Materials. The problem of necessary teaching materials for work experience in teaching is another problem which our Indian Schools are facing. Due to the scarcity of funds we have not been able to convert our secondary schools into multipurpose schools and as such the objective of vocationalization has not been achieved. The same problem is there in relation to work experience. It is very difficult for us to arrange adequate material for work experience in our schools and colleges. For the work experience programme there is need of correlated time-table laboratory, workshop and contact with local industry. How to arrange all these facilities is a difficult task for us.

Solution. Work experience should be correlated to vocationalization of education. The central and state government and local agencies should provide necessary material equipments and other facilities to all the secondary schools for the vocationalization of education. The material should be such as to serve many purposes.

Problem of Evaluation. Our examination system is subjective and it can not be used for evaluating the progress of those students through work experiences. We shall have to device objective and rated evaluating devices for the purpose.

Solution. The productivity of students shall be the guiding force in our evaluation system. More emphasis should be given on practical work. Laboratory, experiments and working in the workshop should be the basis of evaluation of the students. For theoretical things we may have the written examinations but in them too there should be more objective tests. The daily work of students should also be considered in order to evaluate the progress of students.

Unfavourable Attitude of Guardians to Work Experience. In our country the guardians have fully understood the importance of vocationalization of education and so they do not react favourably against work experience. The guardians hesitate to get their wards admitted to those schools where students are required to do manual work.

Solution. There is a great need to change the outlook of guardians. They should be made aware that unemployment problem can be solved only through that education which place emphasis on manual labour. Favourable attitude of the guardians may be developed for work experience through exhibitions, seminars, lectures, radio and television.

5

Training for Teachers

The Background

Teacher Education in Ancient Period. In ancient period a special feature of the teacher education was that teachers used to take a personal interest towards each pupil. Sometimes so many students come to a teacher that he could not fulfil his responsibilities towards them. Hence, he used to seek the assistance of meritorious students of higher classes. They were called 'pattacharya'. They assisted their teacher (Guru) in teaching, used to be his pupils. If the teacher some times went away, the teacher used to entrust the whole work of teaching and schools to such students.

This system was, in fact, the monitorial system in which some meritorious students of the same Class and some students of the higher classes assisted the teacher in the performance of teaching and other allied works. The students, who were entrusted with this work, used to become efficient teachers and school organisers in the course of time. After having been thus trained, they used to devote themselves to teaching work in future.

Teacher Education in Medieval Period. Consequently, excepting a few rulers, they did not devote much attention to education. In such a condition, it was very difficult for them to have any idea of teacher education.

Teacher Education in Modern Period. In fact, teacher education in the systematic form was introduced in the modern times only.

Early efforts of Teacher Education in the Modern Period. In the modern period, the Educational Boards of Bombay, Madras and Calcutta for the first time felt the need of teacher education and they established a few training centres but only the teachers of primary schools were imparted training to these schools. The Native Education Society of Bombay trained 25 teachers and sent them to different parts of the province so that the standard of teaching in the primary schools might be raised. In 1812, Calcutta Society was established in Calcutta. This Society made the provision for the training of the teachers on the basis of monitorial system. In order to encourage the work of the society, the East India Company started giving Rs. 500 monthly aid since 1825. In accordance with the suggestions of Munro, the-then Governor of Madras, a Training School for the training of the teachers was founded at Madras in 1826.

Woods' Despatch and Teacher Education. Wood's Despatch of 1854 mentioned the following, "We desire to see the establishment, with as little delay as possible, of training schools and classes for masters in each Presidency in India." The wish that was expressed by the Directors of the Company in Wood's Despatch in regard to teacher education could not be fulfilled.

Teacher Education from 1859 to 1882. Lord Stanley has mentioned in his Despatch that special attention should be devoted to the training of the teachers. After the transfer of the power it was not possible for the British administrators posted in India to ignore or disregard the orders of the Secretary for State of India. Consequently, they worked with enthusiasm for the establishment of training schools for the teachers of primary schools and as a result of their efforts many Training Schools were established in each province by the year 1882. The number of students studying in these schools was 553. The number of schools in Madhya Pradesh was 44 for men and 1 for women and the number of students studying in these schools was 118.

In 1862, Normal School system was started in Bengal. According to this system the teachers of the native schools or their relations were lent to Normal Schools. In 1874, Campbell, the Governor of the Province, prepared a new scheme for the training of the teachers, and consequently, 46 normal schools were established at the cost of Rs. 1,64,000.

In Madras, there were 32 training schools and nearly 927 students were receiving training in those schools. Likewise, provision of the training of the teachers of primary schools was made in other provinces also. In 1882, there were 106 normal schools in the whole of India and about 3,886 men and women were being trained in those schools, the annual expenditure of these schools was nearly Rs. 4 lacs.

Regular System of Teacher Education. The regular system of teacher education was detailed in accordance with the recommendations of the Indian Education Commission, 1882. Consequently, by the end of 19th century, there were six Training Colleges at Madras, Lahore, Allahabad, Kurung, Rajmundii and Jabalpur and 50 Training schools in the whole country.

Government Resolution of Education Policy, 1904. Lord Curzon devoted sufficient attention towards education and training of the teachers. The Government Resolution of Educational Policy of 1904, after considering all the aspects of the teacher education, made the following recommendations:

(1) Provision should be made for higher training of able and experienced teachers for the Indian Educational Service.

(2) The importance of the equipment of the Training colleges is almost equal as that of General Colleges.

(3) The training period for the graduates should be only one year and therefore they should be granted degree by the University. The knowledge of teaching method and practical training should also be included in the curriculum. The training period for the non-graduates should be two years.

(4) Theoretical training and practical training should be mutually connected with each other and there should be a practising school connected with each Training College.

(5) Training colleges should be connected with ordinary schools so that the teachers may apply the methods teamed in the Training Colleges.

The Government Resolution of Educational Policy. Government Resolution in Educational Policy of 1913 further emphasised teacher education and declared: "Under modern system of education, no teacher should be allowed to teach without certificate that he is qualified to do so."

Calcutta University Commission and Teacher Education. The Calcutta University Commission (1916-17) devoted special attention towards teacher education and made the following recommendations: (1) The number of trained teachers should be increased; (2) Research work in education should be encouraged; (3) A demonstration school should be attached with each Training College so that practical work may be done in it; (4) The subject of education should be included in the curriculum of B.A. and Intermediate classes; (5) Education Department should be established in Calcutta and Dacca Universities.

Hartog Committee of 1929 and Teacher Education. The Hartog Committee emphasised the training of the teachers of primary schools and recommended the following in this connection: (1) Education Standard of the teachers shourld be raised; (2) Training period should be extended; (3) Able teachers should be appointed in training institutions and their number should be increased; (4) Provision of refresher courses should be made from time to time for the teachers of primary schools; (5) In order to attract able persons in the-teaching profession, the conditions of teachers should be improved and made attractive.

Training Institution. In 1947, there were following three types of institutions:

Normal Schools. Teachers of Primary schools were given training in these schools.

Secondary Training Schools. These schools imparted training to the teachers of middle schools only, those students who passed matriculation were admitted in these schools.

Training Colleges. The teachers of High Schools were given training in these schools. Only graduates and post-graduates were entitled to get admission in these colleges.

Training Facilities

Praiseworthy works have been performed in the field of expanding the facilities of teachers training in the post-independent period. Suggestions given by the University Education Commission, 1949, Secondary Education Commission, 1952 and Kothari Commission, 1964-66 are being implemented by the Government. We will now briefly discuss the suggestions made by these three Commissions:

University Education Commission (1948-49). Radhakrishnan Commission for the change in teacher education by telling, "A real education is not so much a matter of lessons to be learnt and memorized as of a life to be lived and purposeful activities to be shared." It made the following important recommendations in regard to teacher education:

(1) The curriculum of training institution should be reformed. Instead of bookish knowledge, importance should be given to the practice of teaching in schools.

(2) While evaluating the work of the students, special attention should be given to their success in teaching works.

(3) Only suitable schools should be selected for practice of teaching.

(4) Most of the teachers of the training schools should have sufficient experience of teaching in schools.

Secondary Education Commission (1952-53). It made the following recommendations:

(1) Training schools should be of two types. (a) First type of schools should be for those students who have completed secondary education; (b) The second type of schools should be for the graduates. For the time being, their training period should be one year but later on it should be extended to two years.

(2) Teacher student should be trained in more than the teaching method.

(3) Provision should be made for Refresher Courses, Short Intensive Courses on Special subjects and poetical training in workshop in the training schools.

(4) No fees should be charged from the teacher-students of the training schools.

Education Commission (Kothari Commission, 1964-66). Kothari Commission made the following recommendations in regard to teacher education:

(1) Extensive Service Department should be established in each Training Institution.

(2) Comprehensive colleges imparting training to the teachers at different stages of education should be established in each state.

(3) A State Board of Teacher Education, which should be responsible for teacher education at all stages and in all the fields, should be established in each State.

(4) The curriculum and courses of the training schools should be changed and re-organised in accordance with the changing times and circumstances.

(5) No fee should be charged from the students of training institutions and provision should be made for grant of stipends and loans to them.

(6) Facilities of correspondence courses and part-time training courses should be made available on extensive basis.

Role of Education Policy

In the Education policy of 1986, due importance was given to teacher-education. It was said that all-out efforts should be made to improve the education and training of future teachers. The appointment of teachers should be on the basis of their abilities and aptitudes. Provision was made for establishing District Institutes of Education & Training, who will cater the need of non-formal education for the workers of adult education. Secondary Teacher Education Institution shall be re-organised.

Training Institution in the Present Period. At present, there are following eight types of teacher's training institution in our country:

1. Pre-primary Training Centres,
2. Primary Teachers Training Schools,
3. Secondary Teachers Training Colleges,
4. Specialised Teachers Training Colleges,
5. Education department of Universities,
6. Special Institutes for Trained Teachers and Research Work,
7. Training Institutes for Women,
8. In-Service Training Institutes.

Here, we are giving a brief account of some of them:

Pre-primary Training Centres. Pre-primary Education is in its early stages in our country. Consequently, the provision of training of the teachers of pre-primary schools is also in its early stage. In the year 1992-93 there were 205 pre-primary training centres in the country. These centres impart training to the matric and upper primary pass students for a period of one year. The curriculums of the training centres are different

Primary Training Schools. There are two types of primary schools in India (i) basic, and (ii) non basic. Consequently, there are also two types of training schools. In the year 1988-89 there were 992 in the whole country. The training period of both these two types issues the following two types of certificates (a) Junior Teachers' certificate is conferred on those students, who take in these schools after passing upper primary, (b) Senior Teachers' Certificate is awarded to the students taking training in these centres after passing matriculation.

Secondary Teachers Training Colleges. They are of two types-some impart training to under-graduates while some to graduates.

In 1988-89, the number of such colleges in the country were 992. The training period of such schools is one year in some States where as it is 2 years in some other States. The successful students are conferred a certificate of diploma by the University or Education Department. The name of the certificates or diplomas are different in different States. The teacher in these institutions perform teaching work in junior high schools and secondary schools.

These institutions are run by Education Department of the States and Universities. In some states such as Uttar Pradesh, these institutions are run by Education Department as well as by the Universities. The training period of these colleges is generally two years and the successful candidates are awarded B.Ed., L.T. or D.P. Ed.

Difficulties and Remedies

Dr. S.N. Mukerji is of the opinion, "The present position in relation to teacher-education is by no means satisfactory, in spite of the rapid progress in recent years. Numerous problems have arisen with this development" Here, we are giving a brief account of these problems and their solution:

Training not Related to School Work. It is one of the chief problems of teacher education that training imparted by the training colleges to the teachers is not related to school work. The conditions and circumstances prevailing in the training institutions are such that the teachers find themselves unable to implement in practice the educational principles which they learn here.

No Diversion Between Theory and Practice. The question arises as to why there is so much difference in practice and the theory and how this difference should be removed. It is not much difficult to find out the reason. There are very few Training Colleges who have some 'Demonstration School' connected with them. Consequently, the teacher-student are not able to determine the educational principles and method for their students. They do not get sufficient opportunity to test in practice the principles and methods of teaching which they have learned and consequently their teaching lacks practical experience.

Consequently, their ideas are not clear and they are unable to impart successful teaching in their schools. What is still worse is that generally their professors are not capable of having a clear conception of things because of the fact that this quality can be developed only when they have the opportunity of testing their principles in practice. Pointing out the solution of this problem, Sri K.G. Saiyadain has aptly remarked: "Practice and theory must both be visualised as growing entities, theory illuminating practice constantly modifying theory.

It is Therefore, very essential that an administration school fully equipped with all the necessary means should be attached with each Training College which should be run on experimental basis. If the teacher-student gets the opportunity of testing into practice the theories and principles of 'teaching learned' in training colleges, they will be able to perform their work more successfully and efficiently.

Undue Emphasis on Theory. Yet another defect of the prevalent Teacher's training is that undue emphasis is given on theory. On the contrary, they are given very little time for practical work. During their training period they teach nearly 50 lessons. As is well-known, generally each teacher has to teach 6 or 7 hours every day. Thus, the teaching of 50 lessons is the work of only one week is completed. In other words we may say that during their training period they are allowed one week for teaching class, whereas they remain busy in study of theoretical subjects from July to April. This clearly shows their lack of practical experience.

Curtailment of Theoretical Courses. The above mentioned problem can be solved only when the theoretical subjects are curtailed. The teacher-student should be taught only those subjects which may prove useful in their teaching life and may help them throughout life. This cannot be said to be a wise practice that they bid farewell to their books and the knowledge acquired after the completion of their examination. The curtailment of theoretical courses will automatically make available to them sufficient time for teaching works. It will be more desirable for teachers to spend 3 to 4 hours every day during the whole of their teaching period so that they may become efficient in teaching profession.

Neglect of Human Aspect. Yet another serious problem of teacher education is that their education neglects human aspect and more emphasis is given on technical aspect. During the training period so much emphasis is given on the methods and capacity of teaching that they do not get proper opportunity to apply their critical mind in solving the problem of education relating to its aim, purpose and values.

Values of Training Centres. It has been unequivocally admitted that there is neglect of human aspects during the period of training of teachers but educational institution do not consider themselves responsible for this. They contend that so little time is given to them for training that they find themselves unable to devote to the human aspect. The argument may appear to be plausible on its face but, in fact it is completely baseless. If we accept this excuse and retain the existing position in the training institutions, it will mean that we believe in the wrong values and do not make any endeavour to reform it. In the works of Sri K.G. Saiyadain, "It is essential for the training colleges to revise their values and avoid the misfortune of the man in the cave who could see nothing of the fascinating vista around because his vision was bounded by the four walls of the prison. There is an adequate appreciation of the social and agricultural background, which must be set right."

Unconditional Environment. The Environment in which the teacher-students study during their training period lacks freedom.

Free Environment. In order to solve the above problem, it is necessary that the Training Institutions should be freed from the binding of strict roles and strict control on the life and activities of teacher student The Training Institution should be organised into such free and active communities, in which the teacher students may work under those circumstances and inspirations which our country wants to establish in our institutions. If this is not done, the teacher student coming out of training college will not be benefited. If they receive their training in unfree and unconductive environment, they will continue the same defective process in which they have received their training. Besides this, they will continue to retain the wrong conception which they have developed during training period.

It is heartening to note that the work of organising the Basic Training Colleges into community centres has started and more freedom is being given to the teacher-students of post graduate training colleges. However, much remains yet to be done to give a real and effective form to this movement.

Selection of Candidates for training. Selection of suitable-candidates for training is also the main problem of teacher education, some years ago when there was not a strong desire among the persons to become teachers; trained teachers were not more than their demand, the position was not as serious and difficult as it is today. There are two aspects of this problem.

(a) The number of persons desirous of seeking admission in training college has unprecedently increased, and

(b) There are not sufficient posts for all the trained teachers. It is, therefore, necessary that only suitable persons should be selected for training in view of the welfare of the teacher as well as the teaching profession.

Some Suggestions. In order to solve the above mentioned problems, K.G. Saiyadain recommended the following:

(i) With the help of training colleges, education Department of each State should ascertain through at least one survey in 5 years as to how many men and women teachers will be required in the State and the scheme of admitting the students in training colleges should be prepared on the basis of this public demand.

(ii) Short-term courses should be organised for old and experienced teachers who on account of some reasons have not been able to take admission in training colleges.

(iii) As regards the persons who wish to take admission in training colleges after completing their education in colleges or universities, only suitable and promising persons who may become able and efficient teachers, should be selected.

(iv) Better and more efficient means should be adopted to select new students for admission.

(v) The person desirous of entering into teaching profession should keep in mind that they should not enter into Training Colleges after acquiring scattered and unconnected knowledge of different things, which may not in any way help them in their future profession.

(vi) For the examination of degree, teaching of science should be made an optional subject as is already prevalent in some universities.

Difference between basic and non-basic courses. At present two types of training institutions are working in our country, basic and non-basic. The curricula of both these courses are different. Basic system emphasises activity, method, community life and practice, its theoretical aspect is weak. On the contrary, the non-basic system emphasises theoretical knowledge and teaching method. The aspect of practice is only subsidiary in this system, thus, there exists defects and weakness in both the systems.

Integration of Basic and Non-basic Courses. The basic and non-basic system should be integrated in such a way so that their defects may be removed and a new and efficient system may be evolved. Keeping this in mind, the All-India Conference of Training Colleges has suggested the following for integration of the said two systems:

(i) The theoretical part of the general training course should be minimised and the desired revision should be made in it.

(ii) More importance should be given to practical work and it should be re-organised in such a way so as to impart training of community life, craft and correlated teaching.

Low Standard of Teachers' Education. The teaching standard of our training colleges is very low and so able teachers are not produced. Kothari Commission was of the view, "Existing programmes of teacher education are largely traditional, rigid and divorced from the realities of schools and existing or proposed programmes of Educational reconstruction.

Re-organisation of Teacher's Education. All out efforts should be made to re-organise the teacher's education so that the standard may be raised. In this connection Kothari Commission was for integrated curriculum of general and technical education in colleges and universities. The curriculum should be framed keeping in view the conditions of the country. While framing the curriculum individual and technical needs of the mind. In training colleges new and progressive means of examinations should be introduced. Keeping in view the suggestions given by the Kothari Commission, in the draft of the fifth plan, it has been said, "The curricula of the training schools and colleges will be reoriented so as to ensure deepening of the prospective teacher's academic and professional preparation."

Conclusion. The problems of teacher education which we have discussed above explicitly indicate that the work of teacher education is not progressing properly in our country and its utility is also doubtful. However, these problems are not such as cannot be solved. The necessity is however this, that the educationists of the country should compel the Government to remove the defects prevalent in the field of teacher education within the shortest possible time. If these defects are not converted into reality. The role of teacher is most significant in educational revival and he can perform his role properly only when he is given proper and efficient training.

6
Higher Education

The History

The system of higher education, which we see today in our country, started after the advent of British in India. The development of this education can be conveniently studied under following four heads:

(a) Periods of Colleges (from beginning of the British rule to 1857),

(b) Period of the first University (from 1857 to 1917)

(c) Establishment of new Universities (from 1917 to 1947)

(d) Higher Education in Independent India

British Period

The higher education was in a very disorganised condition at the time when the Britishers established their authority in India. The British rulers established many Government and private colleges till 1857. The more prominent of such colleges were Banaras Sanskrit College, Hindu College, Calcutta Christian College, Madras and Agra College. There were 23 colleges of general education - Medical Colleges, 1 Civil Engineering School in the year 1857.

First University

Accepting the recommendations of Wood's Despatch of 1855

the Universities of Calcutta, Bombay and Madras were established in 1857 on the model of London University. All universities performed the functions of only conducting examinations. Emulating the examples of these universities, Punjab and Allahabad Universities were established in 1882 respectively. The college education received a great impetus during 1901-02. The number of colleges which were 68 in 1881-82 increased to 179 in 1901-02. University education made a great progress during the reign of Lord Curzon, Viceroy of India. In order to give a fillip to the university education, be appointed the Indian University Commission in 1902 in order to enquire into the conditions and working of the Indian Universities and make necessary suggestions. Two years later, Indian Universities Act was passed. This act brought about many important changes in the organisation. Jurisdiction, powers and administration, etc. of the Universities. Consequently, the expansion of the university education was checked for some time. However, it must be admitted that this act went a long way to improve and reform the conditions and standards of the contemporary universities and colleges.

Later Universities

After the establishment of Allahabad University in 1887, no new university was established for a period of 30 years. However, the number of colleges, increased to 185 during this period. In view of the increase in the number of colleges, it was felt that 5 universities at Calcutta, Madras, Bombay, Punjab and Allahabad were incapable to cope with the increased work. Hence, it was thought necessary to increase the number of universities. The Government Resolution of 1913 emphasised the establishment of new universities. The Calcutta University Commission, 1917 also advised the establishment of new universities. Consequently, following universities were established by the year 1947. Mysore University (1916), Patna University (1917), Banaras Hindu University (1917), Osmania University (1918), Aligarh Muslim University (1920), Dacca University (1920), Lucknow University (1920), Delhi University (1922), Nagpur University (1923), Andhra University (1926), Agra University (1927), Annamalai University (1929), Travancore University (1937), Utkal University (1943), Saugoi-University (1947) and Rajputana University (1947).

Scence after Independence

At present higher and university education is imparted through arts, science and commerce and professional colleges, research institutions and institutions deemed to be universities under the Universities Grants Commission Act, 1956.

In addition to Central universities, State Universities and their affiliated colleges, Indira Gandhi Open University and other open universities are doing a commendable job in the field of higher education.

It is clear from the above discussion that the expansion of higher education has received a great impetus after independence. However, it may be mentioned here that the expansion of higher education has not taken place in accordance with the new needs and interests of the country. Generally, the policy of the government has been to increase the number of institutions of higher education rather than to aim at the qualitative progress of higher education. Besides this, there are multi-lateral problems of higher education, which have not attracted the proper attention of the Government and hence special efforts have not been made so far to remove the defects of higher education. It is good that after the declaration of the Education Policy of 1986, more emphasis is being given to the specialization in higher education.

Difficulties and Remedies

The problems of higher and University education in India is nothing but the problems of Indian society in general. If we wish to establish a society based on the principles of democratic socialism, we will have to reorient the entire educational structure. But unfortunately there is still a lag between our ideal and reality. Our universities have not been able to shake off the heavy load of bookish learning. The Kothari Commission has very aptly quoted Sir Eerie Ash by on the real condition of Indian universities:

"Looking at Indian universities a century after, their foundation, one cannot but help feel that they have failed to adopt themselves sufficiently to the vast and unique opportunities which surround them; they seem to have lost enthusiasm and initiative under the crashing problems which have beset them. Despite three major commissions they have not been able to extricate themselves from their own brief history. With a few notable exceptions they remain examining bodies. As universities multiply in number, their academic standards, relative to those elsewhere, do not improve... the universities remain alien implantations, not integrated into the new India...

This is one reason why, to the observer from outside, the Indian intellectually displaced person nostalgically treasuring his threads of communication with England... Universities have responded to reply to the challenge of Asiatic culture." The main problems of higher and university education in India are as follows:

Purposeless Exercise

One of the chief problems that confronts the higher education in India is its aimlessness. Most of the students are receiving higher education in India without having any definite aim.

Change in Aims. It is most essential that the students receiving higher education must have some definite aims before starting higher education. The aims of higher education should be changed. While describing the aims of University education in 1952, Newmen remarked, "if a practical end must be assigned to a university course, then I say it is training of good members of society." The University Education Commission visited many universities and made the following remark in this connection: "We are everywhere struck by a deep general awareness of the importance of higher education for national welfare and uneasy sense of the inadequacy of the present pattern. The universities as the marks of the future, cannot persist in the old pattern. With the increasing complexity of society and its shifting pattern universities have to change their objectives and methods, if they are to function effectively in our national life."

The University Education Commission has determined many aims of higher education. We have discussed it earlier while dealing with the recommendations and suggestions of the University Education Commission. The aims are no doubt praiseworthy but most of them are based on idealism. It may also be pointed out that these aims have neither been achieved since 1949 to this date nor are they expected to be ever achieved. The aims determined by the University Education Commission are very good but it is not easy to provide facilities, so that the said aims may be achieved.

Defective Curriculum

The curricula of the institutions of our higher education are full of many defects. The subjects of study in most of colleges are old and out of date. The curriculum fails to fulfil the interests of different types of students and consequently their intellectual development is checked. Radhakrishnan Commission has remarked, "A Curriculum which had validity in the Vedic period or the renaissance cannot continue unaltered in the 20th century."

Some Suggestions. As pointed out earlier the curricula of our universities are not in accordance with the interest of different types of students. In order to remove this defect, it is necessary that there should be diversification of courses in curriculum of the universities in the same way as determined by the Mudaliar Commission for the curriculum of the secondary schools. The curriculum of the universities should be flexible so that it may be made in accordance with the changing conditions and need of the changing society. In this connection, the University Education Commission had rightly remarked, "Educational systems are built for the time and not for all time. There are no changeless ways of educating human nature. A curriculum which, vitally in the Vedic period or the renaissance cannot continue unaltered in the 20th century."

Specific Areas

In university education, emphasis is given on the specialisation in different subjects. Consequently, when the students complete the university education they acquire special knowledge and skill in some particular subjects but their view-point remains unbalanced and narrow but they do not become completely educated in real sense. Explaining its reason, K.G. Saiydain remarks, "there is certain narrow, un-imaginative type of specialization which results in the science being complacency ignorant of arts and poetry and social and political problems, and arts students having no appreciation of how science and scientific technique have transformed the world in which they are living."

Suggestions. It is necessary that different branches and experiences of knowledge should be interlinked and harmonious relations established among them. The balanced development of the mind of the students will not be possible unless and until they experience the integration of knowledge and experience. It may, therefore, be suggested that along with the education of art and science in secondary schools, colleges and universities, provision should also be made for imparting general education so that the students of arts and literature may acquire the knowledge of the subjects of science and the students of science and commerce may acquire the knowledge of the subjects of art and literature. Thus, the defect of narrow specialisation can be removed by establishing harmony between general education and specialisation. This will also help the development of personality of the students and they will become able and dutiful citizen. The subjects and curriculum of the general education should be selected in accordance with students of particular fields. It is heartening to note that University Education Commission has suggested the inclusion of general education in the curriculum of the universities. This suggestion has been accepted by some universities, namely Aligarh, Andhra, Banaras, Baroda, Jadavpur, Kanotak, Kerala, Mysore, Poona, Rajasthan, Saugor, S.N.D.T., Bombay, Srivainkateshwara, Utkal and Vishwabharn.

Need for Guidance and Counselling

In the institutions of our higher education, there is no provision for giving proper guidance and counselling to the students. In the absence of such a provision, the students select their courses either according to their own choice or with the advice of some inexperienced persons. Consequently, many students select subjects which are either against their interest and tendencies or they are not capable of studying those subjects.

It is necessary that in the educational institutions of higher education, there should be a provision of experienced and trained persons to provide guidance and counselling to the students from beginning to the end. The suggestions given by Mudaliar Commission and Kothari Commission in this connection hold good for the educational institutions for the higher education also.

Teaching Standards

The standard of teaching in our colleges and universities is very low. In this connection in his book, 'A new deal for our Universities', K.R.S. Iyenger has rightly remarked, "Our standards, whether in scholarship or teaching, were never very high or exacting, are now fast racing to the bottom." It is very difficult to raise this standard as pointed out by Dr. S.N. Mukeqi, "Academic standards once lowered are not retrievable and Gresham's law is applicable to them."

Suggestions. Many suggestions can be given for raising the standard of teaching. The more prominent of such suggestions are increase in the salaries of teachers; not more than 18 hours of teaching work in a week; improvement in the condition of the services of teachers; provision of tutorial classes; well-organised libraries and laboratories and encouragement to debates and discussions. The Kothari Commission has made some praiseworthy recommendations in this connection such as giving professional training to junior lecturers, organisation of Re-orientation Courses for new lecturers etc.

Significance of English

More than 50 years have passed since the attainment of indepen-dence but as yet English continues to be the medium of instruction in the institutions of higher education. Our subservience to the British for a long time has created so much reverence and love for English that we still find ourselves unable to replace English as a medium of instruction with some other Indian language or national language. It is a matter of great regret that due consideration has not been given to the loss which English as a medium of instruction is causing to our youth.

Federal Language as Medium of Instructions. It has become expedient that English should be replaced as a medium of instructions as soon as possible. The University Education

Commission has suggested the regional language or federal language. Most of the universities of the country have been endeavouring to give practical shape to the suggestion of making federal language as medium of instructions so that it would be convenient for the persons of different States of the country to establish contacts among themselves. It would be proper and convenient to conduct the examination of Indian Services in the Federal language.

However, we should not totally ignore English. We should remember the words of Dr. Radha Krishnan, "We might have banished Englishmen, but not their language, and English is not the monopoly of Englishmen."

Faulty Examination System

The present examination system of our universities has been subjected to severe criticism by Indian and foreign educationists. All the Committees and Commissions that have been appointed so far have thrown special light on the defects in the prevalent examination system. Indian University Commission in 1902 pointed out in its report, "The greater evil from which university education in India suffers is, that teaching is subordinated to examination, and not examination to teaching." The University Education Commission of 1949 also pointed out, "If we are to suggest one single reform in university education, it should be that of examination."

Suggestions. The present examination system can be reformed by including scientific methods. In our examination system, examination of students by progressive tests and determination of 70, 55 and 40 per cent marks for awarding first, second and third division to the students is necessary. Besides this, it has also been suggested that abolition of external examination, start of internal assessment or evaluation system and training of teachers with the new system of assessment or evaluation etc. may go a long way to remove many of the defects to the present examination system.

Discipline Problem

The problem of indiscipline among the students has assumed

so much seriousness and complications that it is eating the very vitals of our educational system. Prof. N.K. Siddhant, former Vice Chancellor of Calcutta University has mentioned the following types of activities coming within the indiscipline- (1) Financial irregularity, (2) Minor misconduct, (3) Disorderly misconduct, (4) Theft and burglary, (5) Sex misconduct, (6) Misuse of privilege, and (7) Cheating in examination. As pointed out rightly by Prof. N.K. Siddhant in his book 'Indian University Administration', "The problem of maintaining discipline in the seats of higher education is assuming greater importance every day."

Suggestions. According to Prof. Siddhant the best way of solving the problem of indiscipline is to divert the activities of the young students into healthy channels including sports, games, co-operative living in hostels, self-management of masses debates and symposia. However, the lead in all these matters should be given by the teachers themselves.

Prof. Siddhant had also made the following suggestions for solving the problem of indiscipline among the students:

1. The statistics of different types of indiscipline in each centre of higher education should be maintained.
2. The family and social life of the students and records where the student has studied earlier should be studied.
3. The cause of each crime committed by the students should be discovered.

Interview of indisciplined students should be arranged with an expert who should be acquainted with the seriousness of the crime and should try to explain them that acts of indiscipline and crime which the students were committing were not proper. It has rightly been suggested by the Education Commission that not only the teachers but the students, their guardians and parents, society, Government and the political parties will have to work in order to solve the problem of indiscipline among the students. Besides this, the defects of educational system should also be solved at the earliest possible time. Vice Chancellor's Conference of 1969 suggested, "It is desirable that student is exposed to and acquainted with national development programmes, secularism, national integration, the constitution, and citizenship." Radhakrishnan Commission was of the view, "great literature sets fire to the highest emotion and promotes the highest ideal and aspiration. A study of great books that fills us with hope is essential in university course." Kothari Commission, while giving the various suggestions for removing the indiscipline remarked, "It is necessary to remember that the responsibility for the situation is not unilateral it is not merely that of the students or parents or teachers or state governments, or the political parties, but multilateral. All of them share it."

Role of Societies

The student-societies in educational institutions of higher education also pose serious problems before us. The harms which these student-societies cause to the students are well known. The workers of these societies interfere in each and every work of the college. If the teacher, principal or managers of the college do any work which is against their wish but they want that the appointment of the teachers, their teaching work and all the policies connected with the college should be done with their advice. Thus, these student- societies prove to be scourge for colleges.

Registration of Student's Society. The Indian Educationists are not against the student societies. On the contrary, they want that these societies should be organised because they provide opportunities of exhibition of intellectual powers of the students, develop their qualities of leadership and develop their homely relation. But mostly these societies start working in the wrong direction. In this connection V.K.R.V. Rao has pointed out "Unfortunately, we have in our universities certain very undesirable elements, many of whom are in contact with embassies, planning trips abroad and obtaining money from outside sources. All these have a demoralising effect on the student-community and should be stopped. Again, I should like to suggest that legislation be introduced for the registration of university or college societies to ensure that they observe certain rules in elections, method of keeping accounts and similar other things."

Almost all the above problems have attracted the attention of the University Education Commission, which has made many suggestions to solve these problems. Most of these suggestions have been accepted by the Government and many of them have already been implemented. It may, therefore, be hoped that after being free from the present problems, the higher education will make the complete development of the personality of the youths and by developing their intellectual and physical powers will make them able citizens of the country.

It is a matter of great regret that in the present scientific period, when the standard of higher education should be very high, the standard of higher education in India is declining day by day. K.R.Y. Iyengar is of the opinion, "our standards whether in scholarship or teaching never were very high or exacting are now fast racing to the bottom." There are many reasons for this decline in the standards of our education. Following are some of the main causes which are responsible for the decline of standards of higher education in India.

Number of Students on Rise

The development of education in India is taking place rapidly. The number of students receiving higher education is constantly increasing and it is likely to increase more in the near future. Although the number of students is rapidly increasing, yet it has not been possible to provide them with necessary facilities. The number of able teachers is also not increasing with the same proportion. University Grants Commission is of the opinion, "If increasing number of students continue to be admitted in our universities without corresponding expansion of facilities, there is great risk of the academic standards being impaired further."

Suggestion. In order to solve the above-mentioned problem, Kothari Commission has recommended that selective system of admissions should be adopted in the universities. The number of students in the educational institutions should be determined keeping in view the facilities available in the institutions concerned and the number of teachers. The university should prescribe necessary qualification for admission and the best students should be selected from among them desiring to seek admission in the universities. The new and modern methods should be adopted while selecting the students. Until these methods are fully developed, the percentage of marks secured by the students in pre-university examinations should be made the basis of their admissions. Each university should establish a Board of University Admission which should solve all the problems concerning admission. In order to help the students to select different subjects of higher education, the University Grants Commission should establish Central Testing Organisation.

Absence of Facilities

Yet another reason for the low standard of education in universities is that in universities the students do not have the same faculties which are provided to the students of the universities in other countries of the world. The students have to face the shortage of books. The libraries of the universities are not properly equipped and are not able to make available all the necessary books to the students. The environment and the condition in which our universities are imparting education is likely to lower the standard of education. In many degree colleges, there is not even proper seating arrangements for the students. There are thousands of such degree colleges, which do not possess even playgrounds. In such conditions, the lowering of the standard of the education is quite natural.

Suggestions. To solve this problem, a high level committee should be appointed for providing necessary facilities to the students. The Government of India and the State Governments have been making every possible endeavour to provide grants in order to remove the difficulties of the students and to equip properly the libraries, etc. But it may be made clear that only Government's efforts alone will not solve this problem. The non-government institutions should also come forward and make as much contributions possible in this field. It is the sacred duty of the rich class of the society to spend as much as possible money to raise the standard of higher education. In progressive countries like America, non-government institutions contribute a lot in the field of higher education. The rich class and non-government institutions of India should also emulate the example of America If the big capitalists and industrialist come forward to make their contribution in this field considering it as their sacred duty, this problem can be solved to a great extent

Teachers' Plight

The poor condition of the teachers is yet another reason which is responsible for the low standard of higher education. The teachers of degree colleges and universities get so less salaries that they adopt other means in order to meet their expenses. Consequently, they are not able to devote themselves heart and soul into the teaching work. A teacher who is always busy in finding means to meet his expenditure cannot be expected to render much help to the students in research work.

Suggestions. It is necessary and expedient to improve the financial conditions of the teachers for raising the standard of teaching. The Kothari Commission has made many important suggestions in this connection. The Commission had recommended the salaries of the teachers at different stages. The Mehrotra Commission has recommended new grades for university teachers.

Besides the increase in their salaries the teacher should also be provided with other types of financial facilities. The teachers doing extraordinary work at the University stage should be given promotions. The qualification and the salaries of the teachers of the affiliated colleges as well as the universities should be the same.

Worse Conditions

Another reason for the low standard of education is that the teachers have been burdened with too much work. The condition of working of the teachers are such that they are not able to perform the teaching work properly. At the university stage where prominence is given to the research work, it is completely improper to burden them with too much work. Kothari Commission has remarked, "There is much serious concern that in many places there is too much teaching but relatively too little of good teaching."

Suggestions. In order to remove the above mentioned defects, it is necessary to reduce the hours of working of the teachers. Besides this, they should be encouraged to devote their utmost time in the research work. Each teacher should be given one year leave with salary within a period of five years of service for increasing his knowledge and for travelling to foreign countries. They should have complete freedom in performing the teaching functions. Only teaching work should be taken from them. It is very bad practice to burden the teachers with administrative and other works of educational institutions. The suggestion made by Kothari Commission in respect of the promotion of teachers, improvement in the conditions of their service and other works, etc. are very important and should be implemented in all institutions of higher studies.

Distance between Teachers and Students

Another reason for the decline in the standard of higher education is the fact that there is a wide gulf between the students and the teachers. The number of students in each class is so much that the teacher is not able to recognise each student with much less talk for establishing close contact. Consequently, there exists a wide gulf between the teachers and the students. While in western countries the students and the teachers work together like a family and perform some type of functions in their interests, in India it appeals that the interests of the students and teachers are separate from each other.

Suggestions. In order to establish close contact between the teachers and students, it is necessary to adopt tutorial system. Besides reducing the number of students in each class, at different hours 4 or 5 students should meet a teacher and hold discussions with him in respect of his subject. Debates and discussions should also be organised. These debates and discussions help to establish close relations between the teachers and the students, and the students are able to increase their knowledge with the help of the teachers.

Defective examination system is also one of the chief causes leading to the decline in the standard of university education. It was pointed out by Radha Krishnan Commission "If only one suggestion is made to reform university education, it should be in respect of present examination system. Too much importance is given to the essay type of examinations. Consequently, the students think that they will achieve success by studying some selective questions and so they do not devote themselves heart and soul into the studies throughout the year. Most of the students study only selected questions and thence the standard of education is constantly declining. Besides this, the number of pass mark is so low that they secure it very easily."

Suggestions. To reform the present examination system, it is necessary to give less prominence to the essay type examination and shift emphasis on internal assessment or evaluation. In place of essay type examination, tests would be more useful. So far students securing 60 per cent, 45 or 48 per cent and 33 per cent marks are awarded first, second and third divisions respectively. The above mentioned percentage of marks should be increased to 70, 55 and 40 respectively.

Political Interference

The prevalence of group party-politics is yet another cause which is responsible for the decline in the standard of education in Indian universities. Different political parties endeavour to make their influence in the University. In every province, there are some particular persons who are ever eager to establish their control over universities. Consequently, because of party- politics such teachers are appointed who are not properly suitable for teaching work. The groupism of the teachers also lowers the standard of teaching work. The teachers remain busy in group party-politics and they do not get sufficient time to throw themselves heart and soul into the teaching work.

Suggestions. The need for keeping the colleges and universities away from party-politics need not be over-emphasised. All the political parties and scholars consider this problem seriously. We should think that the future of our country depends upon the progress of higher education. If the standard of higher education goes on constantly declining, we cannot make progress in any field. The conferences should be organised for keeping the universities away from party politics. There should be a free discussion in these conferences over this problem. Thereafter, a date should be fixed on which the suggestions should be submitted in this connection. Government should implement the suggestions of the said conferences. As far as possible, the politicians should not be appointed in the universities. The debates and discussions should also be organised. These debates and discussions help to establish close relations between the teachers and the students, and the students are able to increase their knowledge with the help of the teachers.

Last but not the least, the growing indiscipline among the students is also one of the chief causes responsible for the decline in standard of higher education. This indiscipline among these causes are the social and economic difficulties; growing unemployment; non availability of educational facilities, group party-politics; lack of interesting subjects in the curriculum etc.

Suggestions. To resolve this problem, Kothari Commission has suggested that not only the teachers but the students, parents and guardian, society, Government and political parties should work together to solve this problem. Such type of programmes should be organised in colleges and universities that may keep the students busy in constructive work and keep them away from party politics. Every possible endeavour should be made to solve the problem of unemployment. Unless and until the problem of indiscipline is satisfactorily solved in the colleges and universities, it would be wishful thinking to hope for an improvement in the standard of our higher education. Kothari Commission is of the opinion, "whatever else education may or may not aim at doing, it should at least strive to enable youngmen and women to learn and practice civilized norms of behaviour."

It is explicit from the above discussion, there are many reasons which are responsible for the decline in the standard of higher education. It is not only necessary but also expedient to check the decline in the standard of education and every possible effort should be made to improve the existing standard of higher education. If we intend to come at par with other advanced countries of the world then it should be our sacred task to work sincerely to raise the standard of higher education.

7
Secondary Education

Importance of Secondary Education

Secondary Education has a vital role to play in any programme of education for the community. It provides teachers for both elementary and adult education. It also prepares pupils for the universities and other institutions of higher education. Besides, it is the stage which in all countries marks the completion of education for the vast majority. Even the minority which goes for higher education can not take full advantage of the under opportunities offered by the universities unless they have received their grounding in a system of sound secondary education.

Significance of Secondary Schools

Secondary school is the gift of modern education. This type of schools were not prevalent in ancient and medieval India. This type of schools were started in India for the first time by the foreign missionaries and thereafter, by the Indian education-lovers. These efforts were started in the end of 18th century and in the 19th century. The chief purpose of the establishment of secondary schools in India was to teach English to Indians.

From 1835 to 1854. The report of Lord Macaulay which was accepted by Lord William Bentmok, the then Viceroy of India in 1835, paved the way for the expansion of secondary education.

From 1854 to 1904. Wood's Despatch also contributed much in the development of secondary education in India. It was suggested in the said Despatch that Indians should be made acquainted with the books written by European writers. Wood's Despatch has also credit, of starting the grant-in-aid system, which further encouraged the establishment of secondary schools.

By this time, certain defects had crept in secondary education. In order to remove these defects, Hunter Commission suggested in 1882, that the education of High School should be devised into 2 parts (a) 'A' Course which should be for those students, who wish to take admission in universities to receive higher education and (b) 'B' Course, which should be made more practical and which should prepare young men for professional and non-literary works. Neither the Government nor the people paid any heed to the recommendation of Hunter Commission. Consequently, the secondary education continued to expand in its former way. This process of expansion continued from 1882 to 1902. There were 3,916 secondary schools in 1902. The number of secondary schools increased to 5,124 in 1902.

From 1904 to 1917. Indian Universities Act of 1904 empowered the universities which desired to send their students for matriculation examination, thus, a restriction was imposed upon the secondary schools because they could not send their students for matriculation examination without obtaining recognition from the University. Consequently, many undesirable secondary schools had to be closed down and new schools were established after considering all the facts and circumstances thus created.

From 1917 to 1947. The Calcutta University Commission which was appointed in 1917 made a study of the defects of the secondary education and arrived at a conclusion that unless and until the secondary education would not be re-organized after removing its defects, it would not be possible to make any sort of reform in the University education. The said Commission recommended the establishment of a Board of Secondary and Intermediate Education in each Province. This was a novel thing, which was made for the first time by this Commission.

In 1929, Hartog Committee accepted that as compared to the education of common people, secondary education had made more progress. However, the Committee added that because of large number of failures in matriculation examination, the rate of wastage in secondary education was very high. In 1936-37, Abbott and Wood suggested in their report that upto the stage of High School, Indian language should not be given in literary form. The Sargent Report of 1944 also made many important suggestions in regard to secondary education, such as high school course should be made of 6 years, no students below the age of 11 years should be admitted in high school.

In spite of the suggestions made by the above mentioned Committees and Commissions, no restrictions were imposed on secondary education and it continued to expand in an unrestricted manner. The number of secondary schools, which was 2,953 in 1916-17 increased to 4,883 in 1947-48.

Scene after Independence

Several Committees and Commissions have been appointed in the post independence era. The prominent among them are being described below:

Tara Chand Committee 1948. One of the important suggestion of the Committee was that secondary school should be multi-lateral but keeping in view the local conditions and circumstances unilateral schools should also be encouraged. This Committee also recommended that a Commission should be appointed in order to investigate the problems of secondary education.

University Education Commission, 1948-49. The chief aim of this Commission was to investigate and make suggestion in regard to university education. But it also considered different aspects of the secondary education and made many important suggestions. In the opinion of the University Education Commission, the secondary education was the weakest link in the whole structure of education. The Commission recommended that students should be admitted in the university only after completing 12 years of study in school or intermediate college.

Secondary Education Commission, 1952-53. As a result of the suggestions of Tara Chand Committee and Central Education

Advisory Board, Secondary Education Commission was appointed to study in detail the different aspects of secondary education and to make different suggestions to reform it. We have already discussed in detail in an earlier chapter the different suggestions made by this Commission to reform secondary education in India.

The Evolution

The development of secondary education has received an impetus after the attainment of independence. At present, secondary education is free in Andbra Pradesh, Gujarat, Karnataka, Uttar Pradesh, Kerala, Tamil Nadu, Andaman & Nicobar Islands, Arunachal Pradesh and Lakshadweep and in Government institutions in Jammu and Kashmir, Nagaland, Dadra and Nagar Haveli and Pondicherry. It is free for girls in Madhya Pradesh, Manipur, Orissa, Rajasthan and Tripura.

Under the new educational policy of 1986 emphasis was laid on the new educational policy and for the formal education National Open Schools were established. In 1992 a new workshop scheme was introduced.

Open Schools are contributing a lot in the field of secondary education. By the end of 1992-93, 305 Navodya Vidyalaya came into existence. 17 more were to be established in 1993-94. It was proposed that by the end of 1996, there shall be atleast one Navodya Vidyalaya in every district.

Difficulties and Remedies

Many defects have crept in the secondary education that if they are not solved within a short period of time, the progress of Indian education will receive a great set-back. We will now attempt to discuss the different problems of secondary education and their solution.

Aimlessness. One of the chief problems of secondary education is its aimlessness. It would not be improper to remark that the aim of education in independent. India is the same which was before independence. Education is acquired only with the aim so that the students may get employment or for getting admission in an institution of higher education, which is also sought with the aim of getting employment

Definite Aims. In order to make the secondary education successful and effective, it is necessary to determine its aim. So long as the aims of this education are not property determined, its utility will continue to be doubtful. Now, the question arises what should be the aim of secondary education? The first and foremost requirement for this is that the secondary education should be made an independent unit and not complimentary of higher education. Thereafter, the following aims of secondary education should be determined:

(i) To make students skilled in some work after completion of their education.

(ii) To increase their professional and productive powers.

The secondary Education Commission determined the following aims of Secondary Education:

(a) Development of democratic citizens

(b) Increase in professional skill

(c) Development of personality

(d) Development of leadership.

Unsuitable Curriculum. The curriculum of secondary schools is unsuitable because of being single track. All the students have to study one pre-fixed curriculum. The students do not get opportunity to select subjects according to their interests and desires. Besides this, their curriculum is not related to the environment and practical life. We observe that many political, economic and social changes are taking place in the country but our education in general and secondary education in particular has failed to keep pace with the changes. The curriculum does not appear to be related with the practical life. The pupils read the traditional curriculum, without interest, understanding or appreciation. Their chief aim is to get through the examinations.

Interesting and Diversified Curriculum. In order to remove the defects of the curriculum, it is necessary that it should be extended in different trades, professions and agricultural subjects should be included in it and the help of the experts should be taken in order to cater the interest and aptitude of the students. With these aims in view, the Secondary Education Commission recommended the diversification of courses and in this connection made the following suggestions:

(i) The curriculum should be such as may develop the different abilities and capabilities of the students.

(ii) The curriculum should be diversified and flexible so that it may be according to the needs and intersts of the students.

(iii) The curriculum should be closely related to the social life of the students.

(iv) The curriculum should be such so that the students may not only be encouraged to work but also to make proper use of leisure.

(v) The curriculum should not include such subjects as are not related to each other. Although the subjects of the curriculum should be inter-linked with each other.

Indiscipline. Indiscipline is yet another main problem of the modern secondary education. It is not proper to accuse only the students of being indisciplined. In fact, the present educational system, examination system, aimless education etc. are the factors which are responsible for the indiscipline among the students. It may be mentioned here that the indiscipline among the students is increasing so far that if something is not done to remedy this evil, it will not only be harmful for the students but would jeopardise the whole education system.

There are various factors involved in the causation of indiscipline. Chief among them are as follows: (1) Loss of higher spiritual values, (2) Political changes, (3) Defective mode of examination, (4) Wretched economic condition of teachers.

Besides this, the role of teachers is also of paramount importance. According to Prof. Humayun Kabir, "If education trains the future citizen, it also determines the shape of future society, the value of such education depends upon the character and competence of the teachers who impart it that is why the fate of society depends on the quality of its teachers. It is no exaggeration to say that incompetent and dissatisfied teachers undermine the very foundation of society.

Suggestions. As pointed out earlier, students alone cannot be held responsible for the growing indiscipline among them. Those who hold students alone responsible for this evil, have not cared to consider all the aspects of this problem. Political movements are, to a great extent if not wholly, responsible for the growing indiscipline among the students. Low social values have also influenced the students as the members of the society. Besides this, economically hard pressed teachers have left thinking as to which direction the students society is proceeding to. In addition to this, obscene films, film songs, racialism, favouritism, indifferent attitude of the persons, etc. have also led to the growing indiscipline among the students.

If we want to remove wide-spread indiscipline among the students, we will have to give proper attention to the above mentioned factors which are responsible for growing indiscipline among the students. This herculian task can be achieved only when the government, people and guardian jointly take active and constructive measures in this connection.

Undesirable Growth of Private Schools. After the attainment of independence, there has been an unprecedented increase in the number of secondary schools in the name of expansion of education. But this increase has not only proved to be undesirable but has proved to be scourge for the students, teachers and ultimately for the country. Most of these schools are the private properties of some particular caste, political party or capitalists and casteism, favouritism, etc., are rampant in these schools. We can easily have idea of the discipline of such schools, standard of teaching and the character of the students and the teachers.

Abolition of Private Schools. Private schools are a slur on the fore-head of secondary education. It is necessary to remove this slur as soon as possible. Only the Government is capable of performing this work and nationalisation of education is the only way through which (his slur can be removed. But at present, nationalisation of the entire secondary education does not appear practicable. However government can regulate the management and administration of private institutions. In this connection the Raghukul Tilak committee had recommended that in order to improve the management of private institutions, the managing committees must include one representative of teachers and three other members nominated by the Education Department

Low Standard of Teaching. Low standard of teaching is also one of the chief problems of the secondary education. Government has mainly concentrated their attention towards the expansion of education and have not devoted their proper attention towards the qualitative progress of education. The teachers do not get sufficient salaries to meet their daily needs and requirements. Unless the teachers are given proper facilities and are given the place of respect in society, we cannot hope good performance. Besides this, there are many schools which do not have sufficient funds to make proper provision of building and other necessary things connected with education. These short-comings have also adversely affected the standard of teaching.

Suggestion. To talk of raising the standard of teaching only by spending the money is to build a castle on the sand. The standard of teaching can be raised by taking into consideration many factors, which have been mentioned earlier. The Government should appoint such Inspectors, who would make their contributions in this connection and should make necessary suggestions. Besides this, the teachers should be sent to training colleges from time to time in order to acquaint them with latest teaching methods. It is also necessary that only enthusiastic persons and the persons who wish to dedicate themselves for the service of the society should be selected for the teaching work. They should also be encouraged from time to time by giving them rewards for their meritorious work in this connection.

Shortcoming of Examination System

The system of examination of our secondary education is full of defects. There is the domination of matriculation examination over the whole secondary education. A school, its teachers and its students are tested in accordance with their success in the examination. Examination is not the real test of knowledge of the student and the working capacity of the teacher. According to S.N. Mukeqee "Worse than India's Communality ridden, social and political system is her examination-ridden educational system. In fact, the matriculation Examination dominates the entire work of our secondary schools. The prestige of a school depends entirely upon matriculation results and very little on real education merits of the institution."

New Trends

The suggestions made by the Secondary Education Commission are really praise-worthy. The Commission made the following suggestions to reform the present examination system:

(i) Number of external examinations should be reduced.

(ii) The method of the questions asked in the examination should be changed in such a way so that they may not remain merely essay type.

(iii) While making the final evaluation of the work of the students along with the internal examinations, proper importance be given to the periodical tests, and school records.

(iv) The public examination of the students should be taken only after the completion of the whole curriculum of the secondary schools.

If the suggestions made by the Secondary Education Commission are properly implemented, the defects of the modern examination system can be removed.

Community Life in Existence

There is absence of well-organised community life in the secondary schools of the modern period. The main reason for this is that the sports and games, excursions, physical exercises, social activities etc. which may establish "lose contacts among the students, are not organised in the schools. Besides this, there is total absence of religious and moral education in the schools. Thus, the schools of modern time have just become a factory whose aim is to make the students pass the matriculation examination.

The schools should be the centres of community life. Mudaliar Commission has rightly remarked, "School is a small community within a large community and the attitude, values and modes of behaviour which have currency in national life are bound to be reflected in the school." In fact, school has an idealist epitome of community life. Hence, schools should be a place which should reflect the elements of all the useful activities of the community.

Vocational Problems

For many years, our secondary education is single track. Neither is there diversification in its curriculum, nor has it given any importance to vocationalisation. The form of curriculum which was fixed by the British Rulers keeping in view their own interest generally continues to be the same even today.

Various Provisions

There is great need of vocationalisation of secondary education. The Secondary Education Commission has remarked, "Secondary Education should be vocationalised in a large measure and enrolment in vocational course rest to 20 per cent of total enrolment at the lower secondary stage and 50 per cent of total enrolment at the higher secondary stage by 1986." Kothari Commission also suggested, "The link between education and productivity can be forged through vocationalisation of education especially at the secondary school level." The following suggestions may go a long way to bring about the vocationalisation in secondary education.

(i) Money should be taken from all the rich persons of the country in the form of education cess.

(ii) 50 per cent of the money thus obtained should be contributed by the Central Government and the rest 50 per cent contributed by the State Government.

(iii) In order to impart education of vocational subjects, persons of different profession of the district and the country should be invited from time to time. In this way, problem of the salary of the teachers can be solved for some time.

(iv) The student should be given opportunities for acquiring practical knowledge in the professions which are carried on in the neighbourhood of the school. In this way, the expenditure to be incurred on establishment of different types of workshop in the schools can be saved for some time. If the Government is not prepared to take full responsibility for giving the implements to the students learning different vocations then at least it should make full endeavours to do so. This will attract the students towards professional courses.

School Management

At present three types of secondary schools are imparting education at the secondary stage:

(i) Government school

(ii) District Board and Municipal school

(iii) Schools run by private bodies.

The number of Government schools is comparatively far less than the number of schools run by private bodies. The main cause of this is that instead of taking the responsibility of education the Government has been encouraging the establishment of schools by giving some grant-in-aid to the schools run by private bodies. As compared to the Government schools, the condition of the District Board and Municipal schools is very miserable. So far as the question of schools run by private bodies is concerned, they are run on the principle of business and are the definite means of income of their managers. Since they are run on profit basis, they cannot be expected to render the real service for the cause of education.

Role of Government

The above mentioned problem can be solved if the

Govenomnet takes over the management of all the non-Government schools by making necessary laws in this connection. If this is not done in the near future, this problem would go on multiplying and would cause irreparable loss to the cause of secondary education.

We have discussed in brief the chief problem of secondary education. It need not be over emphasized that these problems should be solved within the earliest possible time. Unless this is done in the near future, it is futile to hope reformation in higher secondary education and subsequently the progress of the country.

8
Elementary Education

History of the Development of Primary Education- We can study the history of development of primary education in India in two parts : (a) Primary education before the commencement of the system of compulsory primary education, and (b) Compulsory primary education.

The History

From 1757 to 1813. After the battle of Plassey (1757), the East India Company started its campaign of expanding its empire and from that time a new chapter started in the history of Indian education. Although by that time the condition of Indian education had become miserable because of the widespread discontent and anarchy, yet there was a net work of educational institutions in the whole of India, which had become a part of social and cultural life of the people. There were about one lac educational institutions in Bengal only. But the Britishers crushed and completely shattered the Indian education in order to establish their trade monopoly and political ownership.

From 1813 to 1854. The modern educational system was started in India by the Christian Missionaries. They built up primary, secondary and higher educational institutions. Indian education was disregarded and ignored under the rule of East India Company. The charter of 1813 provided that at least one lac rupees was to be spent every year on the revival of Indian literature and expansion of scientific studies. But even this amount, which was not at all sufficient for so vast a population, could not be properly used for a period of 10 years. From 1824, some amount was sanctioned for education but it could not fulfil the needs of the education of Indians.

From 1854 to 1857. It was accepted in Wood's Despatch of 1854 that the education of the common people had been completely ignored and disregarded. Wood's Despatch, therefore, suggested that provision should be made to impart practical and useful education to the common people. The number of primary schools should be increased. Native schools should be encouraged through grant-in-aid system. But the officials of East India Company ignored the primary education and spent more money on secondary and higher education. Consequently, the primary education could not make any progress.

From 1857 to 1882. Stanley's Despatch of 1850 recommended that the Government of India should take up the responsibility of primary education and advised that the Government should impose local taxes to bear the expenditure of education. Consequently, primary education made some progress during this period.

From 1882 to 1905. According to recommendations of Indian Education Commission of 1882, the management of primary education was transferred to the local institutions. This new system undoubtedly led to some progress but it cannot be called satisfactory. The real position was that by transferring the responsibility of primary education to the local institutions, the Government wanted to get rid of this responsibility. Lord Curzon, the Governor General of India, admitted that primary education was so far ignored and disregarded by the Government. He wrote: "I am one of those who think that Government has not fulfilled its duty in this respect."

Lord Curzon did praise-worthy works in the field of increasing the number of primary schools and in raising their teaching standards. But the partition of Bengal led to wide-spread discontentment and dissatisfaction among the people and his services in the field of education could not be taken into consideration by the people. At its Calcutta Session of 1905, the Congress decided to launch the National Movement, this Movement created consciousness among the Indians in regard to their rights. The primary education takes a turn from this period and advances towards the stage of compulsory primary education.

Education made Compulsory

Early Efforts. Although no solid efforts were made till the beginning of 20th century in regard to compulsory primary education, yet some Britishers, who were the lovers of education, were inspired to work in the field of intellectual and social development. Some important suggestions were made in regard to compulsory primary education. Baptist Missionary, William Adam, was the first of such liberal persons. Revenue Survey Commissioner of Bombay, Capt. Wingate and educational Inspector of Gujarat and T.C. Hope were the other prominent Britishers who suggested the provision of compulsory primary education but unfortunately, the British rulers did not pay any heed to their suggestions and their suggestions were completely ignored.

Leaders' Role

The National Movement, which was gaining momentum slowly and gradually was bringing about the consciousness among the Indians. The field of education was also influenced by this Movement. Educated Indians, prominent among them being Sir Chimnun Lal Sitalvad and Sir Ibrahim Rahmatallah, started the Movement to make the provision of compulsory education. Since then the movement was limited to Bombay province only, it influenced only the Government of Bombay and in order to investigate the utility of compulsory education in Bombay city, a Committee was appointed in 1906. But unfortunately, this Committee arrived at a conclusion that the provision of the compulsory primary education would not be proper because the people were not prepared for it.

Great Experiment

The king of Baroda, Maharaj Sayaji Rao Gaekwad had the

credit of making the first successful experiment of compulsory education in India. Liberal minded and education-lover king of Baroda declared in 1892 that there would be compulsory primary education in a Talluqa of Amraili City, consisting of 9 villages in his State. All the boys from 7 to 12 years of age and all the girls from 7 to 10 years of age were to receive education in primary schools. This provision was started from November 18, 1893 and met with such an astonishing success that it was extended to 52 villages of the said Talluqa. Thereafter, primary education was made compulsory for all the children of the State by the Act of 1906.

Being inspired with the feeling of nationalism, Gopal Krishna Gokhale presented a Resolution in the Imperial Legislative Assembly in regard to primary education. The Resolution suggested to take steps for making primary education free and compulsory throughout India. On being assured by the Government to consider over the said Resolution, Gokhale withdrew his resolution but the Government did not even dream of giving practical form to its assurance. After seeing the attitude of the Government towards the primary education, Gopal Krishna Gokhale submitted a bill in 1911, in the Imperial Legislative Assembly in regard to primary education. The bill aimed to implement the principle of compulsory primary education through stages. According to this bill, compulsory primary education could be started by seeking prior consent of the Local Councils of their areas where a definite number of children from 6 to 10 years of age were receiving education. But the efforts of Gokhale could not succeed. His bill was strongly opposed in the Imperical Legislative Assembly, and was defeated by 38 to 13 votes on March 19, 1892.

Law for Compulsory Education

Being inspired by the efforts of Gokhale, another great leader, Vithal Bhai Patel presented a bill in the Provincial Legislative Assembly of Bombay. The aim of this bill was to introduce compulsory primary education in the municipal areas of the province. The said bill became an Act in 1918 and was called Bombay Primary Education Act. This was the fast act, which accepted the principle of compulsory primary education by the Government of a Province. This was the pioneer of the revolution in the field of education. Consequently, by the year 1930, almost all the provinces passed the Acts in regard to compulsory primary education. According to these Acts, responsibility of primary education was entrusted to the local institutions. It was the responsibility of these institutions to implement the provisions of these Acts. These institutions were also empowered to impose education cess in order to meet the expenditure to be incurred on education. The Provincial Government also promised financial help to meet the expenditure on education. Only those boys and girls who were ordinarily between the age of 6 to 7 years could take benefit of the provision of compulsory education.

Further Expansion

As a result of Compulsory Education Acts and the feeling of nationalism, the expansion of compulsory education received an impetus. Under the guidance of the father of the nation, Mahatma Gandhi, women also demanded their rights. They organised All India Women Educational Conference in 1927 and demanded the right of receiving education equal to those of men. The efforts of Mahatma Gandhi and Dr. Ambedkar not only brought about consciousness among the Harijans but they also went a long way to expand the education. Because of the efforts of these great leaders, the people started taking interest in primary education. Fortunately for India, the organisation of the provincial education came into the hands of Indian Ministers and Government contributed much for the expansion of primary education.

This progress of compulsory primary education continued till 1930 but thereafter from 1931 to 1937 the development of compulsory education received a set-back. There were two main reasons for this. The first cause of this set-back was the world-wide economic depression, which also influenced India. Hence, it was quite natural that the expensive schemes of compulsory education were postponed. Secondly, the Hartog Committee which was appointed in 1927, emphasised that instead of aiming the quantitative increase in primary education special attention should be given to the qualitative progress of primary education and the policy of consolidation of education should be followed. In spite of great opposition of the people, the Government implemented the suggestions of this Committee, which brought about a set-back in the expansion of compulsory education.

At the time of provincial autonomy in 1937, Congress Ministries were formed in 6 out of 11 provinces. The Congress made vigorous efforts to expand compulsory primary education in their provinces. They established primary schools in those villages, where there were no primary schools. Local institutions were given additional grants so that they could meet the expenditure in making the primary education compulsory. Gut's schools were also opened at the places where people demanded it. These efforts of the Congress Ministries led to a great expansion of compulsory education. By the time independence was achieved, provision had been made for compulsory education of boys in 229 cities and 10,017 villages for girls in 10 cities and 1404 villages.

After Independence

The independent India felt the great need of expansion of education at all stages and specially at the stage of primary education. Therefore, the national Government took active and sincere steps to make the primary education free, universal and compulsory. The principle of compulsory education was declared through Article 45 of the constitution of India. It was also made clear that this education would be of basic type. On this basis, Board of National Education was established. Our Government has been making vigorous efforts to expand compulsory primary education in all corners of the country. Under the different Five-year plans, huge amount has been spent for the development of Primary Education.

Difficulties and Remedies

For the expansion of Primary education, the Central Government has been giving the financial help to the Provincial Governments. The States which intend to expand primary education are given 34 per cent of the total annual expenditure in this connection in the form of financial help. Thus, we see that the primary education has made a great progress, but because of certain reasons it cannot be said to be encouraging and satisfactory. The main reason for this is that there are many problems and difficulties in the field of primary education, which are creating obstacles. We will now discuss the different problems and their solution.

Education Policy: Various Angles

It was made clear in 1950, in the Constitution of the independent India that within a period of 10 years from the commencement of the Constitution, States shall endeavour to provide free and compulsory education to all children until they complete the age of 11 years. It is a matter of great regret that the Government has not achieved complete success in this regard. In 1950-51, 42.6 per cent of the children of the age-group of 6 to 11 years were receiving education. This percentage increased to 83.6 by 1979-80. Similarly in 1950-51, 12.7 per cent pupil in the age group 1-4 were receiving education while this percentage was 4.02 in 1979-80. Till date, the percentage of the children receiving education between the age group of 6 to 11 years is 83 while that of age group of 11 to 14 is 63.

These statistics clearly indicate that the Government has not been able to achieve the prescribed goal. The main cause for this is that the policy of the Government is based on idealism. Basic education has been accepted as the form of national education. Being inspired with this aim, work has been started to convert primary schools into basic schools. But in a country like India which has a vast population and where there is too much shortage of money, the implementation of the expensive scheme of basic schools is difficult. The Government has also accepted the gravity of this problem and has admitted that it is not possible to implement the scheme of basic education in the whole of India within a short period. But, still the Government has been spending most of the money on basic education. In such a situation, we may say that Government policy is based on idealism and is not taking active steps to expand primary education by adopting a practical and realistic attitude.

The first and foremost necessity is this that the Government should first evolve a definite education policy. The Government has already admitted that the national education will be basic type of education. But along with this, it has also been admitted by the Government that it is not possible to implement the scheme of basic education in the whole country within a short period.

In such a situation, the best policy can be that expansion of compulsory education and basic education should be separated from each other. Whatever education that is being imparted in primary schools should be made compulsory. Slowly and gradually according to convenience, primary education should be converted into basic education. If the Government does not build its compulsory educational policy on this principle, it is futile to hope that compulsory education would be universal in the near future.

Political Factors

So far the Government has not been able to devote its full attention towards removing the political difficulties. The main reason for it is that since the attainment of independence the Government had to face many problems and many of them still exist, e.g. the problem of native States, the problem of the refugees, the problem of Kashmir, the problem of different linguistic States, the problem of 100% the problem of China etc.

Government's Role

The political problems that we have mentioned above are mostly such which still exist and may continue to exist for a long time. It is also possible that the Government may have to face some more problems in the near future. However, this does not mean that the Government should not pay proper attention towards public education. If the Government is responsible to solve the political problems of the country, the Government is also duty-bound to solve the problem of public education. In spite of the fact that the Government has to face so many problems, the indifference of Government towards education cannot be justified by any means. Some scholars have even remarked that the political situation also demands that the Government should implement the scheme of compulsory, free and universal education within the shortest possible time. According to K.G. Saiydain, "While the political situation demands the immediate introduction of the scheme, the politicians are not keen enough to take it up." The Government can be exonerated of this charge only when they devote their proper attention and perform their duties towards the expansion of primary education. Nothing less than this will satisfy the people.

Shortcomings of Administration

In most of the States of India, the responsibility of the primary education is on the municipalities and the district boards. At the time when the responsibility and the work of primary education was entrusted to these institutions, it was hoped that these institutions will speed up the work of the expansion of primary education. In the course of time, however, it has become clear that these institutions have not risen equal to the occasion. Ordinarily, there is lack of working capacity, interest and money in these institutions. All the Acts relating to compulsory education have become out of date. There is no such central institution or power which may compel these institutions to implement these Acts.

The Reforms

In fact, it is the responsibility of the nation to educate its citizens. It is, therefore, necessary that the Government of India should take upon itself the sacred work of primary education. If on account of some reasons, the Government cannot shoulder the responsibility, then it should establish such a powerful central institution, which may compel the district boards and the municipalities to start the work of compulsory primary education in their respective areas within a definite period.

Need for Good Teachers

Yet another problem of primary education is the non availability of the desired number of really trained teachers. This poses a very difficult and serious problem before the Government. As compared to the city schools, there is great shortage of such teachers in village schools.

Teachers' Recruitment

As pointed out earlier, the desired number of really trained teachers are not available for making education compulsory but this problem can be solved. In the beginning, the teachers of essential qualification can be selected as teachers, no matter whether they are trained or not. Thereafter, a definite number of teachers from among the above mentioned teachers can be encouraged to increase their qualifications or they can be sent to training schools to undergo the training on Government expenses. It cannot be a wise step to wait for making the education compulsory till the time when the desired number of trained teachers may be available. It is rather more essential that the salaries of the teachers should be increased. They should be provided more facilities and they should be attracted towards teaching work by conferring upon them more honour and respect

Teaching Standards

There is a great shortage of really trained teachers in primary schools. Besides this, the primary schools are not using the proper and necessary implementation of teaching due to shortage of money. It is because of these reasons that the education is uninteresting and its standard is low. Hence, it fails to attract children and their guardians.

Training and Grants

The first essential requirement that is necessary to raise the standard of teaching is that only trained teachers should be appointed in primary schools. To implement this, it is necessary that the number of training schools should be increased. It should also be kept in mind that the training schools should be established not only in the urban areas but also in the rural areas so that men and women of the neighbouring places may be attracted to receive training in them at less expense. Probably, it would be the best if the Government or local boards meet the whole expenditure of the training of the teachers. It may, however, be added that it would be only sheer imagination that only the appointment of trained teachers would raise the standard of teaching. It is also necessary that the primary schools should be given liberal grant-in-aid to enable them to purchase teaching implements. Enthusiastic and trained teachers generally find themselves unable to do much due to lack of the necessary means of education.

Financial Problems

Dearth of money is yet another serious problem that confronts the primary schools. During the British period the Government met 30 per cent of the total expenditure incurred on primary education. In the independ India, this amount was increased to 34 per cent. This scanty help given by the Government cannot be said to be adequate for making education compulsory.

Suggestions. The expansion of primary education is not taking place properly due to shortage of money. It has been estimated that if compulsory basic education for the children of 6 to 14 years of age in the whole country is made, it will require an annual expenditure of about Rs 300 crores. To spend so much money on education is beyond the capacity of this poor country. Rupees 93 crores were spent on primary education in the First Five Year Plan but this amount was reduced to 89 crores in the Second Five Year Plan because of need of money for other development work. In the Fourth plan Rs 241.3 crores were spent while the proposed outlay for the Fifth plan was Rs 743.0 crores. The allocation for primary education in the Sixth Five-year plan was 835.73 and in the Eighth Five-year plan it was 920.14.

In the situation of this shortage of money, our aim should not be to achieve qualitative increase in primary education but we should rather make efforts to educate as many children as possible so as to make them get rid of illiteracy. In this connection, Gokhale has rightly remarked, "Primary purpose of mass education is to banish illiteracy. Quality of education is a matter of importance that comes only after illiteracy has been abolished."

Keeping in view this thing it would be desirable to end partially if not completely the expenditure that is being incurred on converting primary schools into basic schools. The emphasis should first be laid on the compulsory education and not in the form of basic education. Some Indian educationists are of the view that the expenditure of primary education can be met by reducing the term of primary education upto 4 years. Australia, Germany, Japan, Egypt, China and Russia expanded primary education among the common people by fixing the term of primary education for 4 years. Sri Desai, an eminent Indian educationist, has suggested that in order to reduce the expenditure of compulsory education, fees should be taken from the children of rich persons and private primary schools should be allowed to take fees from the students. If the Government accepts these suggestions, the financial problem of compulsory education can be solved at least to some extent.

School Premises

Another problem in the way of compulsory education is the establishment of schools. It becomes very difficult to solve this problem in villages, if not in cities. India is mainly a rural country but still there are thousands of villages where there are no schools. In order to make the education compulsory, the establishment of Primary Schools is necessary in nearly 4 lakh villages including the villages having a population of less than 500. It is not easy to collect money to establish so many schools. Moreover, it would not be beneficial to establish schools in the villages having population less than 500. This poses a serious and complicated problem before the administrators and educationists of the country.

Allied to the problem of the establishment of schools, there is also the problem of buildings of the schools. At present in our country, there are only 20 per cent such buildings of schools which can be called proper and adequate. The rest of the schools are being run in houses, temples, buildings of rich persons, residence of teachers etc. These schools lack sufficient space for seating all the children much less to talk of their games and sports. Many schools are situated in a very busy locality and undesirable environment. Moreover, these buildings are such that adversely affect the health of the students because of inadequate supply and provision of the sun and the air. These problems can be solved only by building new buildings which require a huge amount of money but as pointed out earlier, it is very difficult to collect the amount needed for building schools.

Suggestions. Following suggestions have been put forward to solve the problem of establishing and building of schools:

(i) The problem of establishing schools in rural areas is very difficult. There is great shortage of money for establishing new schools. Besides this, many villages are small and at distant places. If money can be arranged for building schools, then they should be first built in those villages where they are most urgently required. As regards the small villages, some villages in the middle of them should be selected so that it may be convenient for the children of other villages to attend school there.

(ii) Problem of the lack of teachers and schools can be solved through shift system. Although this system cannot be accepted as an ideal one, yet because of the lack of teachers and school buildings for the present it will be better to adopt this system. According to the shift system, different students can be called to receive education into two shifts. The first shift can be run from 7.30 to 11.30 a.m. and the second shift can the run from 1.00 p.m. to 5.00 p.m. Different countries of the world have adopted shift system in their early stage of expansion of education. The more prominent of such countries are Germany, France, Purtugal, United States of America, Japan etc. Even today, this system is prevalent in Australia, Newzealand, Turkey, Egypt, China, Ceylon, Denmark, etc. This system should be made prevalent in India also. If the time of the shifts is kept, keeping in view the season and the needs of the farmers and the workers, then the problem of establishment of schools and buildings can be easily solved in India. Of course, the teachers will have to work more in this system. But if they are given more salaries they will have no difficulty in taking up this additional work.

(iii) In order to speed up the progress of compulsory education, the Indian educationists have suggested that the number of students in each school should be increased. At present, the teacher has to teach on an average 35 students in each class. In many western countries, each teacher had to teach more than 36 students in the early stages of education. For example, till 1922, the number of students in each class was 60 in England and so was the case in Italy upto 1932. The United Nations Organisation recommended 60 students in the primary classes of China. Therefore, in those primary schools of India where one teacher teaches the students of one class only the number of students can certainly be increased. Of course, in those schools where one teacher teaches more than one class it would not be proper to introduce this system.

Defective Curriculum

The curriculum of the primary school is narrow and unsuitable to the local needs. It, emphasis is given on bookish knowledge and the principle of 'learning by work' to develop the constructive powers of the student is disregarded and ignored. In order to remove these defects of the curriculum, the Government has decided to convert primary education into basic education. This will certainly remove the defects of the curriculum but the expensive scheme of basic education cannot be enforced at one time in the whole country and hence the seriousness of the problem cannot be undermined.

Suggestions. As mentioned earlier, the curriculum of the primary schools is one sided and uninteresting. Because of not being related to the local environments, it has no utility. It is true that by implementing the scheme of basic education, the Government is endeavouring to make the curriculum interesting but this work will take a long time. Therefore, for the time being, the education of crafts should be given in the primary schools in accordance with the local needs and requirements. This will not only increase the interest of the children in education, but they will also be benefitted by the knowledge they thus acquire. It is not necessary that the education of crafts should be imparted by some scholars or trained teachers. The services of local and experienced persons can be utilised to perform this work.

Stagnation and Wastage

Another great obstacle in the expansion of primary education is wastage and stagnation. Out of hundred students of class Ist in 1957-58, only 61 students reacted in class II; in 1958-59, 49 students reached in class III; in 1959-60, 42 students reached in class IV in 1960-61. The percentage of wastage and stagnation in these four classes was 58. The recent studies made in some districts have revealed that the wastage and stagnation in class Ist are 46.5 and 43.9 respectively. The rest of the children left studies either after their failure in the examination or in order to assist their guardians in earning their livelihood. Unfortunately, the lack of buildings, etc. are the reasons because of which the schools fail to attract children to complete their education. It is of utmost importance that the wastage and stagnation in primary education should be checked otherwise there will be no possibility for the success of any scheme of expansion of education.

Suggestions. The problem of wastage and stagnation can be solved through the following ways and means:

(a) Educational system should be reformed.

(b) Teaching method should be made interesting.

(c) Good school-buildings should be built.

(d) The environment inside and outside the school should be reformed.

(e) The curriculum should be reformed.

(f) Educational system should also be reformed.

(g) Efforts should be made to develop the health of the students.

(h) The guardians or the parents should also be educated.

(i) Social problems relating to education should also be solved.

We have simply mentioned some suggestions in brief here because later on we will discuss the problem of wastage and stagnation in detail in a separate chapter.

The Hindrances

There are also natural obstacles in the way of expansion of compulsory education. Because of less population in Himalayan region, Kashmir, Garhwal and Almora etc., the villages in these areas are situated at distant places. So is the case with Rajasthan. Besides this, there are many areas in Madhya Pradesh and South India, which are covered with forest and the population of these places is scattered in small and distant villages. There is lack of means of transport in the above mentioned regions and because of the severe cold, heat or heavy rains, their difficulties further increase.

Suggestions. It is very difficult to conquer natural obstacles mentioned above in a big country like India. However, after the attainment of independence, many of these problems have been solved. There has been praise-worthy increase and progress in the means of transport under the Five Year Plans. Roads have been built in many distant villages and the work in large scale is still being done in this connection, but there are many places where the natural obstacles create problems for the children for receiving education. It would be rather more desirable to entrust the responsibility of the education on some local persons in order to avoid the problem of children going to distant places to receive education.

Bad Elements

There is no corner of India which is not infested with social evils such as superstitions, illiteracy, faith in ancient convention and customs, child marriages, untouchability, Pardah system, etc. These social evils create innumerable obstacles in the expansion of compulsory primary education. Without having any regard or care of the Child Marriage Prohibition Act, many persons still marry their boys and girls at a very minor age and deprive them of the fruits of education and knowledge. Although, citizens have been granted the right of equality by law, yet in some schools or the other many Harijan students are still not admitted in many schools. Even today some Hindus and Muslims firmly believe that either girls should be given no education or they should be given only little education. Because of the prevalent pardah system, there are still many persons, who oppose the system of co-education even in primary schools.

Suggestions. It may be suggested that despite the prevalence of these evils, the work of the expansion of education should not be slackened. It should be rather increased because social evils are flourishing because of illiteracy and ignorance. Education develops the mind of the man and his logic power. In the course of tune, education will itself root out all these social problems which appear to be formidable at present. Beside this, the Government and the social workers should try to bring about consciousness among the people in regard to disadvantages because of the prevalence of social evils through the means of pictures, speeches and other such works. Lastly, the educated young men and women should volunteer themselves to remove the social evils around their neighbourhood. This will go a long way to remove social evil from our society.

Significance of Language

Last but not the least is the problem of language. There are about 826 languages and 1952 dialects in the country. It is a serious problem before the administrators and educationists as to which language should be the medium of instruction for the children speaking different languages, and dialects. The Constitution of India mentions 14 languages, which cannot be made the medium of education but there are many other languages, which cannot be given that status.

Suggestions. Kothari Commission has suggested the mother tongue should be the medium of instruction at the primary stage. All the regional languages should be developed. It is also suggested that the teaching of Hindi should be compulsory right from the primary stage so that it can be medium of instruction in all the states in the near future.

Prtoblems of Scheduled Castes

Most of the children of scheduled castes, scheduled tribes and de-notified tribes do not get even the primary education. Though untouchability is prohibited but in remote villages, we still find the caste barriers and children of schedule castes, scheduled tribes and de-notified tribes are subject to hatred and so they are not given due attention.

Schools for Specific Purposes

The establishment of special schools is necessary in the areas where there are the people of scheduled castes and tribes and de-notified tribes. Sufficient attention is being given to this in the independent India. The Government has been taking every possible steps to establish special schools for the students of such tribes and is providing facilities of free education, scholarship, books, writing material, etc. Under the different Five Year Plans huge amount has been invested for the purpose. Although the efforts of the Government are really praiseworthy, but we are disappointed to find that the number of people of scheduled castes and tribes are lagging behind in the field of education. The accountability of education of these castes and tribes who have been staggering under the weight of misery and poverty for centuries should not be left on the Government alone but people should also come forward to assist the Government in this sacred work.

9

Nursery Education

Earlier, In India Pre-primary education was the concern of the family only. It was the duty of parents to impart instructions to their children in the rudiments of their mother tongue and general good behaviour. Now, the families are incapable to shoulder the responsibility and so these things are taught to children at school. Thus, the responsibilities of schools in the field of Primary Education have greatly increased.

Various Levels

Most of the scholars are of opinion that Froebel is the founder of Pre-primary system of education, to 1837, he founded a Kinder-garten school at Blackenberg. This was the beginning of Pre-primary education. Initially the system of Pre-primary education was not so organized as it is today. In the great epic Mahabharata we find the example of Abhimanyu, who was taught the Art of demolishing the Circular Fort while he was in mother's womb. However, with the advent of modern period, in India too, the formal Pre-primary education was begun. For the Pre-primary education we have Proebel's Kinder-garten Montessori system and Nursery system.

Froebel's system of education 'is called the play-way method. In Kinder-garten school, the children of four years of age are admitted. They are taught many things pertaining to good behaviour, through various plays. Children are also taught 3R's, through a psychological method. The first six years of the child's life are very vital. During these years, the child is able to develop many such sentiments which become almost permanent with him. Froebel studied child psychology and made it as the basis of education for children.

Under Montessari System

Mana Montessori was the founder of this system of primary education. In montessori school children from two to six years age are educated. They are imparted education through didactic materials and toys.

Other Schools

Mrs. Margret Macmillan was the founder of Nursery system education. She founded a Nursery school for physical and mental development of children. In Nursery school, children of two to four years of age are admitted. They are provided healthy environment for their development. In these schools, the trained lady teachers are appointed and children get their motherly treatment.

The Pre-primary schools provide good opportunities to young children for their sensory training and education in good conduct and behaviour. In these schools, psychological methods are adopted for the physical and mental development. The impressions and habits acquired during this period of school life last life-long. Pre-primary schools provide medical care, healthy food and healthy environment for physical and character development. Through different types of plays, children acquire many good social traits. Children in these schools are taught language, art, music, dance and rudimentary mathematics on psychological lines.

Scene in India

The system of pre-primary education in India was introduced in the third decade of the twentieth century. By 1952, there were about 330 nursery schools in the country. Upto the end of first Five Year Plan, their numbers rose to 800. Since then their number is increasing day-by-day. At present, there are thousands of pre-primary schools. We find the mushroom growth of such schools. Some of them are of good standard but most of them are befooling the public. Pre-primary schools are individual and voluntary. The government provides very little help to some of the schools. The result is that most of the schools suffer from want of necessary material equipments, good buildings and other facilities. In most of the schools, there are no trained, teachers.

It is most alarming that the utility and importance of pre-primary schools was felt as back as Sargent report of 1944 but the government has taken very little pains for pre-primary education uptill now.

New Experiments and Investigations, As a result of some experiments and investigation, pre-primary education has been divided into the following four stages:

(1) From conception to birth.

(2) From birth to 2 years of age

(3) From 2 to 4 years of age

(4) From 4 to 6 years of age.

From conception to birth, the baby is influenced by the physical and mental dispositions of the expectant mother. So in order to educate baby, mother's welfare is greatly needed, mother welfare centres are established at some places but there are steps to be taken in this field. Through these centres the expectant mothers should be provided good environment inclusive to healthy development of the child.

From birth to 2 years of age, the child learns something under the guidance of the mother. If the mother is healthy and of good nature and culture, the child shall also be influenced by the same. From 2 to 6 years of age, the child should receive education in some good pre-primary school. As we have already said, these types of schools provide the necessary environment for healthy development of children on psychological lines. Children are taught language, music, art, dance, arithmetic, general science along with manners of good behaviour through plays.

Teaching System- In our country, we have adopted the pre-primary system of education on western toes. But the need is that the new techniques suited to our conditions and traditions should be devised. Uptill now we have adopted the Kinder-garten, Montessori and Nursery systems in our pre-primary schools. The need of the hour is that the children should be taught manners and social etiquettes according to our own traditions. So far young children are told stories with themes imbued with European culture. The need is to write new stories with Indian themes. We should not blindly copy the European method but adopt them if they are suited to our culture and tradition.

It is a matter of joy that some pre-primary schools on the montessori lines have started in our country. The Child Education Society of Bhavnagar has been the pioneer in this field. Some other societies have come forward to adopt a new system of nursery education by drawing the best from the Basic and Montessori systems. Sarvodaya Society have also come forward with many good ideas about nursery education. If we embrace a new system of pre-primary education conducive to our society and education, we shall be able to train our babies in the right direction.

10

Professional Streams

Most Required

In modern era, emphasis is given for the inclusion of technical and vocational subjects in the curricula of education. The main cause of this is that the need for vocational and technical education is being greatly felt. Sri Humayun Kabir is of the opinion that the basis of prosperity of any nation is the scientific and vocational education. If this education is successfully imparted in the country, it will certainly achieve progress. The examples of the United States of America, Germany and Japan confirm this view.

In the modern period, here are elements- (1) capital, (2) raw material, (3) materials and (4) technical education are considered the basis of prosperity of a nation. We have to accept without any hesitation that there is lack of capital in India because the foreign rulers have exploited our nation and the natural means of this country have been used by them to their self-interest for a long time. Consequently, India has to face many famines and there prevailed wide-spread poverty in the country. However, our country does not lack raw material and mineral substances. A large quantity of deposits of iron, manganese, oil, eremite, copper, bauxite, mica, etc. are lying in the lands of India. Besides this, there are best means of producing electricity in the country. But the use of these things can be made only when there are large number of persons who have thorough knowledge of technical, vocational subject and different sciences in the country.

In the Science Policy Resolution of Government of India on 4th March, 1958, great emphasis was laid on technical education. It lays, "The wealth and prosperity of nation depend on the qualitative utilisation of its human and material resources through industrialization. The use of human material for industrialization demands its education in science and training in technical skills. India's enormous resources of manpower can only become an asset in the modern world, when trained and educated."

The Background

Technical and Vocational Education in Ancient India. In ancient period, technical and vocational education had expanded greatly in India but this education was not imparted in the schools. The works and professions of different cites were definite, some of these persons had the knowledge of different types of crafts and were engaged in the production of things. Education of different crafts was given by these persons to their sons and disciples. In Muslim period, the form of technical and vocational education was nearly the same as in ancient India.

Detraction of Indian Industries. The technical and vocational education that was being imparted in India in a conventional way was responsible for the progress of different trades and industries. The trades and industries received a major setback under the British rule. The British merchants opened their first factory in Masaullipattam. They acquired political strength after their victory in the battle of Plassey in 1765. From that period to 1947, they ruled unchallenged over the sub-continent of India. A French traveller named Bender who travelled India near about 1700, described the prosperity of Indians during that period. But slowly and gradually, because of the constant exploitation by the British, trades and industries were destroyed and poverty engulfed the majority of Indians. In such a condition, the system of technical and vocational education that was imparted by a father to his son or disciple met with an end for ever. This condition continued for a long time. Thereafter, the condition began to change slowly and gradually.

From 1882 to 1902. The national leaders of India were of firm conviction that technical and vocational education was utmost necessary to remove poverty from the country. This demand was made by the congress in its Session which was held in the year 1887. Later on, the demand was repeated again and again in other Sessions. But the British Government continued to reject this demand because of their vested interest. In 1902 there were only 80 technical and vocational schools out of which only few could be called really technical schools.

From 1902-1921. During this period also, the Government of India did not pay any attention towards technical and professional education. Of course, much was done by accepting the recommendation of Sadler Commission of 1917. Technical and vocational subjects were also included in the curricula of high schools in different provinces.

From 1921-1937. After the establishment of the dual rule in 1921, demand of the people for technical and vocational education received great momentum. It was demanded that the provision of this type of education should be made in India. In order to take a decision in this matter, a special Committee under the Chairmanship of Lord Lytton was entrusted this work.

This Committee studied the problems and difficulties of the Indian students, studying 111 foreign countries and made many suggestions to remove them. The most important suggestion of the committee was that the technical, vocational and industrial institutions should be established in India and provision should be made for imparting higher education to Indians in their own country. Hence, it was necessary that different branches of this type of education should be developed within the shortest possible period.

The institutions that were established in consequence of this recommendation were the following:

(1) Harcourt Butler Technological Institution, Kanpur.

(2) College of Engineering and Technology, Jadavpur.

(3) Government School of Technology, Madras.

There were nearly 535 technical, vocational and industrial schools in the whole of India in 1937.

From 1937 to 1947. As pointed out earlier, vocational and technical education was totally ignored before 1937, but the expansion of this type of education took place with great speed after 1937. The following were three main reasons for this:

(1) Upto the Second World War, the demand of such persons increased who had acquired technical education.

(2) New industries had been established in India for the production of war material and industrial persons having received technical education were required for these industries.

(3) The demand of persons having received technical education increased for implementing the post development schemes prepared the Central and the Provincial Government.

The expansion of technical education was natural in consequence of the above mentioned reasons. But the expansion of this type of education that took place during this period cannot be called satisfactory because in 1941-42 only 264 students and 22 students were studying in graduate courses of technical education and chemical technology respectively.

From 1947 to 1969. The post independent period witnessed the tremendous progress in the field of technical and vocational education along with the rapid growth of industrialisation in the country. There was the provision of imparting vocational and technical education to only 6,600 students in the year 1947. This number increased to 4,35,796 in the year 1963. Besides this, facilities were also provided to 25,000 students for engineering and technical degree and to 49,000 for diploma in the year 1966.

Vocational and Technical Education during the First Five Year Plan. Special attention was given to the expansion of technical and vocational education during the First Five Year Plan. It was decided to develop Indian Institute of Science, Bangalore, to establish 14 colleges of engineering to make provision of teaching of some special vocational subjects and to establish guidance centres for the students receiving professional and technical education. In addition to this, schemes were also prepared for the establishment of Industrial, Technical and professional schools, conversion of crafts schools into Junior Technical high schools, establishment of Junior multi-purpose schools, development of general secondary schools into technical high schools, giving of proper place to agricultural education in the curriculum, conversion of commercial, vocational and technical schools into colleges and grant of scholarship to the students for receiving higher education in foreign countries. Provision was also made for providing more facilities to impart training to the artists and craftsmen and to establish trained centres in villages.

Second Five Year Plan. In view of the increasing demand of the technical and vocational workers, special importance was given to the expansion of vocational and technical education during the Second Five Year Plan. With this aim in view, 48 crores rupees were allotted for technical and vocational education in the Second Five Year Plan. This sum was more than two times the sum (23 crores) which was granted for this purpose during the First Five Year Plan.

During the Second Five Year Plan, the Indian Institute of Technology, Kharaghpur was completely developed for graduate and post-graduate studies. Provision was made for the study of graduate courses of 1,200 students and post-graduate and research work for 600 students. The Institute of Science, Bangalore was developed for Air and Naval Engineering, Power Engineering, Internal Combustion Metallurgy and Electrical Research and other types of vocational and technical education.

In the centres established for vocational and technical education under the First Five-Year Plan, provision was made for the post graduate course in engineering, technological and research work. The work started under the First Five-year Plan for developing degree during the Second Five-Year Plan. The rest of the money was spent in establishing higher institutions of vocational and technical education in western, northern, southern regions of the country. Two of such types of institutions were established at Bombay and Kanpur.

During the Second Five Year Plan, facilities for the education of engineering and technology in Delhi Polytechnic were expanded.

Besides this, 9 other institutions of degree stage and 20 institutions of diploma stage were established in other parts of the country. The scheme of training of foremen was implemented with the co-operation of industrial institutions. The number of scholarships were increased from 630 to 800. Some seats were reserved for meritorious students in technical and vocational Institutions. Hostels were built for 13,000 technical students and for 3,300, students of Junior technical schools, Indian School of Science and Applied Geology, Dhanbad was further developed and expanded.

In consequence of these efforts, by the end of the year 1960-61, 57,000 graduates and 6,800 diploma holders in the engineering and technical education were made available to the country. This number was doubled and tripled to the number of graduates and diploma holders respectively made available during the First Five year Plan.

Third Five-Year Plan. It was envisaged that 45,000 graduates and 80,000 diploma holders would be required during the Third Five Year Plan. This requirement was nearly fulfited. In order to meet the little shortage of the diploma holders, additional facilities were provided in the beginning of the Third Five-Year Plan. During the period of Third Five-Year Plan, the number of students admitting annually in the degree courses was increased by 6,000 by admitting of 5,000 in engineering colleges and by imparting education to the rest of 1,000 through part time or correspondence courses. Thus, number of students admitted every year increased from 13,200 in 1961 to 19,200 in 1966. Likewise, the number of students admitted in diploma courses was also increased by 15,000 by admitting 10,000 students in Polytechnic and education of the test of 5,000 students through part-time or correspondence courses. Consequently, the number of the students, which was 24,000 at the end of the Second Five Year Plan increased to 9,000 at the end of the Third Five Year Plan. A sum of rupees 142 crores was allotted for implementing the programme of the development of the technical and vocational education.

Fourth Five-Year Plan. During the Fourth Five-Year Plan, an additional capacity of 4,000 seats for degree and 3,400 for diploma courses was created. The other programmes implemented during the Fourth Five-Year Plan increase in number of students in technical schools, expansion of technical schools of diploma stage, establishment of close co-operation between the developing industrial centres with the technical institutes, imparting facilities to technical students to achieve practical knowledge in big industries and facility for part-time and correspondence for the persons engaged in technical jobs.

Fifth Five Year Plan. In the Fifth Plan top priority was given to vocational and technical education, the proposed plan outlay for technical education was Rs 164 crores. It was same in the draft of Fifth Five-Year Plan, "The main stress in the Fifth plan will continue to be on the consolidation and improvement of the quality of the technical education system."

The aim was to provide technical education to 25,000 students at degree level and 50,000 at diploma level. In the draft of the plan, it was said, "The main stress will continue to be on the consolidation and improvement of the quality of the technical education system."

Sixth Five Year Plan. The Janta Government under the Sixth Five-Year Plan (1978-83) allocated Rs 150 crores for the expansion of technical and vocational education. The Congress Government in its revised draft allocated Rs 278 crores for its expansion under the sixth plan.

Under the Sixth Five-Year Plan emphasis was laid on maximum utilization of existing facilities, improvement of technical education at all levels and evaluation of the number of technical hands required in the forth-coming ten years.

Seventh Five Year Plan. Under the Seventh Five Year Plan Rs 681.79 crores were allocated for technical and vocational education. The existing institutions were expanded and hectic programme for vocational education upto higher secondary stage was implemented. Efforts were also made to improve the quality of technical and vocational education.

For the vocationalization, a centrally sponsored scheme was introduced. The scheme was implemented in all the states except

Tripura, Daman & Diu, Dadra and Nagar Haveli and Lakshadweep.

Eighth Five Year Plan. Under the Eighth Five year plan Rupees 278.63 crores were allocated for technical and vocational education. Upto the year 1991, 44,000 technical schools and 12543 technical courses were recognised in which about 6.27 lac students were moulded towards technical education of +2 stage.

National Education Policy

In the educational policy of 1986, a well thought scheme of vocational education was propounded, it was proposed under the 10+2+3 scheme that generally the vocational curriculum shall be started at upper secondary (+2) stage but there will be flexibility to start it from class 8. It was proposed that upto 1990, 10% students and upto 1995, 25% students shall receive vocational education. Upto the end of 1991-92, 12,543 schools were allowed to start vocational courses so that at +2 stage 6.27 lac students may get vocational education which was 9.3% of total number of students enrolled at this stage.

Difficulties and Remedies

We will now discuss the different obstacles and problems and their solutions:

Wrong Attitude. In India from very ancient period a very respectful place has been given to intellectual labour and physical labour has been given a very low place. It was only on the basis of work of labour that the caste system had been built in our country. Youths of higher castes and families are generally indifferent to receive technical education. Consequently, this type of education has not made the desired progress.

Solution. The solution of this problem is not easy. If the Government and the social workers start the movement then the youths of this country can be attracted towards the technical and vocational education, but the movement alone will not bring about the desired results. This will certainly bring about the change in the attitude of the people but only this will not be sufficient. The Government will have to provide facilities for the studies of those students who wish to receive technical education. It is, therefore, necessary that the Government should grant scholarships and make proper provision for their employment after receiving tins type of education. It may be mentioned in the end that with the vigorous efforts of the Government and social workers, a significant change has come in the attitude of the people and now a large number of Indian youths are desirous to receive technical and vocational education. Thus, much has been achieved during post-independent period, but much remains yet to be achieved. We should always remember the words of Carlyle, "Labour is life. The true epic of our times is tools and the man."

Dearth of Institutions. Although many technical and vocational institutions have been established after independence, yet their number cannot be said to be sufficient The awakened Indian people have now realised that the young person receiving technical education have a very bright future. But because of the shortage of such institutions and lack of facilities, 60 per cent of the students are not able to get admission and hence they are greatly disappointed.

Solution. This problem can be solved only when more technical and vocational institutions are established in the country and technical education should be imparted at all the stages. At present there are less than 800 good engineering and technical institutions in the country. These institutions are very few for the country like India having so huge population. It is, therefore, the duty of the Government to establish new technical and vocational institutions to cope up with the increasing demand.

Narrow Curriculum. The curriculum of our technical and vocational schools are very narrow because only technical subjects have been included in them. No place has been given to liberal education in them. Consequently, after receiving technical education, the youths are not able to acquire knowledge of human relation and social objectives of production.

Solution. In order to remove the defects of the curriculum, it is necessary that proper place should be given to general and liberal education in it. This is heartening to note that this problem has attracted the attention of the Government and the curriculum of the technical and vocational institutions are being broadened by including the subjects of general and liberal education.

Unsuitable Medium of Instruction. Yet, another serious problem that confronts technical and vocational education the unsuitability of the medium of instruction. In almost all the technical institutions of the modern India, English is the medium of instructions.

Solution. It may be frankly remarked that in order to solve this problem, administrators and politicians of India will have to give-up the dual policy. They will have to make Hindi or regional languages of different States as the medium of instruction of technical and vocational institutions. Of course, it cannot be denied that many difficulties will come in the way because neither do we have books on technical subjects in Indian languages nor have we evolved a suitable vocabulary for it. But if we firmly resolve to solve it and work sincerely for it, those difficulties will be removed in due course of time. We should emulate the example of other countries such as China, Japan, Russia, Germany where the medium of instruction is not English but their own languages. If it has been possible for these countries to adopt their own languages as medium of instructions, why can it not be possible for India to do the same?

Less Importance of Practical Education. In our technical and vocational schools, importance is given to the theoretical education rather than to practical education. Consequently, the graduates of engineering and technology are generally not skilled in practical works. Hence, they have to face many difficulties and have to depend upon their subordinates and less educated officers to learn practical works. This entails loss of their prestige.

Solution. It is necessary that importance should be given to practical education in our technical and vocational institutions. We should follow the example of technical and vocational institutions of Europe and America in this connection. In these countries, the students are given adequate knowledge of practical works by sending them in workshops, factories etc. and when they enter into their career they do not have to depend upon others.

Lack of Continuation of Education. After having completed their technical and vocational education the young persons are employed in some industries, etc. For some time their minds are full of knowledge which they have recently acquired but slowly and gradually they begin to forget many things. This brings about lack of efficiency in their work. The efficiency of technical personnel depends upon the quality of industrial technical knowledge that he possesses. But he lacks the knowledge, or forgets much of the things that he learned, then his efficiency will naturally decline. This is due to the fact that there is no provision for continuation of education after completion of their education.

Solution. This problem can be solved through the following two methods:

(a) Provision should be made for part-time instruction to the person engaged in technical and vocational works. Prominence should be given only to theory in this education because the persons concerned become efficient in their practical works by doing work in the factories and the workshops in which they are employed.

(b) Another method of solving this problem is through the method of providing refresher courses to such persons. It is remark to suggest here that each skilled or semi-skilled person should be compelled to take benefit of this type of profession at least in a year or once after two years.

Dearth of Teachers. Main problem of technical and vocational education is the dearth of teacher. Kothari Commission was of the view, "The existing shortage of teacher in engineering colleges is disturbingly large." The main reason for this to that the meritorious and able persons, having received technical and vocational education. Besides this, sufficient respect is not accorded to nteleacoers in the society.

Solution. This problem can be solved only by the Government. It is the responsibility of the Government to give due importance to this problem and do the needful to make available the services of good and skilled persons in these institutions. This can be done only when the scales of pay of such teachers are increased and the conditions of their services are improved and made more attractive, for encouraging to note that this problem has attracted the serious consideration of the Government and the Government is making every possible endeavour to solve this problem.

Special attention proposed to be given to solve this problem under the 8th Five-year Plan. It has been decided to increase the faculties of post-graduate courses and research work and the teachers, who have been doing teaching work will be given financial help by the Government to improve their educational qualification. The scales of salaries of such teachers have also been increased but much remains yet to be achieved in this connection.

Role of Kothari Commission

The Kothari Commission has recognized the importance of indust-rialisation and has discussed the steps to be taken for industrialisation and prosperity of the nation. The success of industrialisation depends upon the ability and skill of the workers. Hence, while emphasising the development of vocational, technical and engineering education the Commission has made many important recommendations. According to it, 20 percent of the students after receiving their education at the secondary stage and 50 per cent of the students after receiving education after class X must adopt professional courses by the year 1986. It is clear from the determination of this objective that the Commission laid down a great emphasis on vocational and technical education. We will now briefly discuss the suggestions of the Commission in regard to different aspects of vocational and technical education.

Training of Semi-Skilled and Skilled Workers. In regard to training of semi-skilled and skilled workers, the suggestions of the Kothari Commission are as follows:

(i) Facilities already existing in the industrial training institutions should be further extended and the minimum age of students admitted in these institutions must be of 14 years.

(ii) Junior Technical schools should be renamed as technical High School and they should organise such courses which should be terminal in their nature.

(iii) Emphasis should be given on production in the training given in Industrial Training Institutions and Technical Schools. For training courses of the skilled workers the qualification for admission should be below high school and for proper utilisation of the existing facilities, they should be connected with polytechnic schools.

(iv) For the students who leave schools, faculties should be provided for part-time professional and technical training through Correspondence Courses and Short Intensive Courses, etc.

Technical Training. The Kothari Commission was of the view that the need of technicians is as much as that of engineers for industrialisation. With the aim in view, the Commission has made the following recommendations in regard to the expansion of training for the technicians:

(i) At present the proportion of the technicians and engineers is 1 : 1.4. This should increase to 1 : 2.5 and 1:3 and 1:4 in the year 1975 and 1986 respectively. The curriculum of the technicians should be re-organised and extended.

(ii) More importance should be given to practical works in the schools conducting diploma courses. Emphasis should also be given in industrial experience in diploma courses.

(iii) Polytechnics should be established for industrial schools. In the polytechnic schools established in the rural areas, education connected with agricultural industries should be imparted.

(iv) The teachers of the Polytechnic schools should be appointed from among the workers of the different industries and the educational qualification for the appointment of such teachers should be fixed comparatively lower than other teachers. The salary of the teachers should be based not only on the basis of their ability but due consideration should also be given to their industrial experience.

(v) Training should be imparted to the students in suitable environment. The students and teachers should be encouraged to make small things during vacation to decorate the laboratories of the schools.

(vi) Emphasis should be given on the education of science and mathematics during the first two years in the Polytechnic schools and their curricula should be developed. The subjects of natural psychology and management, costing and estimating etc. should be included in the curriculum of the technicians.

(vii) The curriculum of the Polytechnics should be reorganised under the Fourth and Fifth Five-Year Plans keeping in view the regional and national requirements.

(viii) At certificate and diploma stages in polytechnics, provision should be made for the courses according to the interests of the girls and they should be encouraged to take the subjects after passing the lower secondary stages.

(ix) Every possible effort should be made to check and minimise the wastage taking place in the polytechnics and they should be made more useful.

(x) Provision should also be made for post-diploma courses in some polytechnic schools. Only those technicians should be admitted in these courses who have acquired industrial experience for some years after having passed diploma courses.

Other Types of Vocational Education. In this connection Kothari Commission gave the following suggestion:

(i) Different Types of courses should be introduced at the higher secondary stage. At this stage along with the polytechnics, scientific, commercial and other courses should be organised. Education of home science, nursing, social work, etc. should be imparted to the girls.

Education of Engineers. In regard to the education of Engineers, the Commission has made the following recommendations:

(i) The conditions of such schools connected with the education of engineering whose standard has declined should be improved and they should be converted into the institutions of training of technicians. If their condition has deteriorated beyond repair then they should be closed down.

(ii) For the education of some branches of engineering such as electronics and instrumentation, etc., only able and talented B.Sc. pass students should be selected and their curricula should be properly modified.

(iii) Practical training should be imparted in the third year to the students of degree courses.

(iv) In workshops, emphasis should be given on production works.

(v) The curricula at the degree and diploma stage should be determined keeping in view the changing needs.

(vi) Subjects of courses should be modified according to the advice of the expert committees. The subjects of chemical technology, aeronautics and astronautics should be developed.

(vii) Provision should be made for the organisation of Extensive Summer Institutes for the teachers.

(viii) In engineering colleges, the teachers of science and technological departments should be given the same salaries as are given to the teachers of other departments.

(ix) In order to make the teaching profession attractive, proper scales of pay should be introduced and able Engineers should be encouraged to do research work along with their teaching work.

(x) The system of frequent transfers of teachers in Government Engineering Colleges should be stopped.

(xi) In technical institutions, teaching and training programmes should be organised on extensive basis for graduates and post- graduate students.

(xii) Conventionally should have no place in the post-graduate course. The students admitted at the post-graduate stage most possess at least one year's industrial experience.

(xiii) Special courses of higher stage should be organised of national level.

(xiv) The system of admitting students in engineering schools by taking money should be completely abolished.

Man-power requirement. Provision and organisation of vocational, technical and engineering education should be made keeping in view the requirement of man-power. The wastage taking place in this education should be checked and the interesting distinction and discrimination on socio-economic background should be removed.

Medium of Instruction. At the Polytechnic stage, regional languages should be made the medium of instructions. At the higher stage, the medium of instruction can be determined keeping in view the conveniences of the students. Provision should be made for preparation of good text-books in regional languages.

Practical Training. For practical training scheme, the selection of the students and the trainees should be properly made. The number of training centres should be increased. If on account of some reasons, some public apprentice schools are being closed, then the Central Government should take them into their own hands.

Co-operation with Industries. In the view of the Kothari Commission, co-operation of the industries is necessary for vocational, technical and engineering education. At present, more than 3000 trainees are receiving training in different industrial institution. Their number should be increased to 5000, the Central Government should render necessary help to the industrial institutions so that they may appoint able training officers, who may impart best type of training to the student trainees.

Correspondence Courses. The Kothari Commission was of the view that the work of imparting vocational, technical and engineering education through correspondence courses should be immediately started. However, the Commission hastened to add that complete and proper arrangements should be made before the start of the work and these courses should be started only after properly testing preparations and arrangements.

Administration of Vocational. Technical and Engineering Education- In this connection, the commission has made the following suggestions:

(i) An institution such as University Grants Commission should be established for this type of education, in which representation should be given to vocational, organisational, industrial institutions and concerning ministries.

(ii) This institution should work in co-operation with Planning Commission and the Institute of Applied Man-Power Research.

(iii) The Industrial Institutions should be accorded the status of universities but their individual names and special features should not be changed.

(iv) The Directorate of Technical Education should be established in each State under the Board of School Education.

(v) Eminent educationists should be appointed on the post of the President of the Board of Governors in Regional Engineering Colleges.

(vi) The Principals of the colleges should have full authority to provide educational facilities in their institutions.

11

Female Education

The women of any country have a significant contribution in the progress of the country. It is the women who are capable of building such children who may lead the country to the path of progress and prosperity. Educated women makes the family and the society cultured. Munu has therefore rightly remarked that God resides at the places where women are worshipped. By worship of women we do not mean the worship through conventional means, but we mean where women are respected, proper provision of education made for them and they are given freedom equal to those of men in the society. The utmost expansion of women education is necessary for the achievement of all-sided development of India.

The Background

Ancient Period. In ancient India, education of women had made a great progress. Women not only studied the Vedic literature, but famous women such as Maittreyee, Gargi, Ghosha, Lopa Mudra, etc. had themselves composed Vedic verses. Women of the ancient period had acquired great knowledge in different Shastras and sometimes they not only participated in the Shasthraths (learned discourses) equal to those of men but also acted as judges or mediators. According to Upanishads, being confused with sharp question of Gargi, Yajnavalkya had requested her not to ask questions and Mandan Misra's wife Bharti had acted as a mediator in the 'Shastrarths' that took place between Mahdan Misra and Shankaracharya.

After the Vedic period, the Education of women received encouragement during the Buddhist period also. Scholars are even of the view that it is the Buddhists who have the credit of making the first organised effort in the field of women-education because they made proper provision of education for the Buddhist female monks. But this condition of women-education could not continue for a long time. After the decline of Budhism, when the revival of Hmduism started, women education received a major setback became Shankaracharya, the leader of the movement of the Revival of Hinduism, was against the Education of women.

Medieval Period. After the establishment of the rule of Muslims in India, Parda system became prevalent both among the Muslims as well as Hindus. The system of child-marriage also became very much prevalent among the Hindus. Hence, only the few gifts acquired some knowledge in their early childhood and most of the women were all together deprived of higher education. There was however, the provision of education for the women of royal families and rich persons at their houses. There was no provision for the education of common girls and women. That is why, only a few famous women such as Razia Begum, Gulbadan, Noor Jahan, Jahan Ara, Zebunnisa, Muktabai, Jijabai etc. could acquire higher education and learning.

East India Company and the British Rule. After the Muslims, East India Company established its rule over India, since the Company did not require educated women in its offices, it showed an apathy and indifference towards education of women. The description of the primary schools made by Munro and Adams makes it obvious that there was provision of education of only boys in primary schools.

Only some individual efforts were made for expansion of women education and the first important endeavour was made in this connection in 1818 at Chinsura. But the school which was started at Chinsura had to be closed after sometime on account of certain reasons. However, there are evidences to show that in 1851, 371 girl's schools were being run by Protestant Missionaries and total number of girls studying in these schools was 11,293. Nearly 2,274 girls were also living in hostels.

Likewise some schools were also organised by Roman Catholic Missionaries. Some Government and non-government educational institutions had also been established. Among such schools, a Girls', schools started by Sri J.E.D. Bethune, President of the Education Board of Bengal, in 1849, deserves special mention. He himself met the whole expenditure of this school. In Bombay, Deccan Education Society was also making vigorous efforts for the expansion of women education. Despite all these efforts, the Government was still indifferent and apathetic towards the education of women. Bombay and Madras Universities did not allow women candidates to appear at the entrance examination for a long time. This restriction continued till 1876, 1877 and 1883, in Madras, Calcutta and Bombay respectively. It may also be mentioned that Wood's Despatch of 1854 bad also advised the Government to come forward to shoulder the responsibility of women education. But the Government did not do much in this field except establishing a few girl's schools.

In 1858, the British Government took upon itself the direct responsibility of the administration of India. But inspite of this, the Government did not pay any attention towards the education of women in this country. Hunter Commission of 1888 did not make any important suggestion in regard to the education of women because neither did it recommend the Government patronage in the field of women education nor 'did it emphasise compulsory education of girls. Thus, the education of women could not make any significant progress till 1902 A.D. In 1902, there were only 12 colleges, 457 secondary schools and 5,628 primary schools in which nearly 4,47,470 girls were receiving education. However, the Indians realised the need and importance of the education of women and made some-significant work in this connection. The establishment of Maharashtra Women Education Committee in 1883 at Bombay should be reckoned as a land mark in this connection. Important contributions were also made in the establishment of girls' schools by Arya Samaj of Swami Dayanand in North and Western India, by Brahma Samaj in Bengal and by Professor Karve and Ramabai in Bombay.

Lord Curzon, the Governor-General, laid emphasis on the establishment of some ideal schools with a view to reforming and improving the education of women at all the stages in accordance with the recommendations of the Government Resolution on Education Policy of 1913. This led to some progress of women education not only in the primary and secondary fields but also in the field of higher education. In 1904, Annie Beasant established Central Hindu Girl's School at Banaras and Professor Karve established S.N.D.T. Women's University at Poona. All India Women Education Conference was organised in 1927 and demands were made for providing different types of education to women. Now the attitude of the public towards co-education has also softened. In 1937, there were nearly 33,989 girls' and women's schools in which nearly 29,67,598 girls and women were receiving education. However, it must be mentioned here that at that time the literacy of women was only 3 per cent. Thereafter, a great progress was made in the field of higher education of women during the next 10 years because women had also started working in Government Departments and the attitude of the Indians in this connection had also undergone a significant change.

Because of this changed attitude the expansion of women education took place with great strides. In 1937, nearly 1,48,687 girls were receiving education at primary stage. In 1947, this number increased to 1,61,226. Similarly, at the secondary stage there were 398 schools imparting education to 1,08,660 girls in 1937. In 1947, the number of these schools and the girls increased to 725 and 2,32,166 respectively. In 1937, there were only 32 colleges imparting education to 14,435 girl students in the country. In 1947, the number of such colleges and the students receiving education increased to 59 and 24,466 respectively.

Independent India. After the independence of India in 1947, our leaders paid special attention towards the expansion of women education in the country. In Article 15 of the Indian Constitution, it is written, "The state shall not discriminate against any citizen on ground only of religion, race, caste, sex, place of birth or any of them." Government has encouraged the education of women, by declaring the equal rights of women in this field.

Radhakrishnan Commission of 1948, Mudaliar Commission of 1952 and National Committee of Women Education useful recommendation for the expression of women education. In 1959 National Council of Women's Education was established under the presidentship of Mrs. Deshmukh to suggest the government in the field of women education. The committee was re-organised in 1964. In 1962, Hansa Mehta Commission recommended that there is no need to differentiate curricula on the basis of sex. It also recommended that care should be taken to see that no step is taken which will tend to perpetuate the existing difference between men and women. Kothari Commission made many useful recommendations for women at all stages. It was of the view that existing difference between girl's and boy's education should be removed.

Under the Five Year Plan hectic efforts have been made for the expansion of women education since the First Five Year Plan.

There was great expansion of women education under our Five Year Plans. In year 1950-51,58.3 lacs girls at the stage of class I to V, 5.3 lacs at the stage of class VI to VIII and 1.9 lacs at the stage of class IX to XI were receiving education. Their number grew up to 435 lacs, 112 lacs and 40 lacs respectively up to the year 1991-92.

In the Education Policy of 1986, it has been said that the curriculum of women-education shall be restructured in such a way that it may develop women values. All out efforts shall be made for technical and vocational education for the girls.

Practical Aspects

As discussed above, expansion of education has taken so place with great strides after independence. Yet there is great disparity between men and women in the field of education. In India, the population of men and women is nearly equal but the number of educated men is several times more than the number of educated women. We will now briefly discuss the obstacles that are confronting the expansion of women education and the suggestions to overcome arose obstacles:

Social Evils and out-dated Conventions. Our country is beset with many social evils and superstitions. It is because of the lack of education that most of the Indians are still the victims of many social evils and old and out-dated conventions. There are still many Indians who are of the view that there is no need of educating the girls because ultimately they are to be married and have to go with their husbands to do domestic work thereafter. It is also contended that if educated women become free and characterless. Besides this, in many Hindu and Muslims, the social evils such as child marriages and 'Pardah system' are still prevalent. These are proving to be great obstacles in the expansion of women education. In our society, more emphasis is given on the marriage of women rather than on their education. Considering the girls as the property of their would be husbands, they consider it extravagant to educate them. It is therefore, quite obvious that unless this attitude of the people is changed, sufficient expansion of women education is not possible. The women-organisation must come forward to remove these out-dated conventions. Muriel Wasi rightly remarked, "Upon their determination, compactness and good sense and efficiency rests the future of education of women in India."

Disregard for the Importance of Education. In fact, our country is still groping in the dark because of lack of education and the majority of Indian people still do not understand the social and cultural importance of education. Hence, the majority of countrymen consider it a wastage of time and money to give education to their children. Likewise many people are of the view that education is received only for professional or practical gain and they are of the view that it is proper to educate the boys but it is useless to educate the girls because after their marriages they have to look after domestic works. As a matter of fact, this wrong attitude is proving to be detrimental for the development of women education. The guardians should be made to understand that the aim of education is not only to obtain Government or other services but it is the education which can help the girls to make the complete development of their personalities. Even if they have to look after domestic works after marriages, education will make them better wives and better mothers and will help them to build up able and dutiful future citizens of the country.

Undeveloped Conditions. The financial condition of Indian people is very poor and majority of the rural areas are in so underdeveloped condition that it is difficult for the people living there to make arrangements for even the bare necessities of life. In such places, it is very difficult to establish schools. Since the parents are not able to collect even the minimum possible money to meet the bare necessities of life, the question of sending their children to schools does not at all arise for them. Thus, it is necessary that our Government should pay special attention to the upliftment of rural people and to give prominent place to women-education in their development programmes. A huge money is required to bring about the desired results in the field of women education. National Committee of Women Education had demanded that the Government should take up the work of expansion of women education on priority basis.

Lack of Girls' Schools and Women-teachers. There is a great lack of Girls' Schools at all the stages of education and there are villages where there is no provision of primary education for girls. In the majority of the villages the girls have to receive primary education along with the boys and the same condition prevails at secondary and higher stages. Co-education is proving an obstacle in the way of expansion of women education, because even today many parents are strongly against co-education and do not like to send their daughters to schools where the girls have to study with the boys. Some educationists have also not supported the idea of co-education and Mudaliar Commission has emphasised on the establishment of separate schools for the girls. It is, therefore, necessary that the Government should establish as many numbers of separate schools as possible for girls. Likewise, there is also a great lack of women teachers in the country. Many educated women do not like to work as teachers because of fear of their husbands and parents, etc. It is necessary to change this attitude. The Government should devote their attention to solve this problem. Women can be attracted to do teaching work by giving them better salaries. The educated wives of the teachers should be encouraged to take up teaching profession. The service conditions of women teachers should also be made liberal and attractive and more facilities should be provided to them.

Defective Curriculum. At all the stages of education the curricula of girls and boys are almost the same. Dr S.N. Mukerji writes, "Education of girls in India today is mere replica of the education given to boys. Practically, there is no provision for teaching the girls anything outside the boy's curriculum." Most of the Indian people do not consider this education suitable for girls for their social and family life and their physical, cultural and social needs are different from the boys. Thus leaving only the curriculum of primary education, significant changes are necessary in the curricula of women at the stages of secondary and higher education. Keeping this thing in mind Mudaliar Commission has recommended that home science should be made compulsory for girls and women and with a view to increasing the utility of women education. Spinning, Weaving, Embroidery in the secondary classes and Painting, Music, Home Science, Economics etc., should be included in the curriculum of higher education.

Indifference of Government and Defective Educational Administration. In fact, our national Government have not been devoting their full attention towards the expansion of women education of boys. Less money is allotted for the education of girls and women. Besides this, the administration of women education is also defective because excepting a few States, in all other states the administration of women education is looked after by men. Proper and sufficient development of women education is not taking place because the administrators are not properly acquainted with the problems of women education and because sufficient money is not being spent on it. In order to encourage women education, able and talented women should be appointed on high administrative posts.

Wastage. As compared to the boys, the rate of wastage is more in the field of women education. This is proving to be a great obstacle in the expansion of women education. Because of the uneducated guardians, social evils and out-dated conventions, lack of money and of facility etc., many girl students leave their studies in the middle. Many parents break the education of their daughters only after giving them education upto classes III or IV. This wrong attitude is causing great wastage in the field of women-education. In order to check this tremendous wastage, it is necessary to bring about a change in the attitude of the parents. In order to change the attitude of the parents to the rural areas, village workers should be appointed who should try to bring about a change in their attitude by telling them the social and cultural importance of education.

Conclusion. Our aim is to bring the women of this country at par with men in the field of education. Each man and woman of this country should become educated. A country, where women education is disregarded can never make progress. The western countries have achieved so much progress because equal importance has been given there to the education of women. Educated women should be given equal opportunities of employment with men in Government and non-government institutions. Consequently, all the women of the country will he encouraged to receive higher education. Our aim should, therefore, be to build a society where these should not be any discrimination based on caste, religion or sex. The discrimination which was shown to women before independence on the basis of sex is also found in the country, though a lesser degree. All signs of discrimination should be removed for ever and impetus should be given to the expansion of women education in the country so that they may come at par with men in the near future. The expansion of women education will lead to the disappearance of several superstitions that are still prevalent in Indian society.

12
Schools for the Elite

Some people think that the Public Schools are those educational institutions which have been established with the public help in different regions and which provide educational facilities for all children without any distinction of caste, colour, community or belief. The name of these schools also gives the impression that they are run on democratic principles and they will be providing better facilities of education to common and poor children than other schools and colleges. But in reality, these schools are just opposite to these pre-suppositions. These schools have been established according to the whims of the founders at selected places without any consideration of the place. Generally, these schools have been established by big industrialists and wealthy people and now they are run by charging high tuition fees and help by the founders from time to time.

Public schools in India have been established on the pattern of the public schools of England. In England this tradition may be said to have started with the establishment of the outlet public schools in the later part of the fourteenth century. Other schools of this type were established in the fifteenth and sixteenth centuries. In the beginning, the form of these schools was almost like other schools. The only difference was that these schools were run without any Government help. Their main aim was to prepare Christian gentleman of desirable behaviour for social, religious and political leadership in future life.

When the British empire established itself firmly in India,

some children of wealthy class in India began to go to England for study. These children were generally sent to public schools. But they had to face great difficulty due to the educational standard and other provisions there. The children of some Rajas, Maharajas and Talukdars and other rich people thought of establishing public schools in India on the pattern of British public schools.

The famous advocate of Calcutta, S.R. Das, first of all thought of establishing a public school in India. He wanted that children of all classes of society should be admitted in this public school. For this purpose in 1929, he established Indian Public Schools Society and collected 14 lakh rupees. But due to his death the plan could not be implemented. However, it was due to his influence that first School was established in 1935.

In India, Chiefs Colleges on the pattern of Public Schools of England were giving education to the children of princes. Rajas, Maharajas and Talukdars and wealthy people at several places. These colleges were also given Government grants, by 1930, in the wake of freedom struggle, the voice was raised as to why the public schools be given any grant from the public exchequer when those colleges did not admit the children of common people. Consequently, the Government was forced to stop the grant. As a result, the Chiefs Colleges had to face financial difficulties. In 1939, they called a conference in Simla. It was decided there that chiefs colleges be called Public Schools in future. It was also decided to incorporate Indian culture in the educational system and establish a body to be named as Indian Public Schools Association. In 1939, a meeting of the Headmasters of Public Schools was held in Gwalior. Indian Public School Conference was organised in this meeting and the headmasters of public schools became the members of this conference. The education Commissioner of the Indian Government Sir John Sargeant was present in both meetings held in Simla and Gwalior. He considered that the establishment and development of public schools in India is important. He stressed the need of developing public schools in India for the development of qualities of leadership in Indian children because he thought that India had to run her own administration some day.

It may be remembered here that even after the establishment of Indian Public School Conference many Chiefs colleges did not like to become its members. Daily College, Indore; Admission College, Lahore; Bhonsia Military School, Poona; Rajkumar College, Rajkot; declared themselves as public schools. These schools wanted to gain the support of the leaders of Indian National Congress. The headmaster Smith of Prince College, Rajpur invited Gandhiji in his school. But Gandhiji did not agree with the policy of maintaining public schools. So he did not accept the invitation. Even so Smith continued to have faith in the utility of public schools and he continued to remain active to get the support of other leaders. He believed that many Indian leaders did not agree with the Basic Education of Mahatma Gandhi So he thought that he would get the support of such leaders.

It has been stated earlier that most of the Chiefs Colleges did not accept the membership of Indian Public School Conferences. The Principal of Mayo College, Ajmer, Mr. Sto expressed the opinion that his college belongs to a special category and hence he and other colleges too, had the same motion. In 1940, a meeting of Public Schools was held in Raipur. In that meeting the conditions for membership of the Indian Public School Conference were determined and it was also decided that the study of Indian languages should be made compulsory for public school students. After this, the public schools of Delhi and Bikaner became the members of the Conference. After recognition of Public School Conference, public schools were opened in some other places also. Among them, the Yadvendra Public School, Patiala (1948), Pilani Birla School (1944), Maharani Gayatri Devi School of Jaipur (1943) and Birla Vidya Mandir, Nainital (1949) are worth mentioning. The Education Ministry of the Government of India took over the administration of Lawrence School of Sanavar and Lawrence School of Lavdel from the Defence Ministry, but handed over to some committee in 1953.

Thus, public schools continued to develop in India. But after the attainment of freedom in 1947 it looked as if the future of public schools in India was dark because they began to be considered as an obstacle in the development of the growth of democratic system in the country. They were considered as symbols of British empire and foreign culture. The continuance of English as medium of instruction and neglect of Indian culture in these schools became a matter of concern for everyone. But some supporters of English mode of living tried for preserving their vanity and the greed for maintaining of high posts began to give shelter to public schools. As a result, public schools continue to exist even today.

In 1952-53, the Mudaliar Commission studied the working of Public Schools and recommended to continue them although it gave several suggestions for improvement. In the opinion of the Commission, the public schools develop qualities of leadership. So it is better to improve them rather than to close them. This recommendation of the Mudaliar Commission has given them much support.

The Kothari Commission of 1964-66 has recommended for the abolition of public schools. In the opinion of the Commission, it is not fair to maintain public schools in the democratic system of India. Public Schools pointed out to a special class system. But those who rule the country used to be sent to those schools.

Prominent Schools

At present there are more than fifty public schools in India. Some military schools established in India may be counted as public schools. It is to be remembered that only fifty percent of public schools have accepted the membership of Indian Public Schools Conference. Some missionary schools in the different parts of the country also work on the pattern of public schools. Some notable public schools are as under:

1. Scindia School, Gwalior, 2. Daily School, Indore, 3. Raj Kumar College, Rajkot, 4. Raj Kumar College, Raipur, 5. Doon School, Dehradun, 6. Birla Vidya Mandir, Nainital. 7. Modern School, Delhi. 8. Yadvendra Public School, Patiala, 9. Birla Public School, Pilani, 10. Mayo College, Ajmer, 11. Sardul Public School, Bikaner, 12. Maharani Gayatri Devi Girls' Public School, Jaipur, 13. Hyderabad Public School, Hyderabad, 14. Shivaji Preparatory

Military School, Poona, 15. Lawrence School, Lovedale, 16. Vikas Vidyalaya, Ranchi, 17. Lawrence School, Sarnavar.

Common Aspects

In accordance with the rules of the public school every student. has to live compulsorily in the school hostel. During the six working days of the week, there is teaching work for six hours daily and the rest of the time is to be spent by the students in the schools or hostel or co-curricular activities. He remains under the control of school authorities all the time. The school determines the daily programme of 24 hours for the student. Generally, the student has to get-up between four and five O'clock in the morning and he has to take part in one activity or the other till eight or nine O'clock at night. The time for bath, food, sleep, rising and study etc., is fixed.

Mathematics, language, literature, history, geography and science are the main subjects of study. Commerce and agricultural subjects are not encouraged. Besides study, facilities are provided to the students for their development in hobbies like swimming, horse riding, wrestling, gymnastics, games and sports, photography, crafts, etc. The supervision and control of teachers can be seen in all the activities. The students of higher classes work as monitors or prefects for junior classes. Like the teacher, the students of higher classes keep control on co-curricular activities of junior classes. But this control is exercised according to a systematic plan under the supervision of a teacher. The feeling of co-operation, responsibility and competition is developed in the students. For these activities like excursions, scouting and volunteer corps are organised. It is expected of the students that they will follow their teachers. Thus the responsibility of the teacher is very much increased. The students are divided into several groups. These groups are called 'house'. The leadership of the house is entrusted to students. Thus, qualities of leadership are inculcated in them. The atmosphere of the 'house' is like that of a family. The warden of the hostel behaves like a father. Thus the atmosphere of the 'house' is made cordial.

The public schools generally possess all necessary resources and equipments. One cannot think of their beginning in the absence of necessary equipments. A big school building which includes different class rooms for different subjects, big hall, library, laboratory, hostel, play ground and necessary material for cultural activities are all available there. In order to maintain their autonomy, the public schools do not take any government help. The headmasters and teachers are paid high salaries. The arrangement for their boarding and lodging is generally made by the public school. Thus the standard of the teachers is generally high.

The Significance

Some people have praised the public schools very much. According to them qualities of co-operation, leadership and shouldering responsibility are developed in the student after studying in these schools. In the free atmosphere of public schools, the students get opportunities for the development of personality, because the students are not prepared for the examination alone. The aim of education there, is the development of personality. All kinds of necessary resources are available there. The teachers and students do not face any difficulty in their work. The condition of ordinary secondary schools in our country is not good. They face sacristies in many ways. So, in a way public schools are ideals for them. Because of this, any school showing better performance compares itself to a public school.

The Shortcomings

The public school has also been very much criticised. Some people are of the opinion that the public school system is against democratic view point. Children of ordinary people do not get admission in these schools because they are so expensive that children of only millionaires, multimillionaires or high officials of government, ministers and other administrators can study in them. These people consider it against their dignity to send their children to ordinary schools. Thus, the children of a special class study in public schools whether they are capable or incapable. They lead their life in an atmosphere of luxury and affluence. This school life leaves a peculiar impression on their personality. They become accustomed to luxurious and affluent life even after leaving the school. Consequently, tendency of exploitation develops in them. They will not hesitate to exploit any one for the satisfaction of their wants in their future life. The children who have studied in public schools consider themselves superior to the children of ordinary people although they may be inferior to them in ability. Thus, undesirable complexes may be developed in their personality. The students of public schools try to maintain a distinction in society because they think that their status is higher than those of other in the democratic India of today where people find it difficult even to got two square meals a day, the maintaining of public schools is a mockery of humanity.

If during the period of education the children of the present day India are not able to understand the magnitude of poverty in the country and if they are not able to understand the fundamental problems of the country, it will be a waste of educational efforts. In that case, through education, we will be making them hypocrites, deceitful, un-Indian and of diffused personality. Needless to say that the public schools running in the country are moving in this direction. So in the present Indian society, public schools should not be encouraged did the sooner they are closed the better it is.

Various Problems

Due to the above demerits, the public schools have created some complex problems. Some of these are being indicated below:

Creation of a Special Class. The atmosphere of public schools gives rise to such a special class which cannot be reconciled with out democratic system and present social and economic conditions prevailing in the country.

Neglect of the Principle of Equal Opportunity for Development. In a democratic system the principle of equal opportunity for development is recognised. Public Schools clearly neglect this principle. Only children of rich people can study there, whereas many able children are deprived of such facilities.

Public Schools, a Cause for the Poor Conditions of the General Public. Children of rich people, ministers and other influential persons and high officials study in public schools. When their children are able to get educational facilities in well equipped public schools why should they bother for the education of general public. This is one of the reasons that the condition of general schools is very miserable. They have neither good buildings or furniture nor other necessary equipments.

Complexity of Language Problem and to the Encash Medium of Public Schools: English is the medium of instruction in the public schools. So the people who have studied in these schools have a good command over English. They do not have good command over the mother tongue. Such people support English for use in future life. Thus, a special class of the supporters of English is being created due to public schools. This class is not in favour of giving due place to the another to ague to educational and administrative fields.

Public School's another System of Secondary Education. In our democratic country, the citizens are getting two types of secondary education. Those who are specially well off are getting education in public schools and the rest of the children go to general schools. Thus the public schools, present another system of secondary education, in a democracy, two types of educational systems at the secondary level will be harmful because they encourage groupism.

The Remedies

(1) The admission in public schools should be opened to the children of general public also.

(2) Public Schools should be run on the basis of Indian background and culture. So far they have been copying the public schools of England. The medium of instruction there should be mother tongue instead of English.

(3) To enhance dignity of labour, crafts and other ordinary crafts should find a place in the education of public schools.

(4) The expenditure of public schools should be reduced. The fees charged in these schools should be reduced so much so the children of general public may take admission in them.

(5) The name of the public schools should be changed to Janta Schools. They should be considered Janta Schools rather than private schools. Indian educational system, Indian culture and Indian problems should receive special attention there.

(6) The students for admission in these schools should be selected on the basis of merit. For this, emphasis should not be laid on the knowledge of English. This selection should be opened to the students of all classes of society.

(7) It is good that provision for good education is made in public schools but their pomp and show, luxury and wastage should be stopped. They should not have more than the needed resources. Simple standard of living should be encouraged there.

(8) The salary of public school teachers should not be more than the salary of general secondary school teachers.

(9) Public schools should be made available with all the facilities by the government but in order to maintain their usefulness, it is necessary that they are kept away from the red-tapism and pressure of educational authorities, otherwise there will be no difference between them and the general schools.d

13

Education for Adults

The Background

Before making a brief discussion of the history of Social Education, it may be made explicit in the beginning that the education which we call social education since 1949 was previously called adult education.

Adult Education Before 1921. Efforts made for the expansion of adult education before the year 1921 were just negligible. Of course, some night colleges were established in different parts of the country but their aim was to impart primary education to the children who worked in the factories and did not get time for studies during the day-time. In 1901-02, there were night schools imparting adult education in Bombay, Madras and Bengal only. But these schools could not flourish because of the indifference and apathetic attitude of the Government and the number of such schools continued to decline by the year 1917. The Government of India Act, 1919 granted extensive rights of vote to the Indians. Hence, adult education naturally increased among the common people because it was felt that Indians could not exercise properly their franchise due to lack of education, consequently, night schools and night classes were organised in United Provinces, Punjab, Bombay, Madhya Pradesh, Bengal and Madras.

From 1921 to 1937. The Government of India Act, 1919 was enforced in 1921, and the 'transfer' subjects were entrusted to the Indian Ministers. Education was also a transferred subject. Indian

Ministers took deep interest in resolving the problem of adult education.

In Various Regions

Consequently, entering efforts were made in different provinces to make the adult literacy popular among the people. Not much time had passed since sincere efforts had begun in respect of the expansion of adult literacy, these efforts received a major set-back because of the world-wide Economic Depression of 1927. Because of the lack of money, both the Government and the people lost inspiration and encouragement to work for expansion of adult education. Consequently, the number of adult schools continued to decline. In the year 1937, the number of men and women schools of this type was reduced to 20 and 11 respectively.

From 1937 to 1947. The fate of adult education again took a turn for betterment when Congress Ministries were formed in 1937. In their programme of expansion of education, the Congress Ministers gave an important place to adult education. Being encouraged with this, the Government of India also showed its interest towards the expansion of adult education for the first time by appointing an 'Adult Education Committee' in 1939.

A brief discussion of the efforts made by the Congress Ministers in different provinces for the expansion of adult literacy is given below:

Assam. The work of expansion of adult literacy was entrusted to Education Department in the province of Assam. With the help and cooperation of its subordinate offices, the Education Department of Assam made proper provision of adult education.

Bengal. In this province the Government granted financial help to the schools organised by the Gram Sabhas and thereby encouraged the adult education.

Bihar. The movement of adult education made great progress in the province of Bihar. The movement named 'make your home literate' was launched and libraries and reading rooms were opened in thousands of villages.

Bombay. In 1917, 'Provincial Adult Education Council' was established in the province and under its supervision the work of adult education was started in the city of Bombay. This scheme achieved so much success that with the aim of the expansion of adult literacy in the city of Bombay, Bombay City Adult Education Committee was also established. In 1938, Bombay Government appointed an Ad-hoc Education Advisory Board which rendered praiseworthy service in removing adult illiteracy in the province of Bombay. Sri S.R. Bhagat was the Chairman of this Board.

Orissa. The work of adult education received a great impetus during the rule of Congress Ministries in this province. But the work of adult education received a set-back immediately after the resignation of the ministry.

Punjab. The work of adult literacy could not make much progress in this province. However, the Government distributed thousands of books among the adults free of charge.

Uttar Pardesh. The Congress Ministry of this Province gave a great impetus to the work of expansion of adult education. Centres of adult education were established at different places and provision was made for the reading rooms, libraries and other types of facilities in order to encourage and inspire the adults to become literate.

Scene after Independence

Adult education has been given a place of priority in the independent India. By changing the name of adult education to social education, not only its nature but its scope has also been extended. It was decided that along with making the adult illiterates literate, they should also be given the education of citizenship. Thus, under the social education the scope and view of adult education was made wide and extensive.

Special Scheme

In order to develop the qualities of citizenship among the adult illiterates and to make them conscious of their rights and duties and to expand their knowledge, the education minister of the government of India presented a twelve point scheme in a press conference organised on May 31,1948.

Conference of Provincial Education Ministers. A Conference of Provincial Education Ministers was organised in February, 1949 at Delhi to discuss the Twelve Point Programme mentioned above. After a thorough and detailed discussion in the conference, it was decided that within a period of three years at least 50 per cent of the adult persons belonging to the age group of 12 to 50 years should be made literate but this programme could not be implemented because of the financial difficulties of the Central and the State Governments.

Specific Programme

The Government of India made a Five Points Programme:

(1) Expansion of literacy;

(2) Propagation of the knowledge relating to rules of health and sanitation;

(3) Financial upliftment of the adult persons;

(4) Consciousness or awakening of the people towards the feeling of citizenship, rights and duties,

(5) Provision of healthy entertainment in accordance with the need of the society and the individual.

First Five Year Plan. It was decided to spend Rs. 7.5 crores for social education in the First Five Year Plan. Many provinces made the provision of social service works and some provinces even made a commendable progress in this respect. The work of social education received an impetus in public work organised with this aim in view. For example, many such work organised by Gram Panchayats, Cooperative Societies and Professional Unions or Associations, etc.

Second Five-Year Plan. Under the Second Five Year Plan besides improving the methods of social education, classes of social education were expanded at different stages. The State Government started many centres of literacy and social education training institutions of workers and organisers of social institutions and established libraries, colleges and audio-visual institutions. A sum of Rs 10 crores was provided for social education under the

Second Five Year Plan. Besides this, a sum of Rs 10 crores was spent on social education through National Extensive and Community Development Schemes.

Third Five-Year Plan. A sum of Rs 15 crores was spent on social education under the Third Five-Year Plan. Under this plan also, efforts were made to expand and encourage social education. In villages, schools, Panchayats and voluntary organisations, work in the field of social education was done.

Fourth Five-Year Plan. Under the Fourth Five-Year Plan a movement on extensive basis was launched for the development of adult education. It was decided to connect the adult literacy with the life and activities of the people so that villages may be developed. A special emphasis was given on expanding literacy by creating awakening for its utility. In order to make the drive of literacy effective, the provision of libraries was being organised to rural areas and a large number of schools were being established for expanding literacy in different languages. As special emphasis was given on the following things during the Fourth Five-Year Plan, training of workers of literacy and library; establishment of adult schools; night schools and colleges for training of the workers, establishment of National Adult Education Board and thereafter State Boards. A sum of about Rs 64 crores was spent on the scheme of social education under the Fourth Five-year Plan.

Fifth Five Year Plan. The Non-formal education Programme was introduced for the first time in the Fifth Plan. Full time institutional education was introduced to meet the requirements of illiterates and semi-illiterates. This programme was integrated problem-oriented, environment and how the young could adjust to it, family life, education, health and hygiene, literacy skills and initial functional training leading to employment and self-employment. In the Fifth Plan the proposed outlay for social education was Rs. 3,500 crores.

Sixth Five Year Plan. Due to the fall of Congress Government at the centre in the year 1978, the draft of the Sixth Five Year Plan (1978-83) was prepared by the Janta Government. The Government allocated Rs. 200 crores for the progress of social education. On

October 2, 1978, the National Social Education Programme was introduced in the formal manner. The aim of this programme was to provide social education to 10 crores illiterate people by the year 1983-84. There was again a change of Government at the centre in the year 1980. The Congress Government prepared a new draft for the Sixth Five Year Plan (1980-85) and Rs 128 crores were allocated for the expansion of social education.

Seventh Five Year Plan. Under the Seventh Five-year Plan Rupees 360 crores were allocated for social education and decided to complete the unfinished programmes of Sixth Five year Plan. The target was to make every adult literate, which however, could not be achieved. Under this plan the programme of continuing education was implemented and it was connected with Industrial Rural Development Programme.

Eighth Five Year Plan. Rupees 184.76 crores were allocated for the development of Social Education under Eighth Five-year plan and it was decided that adult illiteracy shall be definitely removed from the country. It was also decided to make hectic efforts for continuing education.

In the education policy of 1986, it was declared that social education should be according to the national objective. More educational centres shall be opened in rural areas, programme of continuing education shall be properly enforced and full use of radio, television and film shall be made for collective teaching.

Social Education

A National Centre for Fundamental Education was established at New Delhi for imparting social education to higher officials and for doing appropriate research in the chief problems of social education. The Library Institution of Delhi University performs the same function in the field of libraries. A Social Education Institution for workers was established at Indore. A provision has also been made for providing constant educational facilities for the establishment of public colleges and Vidyapeeths for imparting education to the adults in rural areas. A Central Film (Documentary) Museum was established which has more than 4974 films on different subjects of education and culture and which are provided to the members of educational institutions free of any charge. Nearly, 1,045 educational institutions and social organisations are the members of this Museum. A quarterly magazine entitled 'Audio-visual education' is also published.

The Central and the State-Government also organised Conference of Audio-visual workers. A Central Audio-visual Committee has also been established. Besides establishing training institutions, public centres of literature and research centres have also been established. This institution also makes available knowledge and information regarding Audio-visual education. Under the National Council of Educational Research and Training, a department of Adult Education has also been established. This department performs the functions of imparting training to the higher officials involving in the work of social education, helps to develop suitable teaching methods, conduct research work on selected problems and furnishes different types of information.

The Fundamentals

The meaning of the phrase, 'Adult Education' has been defined in different ways. As is very clear from the phrase, adult education means making the adults literate. As a matter of fact, the meaning of adult education is much wider than this. While clarifying this, Sri S.N. Mukherji has remarked, "Adult education may be defined very broadly so as to include all instructions, formal or informal imparting to adults. In India, adult education has two aspects- (1) Adult literacy, i.e. education of those adults, who never had any schooling, and (2) Continuation of education of the literate."

(*Education in India Today and Tomorrow*)

According to K.G. Saiyadain, "Adult education ... includes political and civic as well as moral education."

New Trends

In the 15th Session of the Central Advisory Board of Education, which was held in Allahabad in January, 1949, Maulana Abul Kalam Azad expressed the new view- point of the Government of India towards adult education. According to him, the aim of adult education should not be confined only to run adult illiterates into literates but it should extend to make each citizen a wise member of the democratic set-up. The view-point of adult education underwent a change and from that time it was called social education. A great change has come in the meaning and definition of social education. The scope and range of adult education has greatly extended and it has now assumed the form of social education.

While clarifying the meaning and definition of social education Maulana Abul Kalam Azad expressed the following words while delivering the inaugural address to UNESCO Seminar on rural adult education, held in December, 1949 in Mysore, "By social education, we mean education for the complete man. It will give him literacy, so that knowledge of the world may become accessible to him. It will teach him, how to harmonise himself with his environment and make the best use of the physical condition in which he resides. It is intended to teach him the unproved crafts and modes of production so that he may achieve economic betterment. It also aims at teaching him the rudiments of hygiene both for the individual and the community so that our domestic life may be healthy and prosperous. Last but not the least, this education should give him training in citizenship so that he obtains some insight into the affairs of world and can help his Government to take decision which will make for its progress."

According to Humayun Kabir, "Social education may be defined as a Course of study directed towards the promotion of consciousness of citizenship among the people and the promotion of social solidarity among them. It is not content with the introduction of literacy among the grown-up illiterates but aims at production of educated mind among the masses. As a natural corollary, it seeks to inculcate in them a lively sense or rights and duties of citizenship both as individuals and members of the community."

It is clear from the above mentioned definition that social education is a regulated subject which increases the capacity of the individual for participating in collective works. It creates consciousness among them for a proper evaluation of citizenship. It attracts them towards duty and behaviour. It is only through social education that the adult can increase his income within his limited means and can make his contribution in the building of society.

Objectives and Aims

Aim of Social Education. Since the attainment of independence, it has been sincerely felt that for the establishment and stability of democracy in India, it is necessary to educate the Indian people. Consequently, the newly established first Education Ministry of the independent India gave an important place to the education of adults in its programme. Consequently in 1949, a Committee headed by Sri Mohan Lal Saxena was appointed to advise the Government in connection with the expansion of adult education. Having found the aims of adult education narrow, this Committee advised the Government that this education should be called 'Social Education'. This suggestion of the Committee was accepted by the Government. This Committee determined the following aims of social education:

(1) To awaken the adults towards their rights and duties and develop the feeling of social service in them.

(2) To create love in them towards democracy and to educate them the administrative system of Government,

(3) To acquaint them with the existing problems before the country and the world.

(4) To develop the feeling of glory towards Indian culture through the education of history, geography and culture.

(5) To provide them the opportunities of pleasure and cultural acquaintance through music, dances, poetry and dramas.

(6) To make them aware of moral values throughout the medium of collective discussion and reading and writing.

(7) To impart them proper knowledge of reading, writing and ordinary mathematics and encourage them for expansion of knowledge.

(8) To teach them to utilise their leisure properly to achieve

their economic progress through the learning of different handicrafts.

(9) To continue their education through libraries, debates, discussions, Education Committees and public colleges.

(10) To develop in them feeling of cooperation.

Purpose of Social Education. The purpose of social education has been divided by the Government into two categories:

(a) Individual, and (b) Social.

Individual Purposes. (1) Mental development; (2) Development of professional capacity; (3) Physical development; (4) Development of Social Skill; (5) Cultural development; (6) Self Development

Social Purposes. (1) Promotion of Social cohesion; (2) Conservation and improvement of national resources; (3) Building of co-operative groups of institutions; (4) Inoculation of social ideology.

Need of Social Education. The above-mentioned aims and purposes have not been determined as a result of any chance or incident but after having seriously considered the needs of the individual and the society of the country. In consequence of these needs, the need of social education has been felt According to Dr. R.S. Pani, "Social education is a many-sided endeavour, since its aim is primarily to develop in an individual a live sense not only of the privileges but of the responsibilities of citizenship him a democratic secular state like India." We will now briefly discuss the need of social education.

Need of Illiterate Adults. Indian Constitution has granted the right of equality and equal rights of freedom to all the citizens but many of the citizens are not able to exercise their rights on account of their illiteracy. Keeping in view of these requirements of the illiterate adults, provision of social education has been made and the chief purpose of social education is to make illiterates the literate adults.

Need of Complete Education. The education which is imparted in the schools and institutions of higher education cannot be called complete because it does not develop the necessary abilities in the persons that they may lead their lives successfully in all the fields. The main defect of the education imparted in the schools is that it does not give any type of training in respect of health, family and proper utilisation of leisure. After entering into life the individual feels, the need of this type of training. Social education fulfils this need of persons.

Need of Recreation. In the modern period, like the citizens of other countries, the needs of Indians have also increased. In order to fulfil these needs, they remain busy to earn money from morning till night. After the hard labour throughout the day, it is quite natural that these persons should have a wish to have means of some type of entertainment. So far as the cities are concerned, lack of means of entertainment is not a problem. There is great lack of means of entertainment in the villages. Social education has also taken upon itself a task of providing different types of entertainment to the rural people.

Political Need. The present time is the period of reorganisation, rehabilitation, development and progress for our country. We have established a secular welfare democratic state in our country. We have to make it strong and stable which can be possible only when its foundation is fine and strong. This foundation is, in fact, the whole people of the country, on whom depends the responsibility to elect able State Governments and it is only on them the welfare of the nation depends. To achieve this aim, it is necessary that the common people of India should be given proper education and proper literature should be made available to them for study. As we emphasise the education of boys and girls and youths, in the same way, we will have to make proper provision of education of adults of India. Unless we are able to bring about the consciousness among the adults, we will not be successful to achieve our cherished goal. Therefore, the social education, which has taken upon itself the task of educating the adult Indians is of utmost importance.

Social Need. It is clear from the definition of the society that co-operation is an essential element of society. The whole structure of the society rests on the foundation of co-operation. It is only this co-operation which not only protects the society but also builds and develops it. The existence of all the institutions, committees and organisations of the society depend upon co-operation. We can be successful in making the society progressive only with the help of co-operation.

Economic Need. The majority of Indian people is poor. The condition of the rural people is comparatively poor and more miserable than the urban people. They do not have even sufficient means to fulfil men-needs of clothing and food. Unless we are able to remove the slur of poverty from the forehead of our country, we are not entitled to call ourselves progressive. Being inspired with these ideas, the Government of India has devoted their attention to the financial uplift of crores of poor Indians and keeping in view this need it has been decided to raise their economical status by giving them different types of training through the programme of social education.

Need of the Country. If the people of the country are not educated, then it is not possible to make a full use of constructive power of the country. There is great need of education for acquiring strength and then making use of it. An uneducated person does not know as to what powers he inherits in him and how can he make use of them. It is completely true in regard to India that huge public power of this big country is not being properly used. The provision of social education has been made keeping in view this need in mind.

Difficulties and Remedies

We will now discuss the different problems confronting social education and some suggestions to solve them.

Illiteracy. India is the second most populated country of the world, next only to China. According to the census of 1991 population of the country is 84.39 crores and out of them only 52.11% are literate. Thus huge population of Indian people are growing in the dark because of their illiteracy. In view of the existence of so widespread illiteracy, to hope any type of social, economic and political development is just like to build a castle on the sand.

Liquidation of Illiteracy. Although the liquidation of illiteracy of the adults is not a simple task yet success can be achieved by adopting some methods. We can resolve this problem only when we stop having golden dreams of placing them on the high peak of culture and humanism and make up our mind to make them literate within the shortest possible time.

Moreover, in the beginning we should concentrate on teaching of writing and simple mathematics. In the 5th Educational Conference held at Washington on October 29 and 30, 1936, Dr. Edwin Embree rightly remarked:

"Reading is the first commandment even among the basic three R's."

In order to teach reading and writing to the adults, it is not necessary the method which is adopted should be proper and complete from the scientific point of view but we should adopt the method, which may give equal and best results.

This type of method was discovered by a Missionary of America named Dr. Frank Laubach to educate the people of Moros tribes of the Phillipine archipelago. First he selected 5 to 6 such words which were generally used. Thereafter, he selected some more words and with their help build sentences. Thus, with the help of the charts he taught 17 letters within a day to each adult. Each family adult who learned the chart was sent to teach the members of his family and his neighbours. Thus, within a period of 5 years, 70,000 adults out of 1,50,000 adults of the province of Lana were taught not only to read but also to write.

Dr. Laubach visited India in 1935, 1937 and 1938 and demonstrated his method for teaching in Marathi, Telugu, Bengali, Hindi, Tamil and Gujarati languages. The Missionary of Moga in Punjab achieved tremendous success by adopting this method. It is a matter of great regret that this method propounded by Dr. Laubach is out of the country now. If the method propounded by Dr. Laubach is adopted by the people, India can be made literate within a very short period.

Obviously, the liquidation of illiteracy is the responsibility of our Government. It is, therefore, necessary that either through the successful method experimented by Dr. Laubach or any other method which is seemed to be proper should be adopted to completely liquidate illiteracy from our subcontinent.

Kothari Commission has suggested for compulsory National Service Programme for adult education for all the schools and colleges. The Commission has also suggested for the appointment of village sisters, introduction of condensed courses and follow up programme.

Curriculum. The second problem of social education is of its curriculum. Because of the improper and unsuitable curriculum, the work of social education is not making much progress. The curriculum which is used for the education of the children cannot be used for the adults because their interests, needs and view-points towards life are completely different. Again, same curriculum cannot be determined for all the adults because some of them are totally illiterate and for the curriculum which can teach them the knowledge of the letters is necessary; some are half illiterates and for them teaching of some special subjects is necessary; and lastly there are some non-literates who know some reading and writing and in order to inculcate the feeling of citizenship in them, the curriculum including subjects such as civilization, culture, history, geography, civics, etc. is necessary.

Construction of Curriculum. The proper and suitable curriculum can be prepared only after carefully and minutely studying and considering the needs of complete illiterates, and non-literates because the aim of social education is not only to expand literacy but also to achieve the complete development of the adults. Hence, the curriculum should include all those subjects which may ensure their political, economic, social and cultural development. Not only one but several curriculum will have to be prepared keeping in view the needs, interests, mental tendencies and standards of the adults of different ages. Although the curricula will be different yet their subjects will ordinarily be the same, subject to their short or detailed studies keeping in view the needs of adults of different age group.

It has been pointed out by several educationists that it would be proper to prepare the curricula considering the curricula of some such countries where the conditions of adults are generally similar to that of Indians. From this point of view, the curricula of Denmark and China can be accepted as ideal.

In the curriculum of adult education, the first importance should be given to the teaching of writing and reading. When the adults acquire sufficient knowledge of writing, and reading then provision should be made for imparting education of mother tongue, mathematics, history, civics, economics, geography, culture, animal husbandry, general science, hygiene, literature, physical education, etc. The education of some other subjects may also be imparted in accordance with the local needs. Each adult should be trained in some or the other crafts, so that be may he able to make it a means of additional means of his income.

Method of Teaching. The problem of determining a suitable method of teaching adults is also not less complicated. If the teaching method has any element which appears to them uninteresting or which is against their reeling of 'self, freedoms, principles or habits then such a teaching method will certainly prove to be unsuccessful. Dr. V.K.R.V. Rao is of the opinion, "An adult may be illiterate, but his mind is grown-up and his interests are already cultivated. We are not writing on a blank slate, when we are dealing with an adult." That is why, so far it is not possible to determine a single method of teaching for the adults.

Suitable Method of Teaching. In order to determine a suitable method of teaching for the adults, it is necessary to study minutely their psychology. The teaching should be such as may be interesting and may attract them to receive education. The educationists of our country are very much active in this direction and they have evolved some suitable methods. We will now briefly discuss some of such teaching methods:

Letter Acquaintance Method. In this method the adults are first made acquainted with the knowledge of the letters. This system is prevalent in our primary schools.

Sentence Method. In this method the adults are first made acquainted with the knowledge of two words and thereafter by joining them the letters, given in the form of different sentences.

Laubach Method. A Missionary named Dr. Laubach has evolved a new method which is known as chart method. This method has been experimented in different parts of the world, to this method education of the whole sentence is given with the help of the chart.

Story Method. Sri Sangam Lal Agarwal has the credit of evolving this method. In this method, the education of the letters is given through certain stories based on the construction of letters.

Simple Word Method. This method has been evolved by Sri Pathak. In this method, prominence has been given to the songs. The songs are first sung and then the letters and the words are recognised by seeing them in the charts.

It is generally accepted that all these methods are suitable for the education of the adults. While adopting all these methods, it is necessary that the letters of Indian language should be made easy so that the adults may have convenience to write, understand and recognise them. It is also pointed out that Roman letters should be used for all the Indian languages. This will give the adults the knowledge of European languages along with their own languages and the obstacle which are there in the unity of the country on account of diversity of the languages will also come to an end. Kamal Ataturk solved the problem of illiteracy of the people of Turkey by making use of the Roman letters and thereby developed the feeling of unity in them.

Dearth of Teachers. Yet another problem confronting the expansion of social education is the dearth of teachers. The teachers who are appointed in the adult schools, are ordinarily the teachers of primary schools. They do not possess necessary ability to teach the adults. They are ignorant of the psychology of adults. They are not trained in the suitable teaching method of the adults.

Supply of Teachers. Although it cannot be denied that the problem of having a desired number of suitable teachers is in fact, difficult but at the same time it may be contended that this problem can be resolved through constant and firm efforts. The first and foremost work in this connection is that the teachers to be appointed for imparting of adult education should be acquainted with the psychology of the adults. Besides this, the teachers to be appointed in the adult schools of villages, should have sufficient knowledge of agriculture, animal husbandry, cottage industry, hygiene, spinning and weaving etc., so that the rural adults may benefited by their teaching.

It will take a long time before we can have the supply of the desired number of teachers for adult schools. However, it would not be proper to postpone the work of social education until the desired number of suitable teachers are available. The volunteers should be invited to do teaching work in adult schools.

Under the guidance of Mahatma Gandhi, the volunteers successfully and properly performed the work of imparting education to children of the village in the District Champaran. The same ideal can be adopted for educational institutions, employees of the offices, members of N.C.C. and A.C.C. and other selfless social workers take inspiration from the example of Mahatma Gandhi and adopt the principle of 'teach one each one' then in the interim period we will have sufficient number of teachers for the adult schools and the problem of liquidation of illiteracy will be successfully solved in the near future. Dr. Kothari has suggested for compulsory National Service Programme at all the levels of studies for the expansion of adult education.

Suitable Literature. The responsibility of social education cannot end only by making the adults literate. It is not sufficient only to teach reading and writing and simple mathematics to the adults. If they stop receiving regular lessons after having received this type of education, then they will again become illiterate after some time. It is, therefore, necessary that after giving them preliminary education some literature should be made available to these Neo-literates. The Neo-literates should be made available to such type of literature as may develop their capacity to examine things, power of criticism and the social feelings, so that they may be able to distinguish between the best and worst in the field of art, truth and untruth in the field of knowledge and good and bad in the field of conduct. It is a problem to prepare such type of literature of the Neo-literates.

Production of Suitable Literature. According to K.G. Saiyadain, "The work of social education is greatly handicapped by the paucity of suitable reading materials, graded to appeal to the adults." There is urgent need for producing large number of booklets, folders, charts, journals, newspapers, wall papers and other illustrated material which will capture adult's interests.

This work can be performed and completed with the help of learned writers. They should be encouraged with every possible way to prepare suitable books and booklets for the adults. Illustrated newspapers and magazines should be published. Monthly magazines should be published containing news relating to games, health, culture and news of the world because there is utmost need of such magazines for the neo-literates. All the State Governments of our country are taking active steps in this direction. The report of the Literary Work in the production of Literature for Neo-literates 1958 of U.P. has made some important suggestions in this connection. According to the said report, while preparing literature for the Neo-literates following 5 things must be kept in mind:

(a) Aims of social education; (b) distinction of age; (c) distinction of sex; (d) distinction of religion; and (e) demand and need.

'Literacy House', Lucknow, 'Adult Education Council', Mysore and 'National Education Council' are doing commendable Job in this direction.

Agencies of Education. According to "Teacher's Hand Book of Social Education", "By agencies of social education is meant the bodies or institutions which deliver the goods, which contract the 'consumer' of social education and satisfy their needs." A special caution is required for selecting these means of social education because if they fail to attract the ' attention of the adults then they will prove to be completely useless. A wise selection of the means is not simple task. That is why, persons having specialised knowledge of adult psychology, are engaged to solve this problem.

Proper Agencies of Education. Different types of suitable means can be suggested for increasing the knowledge of the adults. In this connection. Report of the Literary Workshop in the Production of Literature for Neo-literates 1958 of U.P. has suggested the following: (a) descriptive prose, (b) poetry, folk- song and riddles, (c) drama, dialogues, (d) Stories, (e) Newspapers, (f) interesting discourses, and (g) reading, etc.

The utility of the above mentioned means of education cannot be doubted but we have to admit that the chief aim of these means is only to achieve intellectual development of the adults. But, if the work of social education will be confined only to this, then it will not be possible to achieve the complete development of the personalities of the adults and which is the main aim of social education. Therefore, other means will also have to be used for giving education to the adults. The following means can prove sufficiently effective:

(a) Audio-visual aids, radio, cinema, gramophone, dramas, etc.

(b) Collective songs and dances

(c) Literary and debating conferences and seminars

(d) Historical and cultural programmes, etc.

The Central Ministry of Education has laid special emphasis on the use of the audio-visual aids.

Lack of Funds. According to Census of 1991, the total population of India was 84.39 crores and out of them only 52.11 per cent were literate. We can Just have an idea as to how much money is required for making so many adults literate. Suppose one teacher can make 30 adults literate within 6 months. Thus, he can teach reading and writing to 60 adults in a year. Consequently, for making all the persons adults literate we will need lakhs of teachers and a large number of adult schools. It is clear from this that the availability of funds is a great problem for making adults literate.

Solution. Generally this argument is put forward that sufficient money cannot be made available for making literate all adults in our poor country. Shri K.G. Saiyadain has rejected this argument. According to him, there is only one type of poverty which cannot be removed and that is the poverty of enthusiasm. If we make sincere efforts, other types of poverty can be removed. It is the responsibility of the Finance Department of the Government and the farmers of the National Schemes to make provision of the necessary money required for the purpose of adult education.

Responsibility. Another problem of social education is as to who should be responsible for social education- Central Government, State Government, Education Department, District Boards or Public Educational Institutions. The Central Government has shifted this responsibility on the State Governments and thus they have tried to free themselves from the responsibility of 'social education'. But the solution of the great problem of social education does not seam possible through this shifting of the responsibility.

Joint Responsibility. All the defects and complicated problems of social education cannot be solved by the Central Government, State Government or any other institution alone. It would be the joint responsibility of the Central Government, State Government and the different institutions of the people of the country. It is only then this problem can be solved satisfactorily in a near future. According to K.G. Saiyadain, "It is obviously a responsibility which neither the Education Department nor the Government Machinery as a whole can take on by itself, and needs the closer and most cordial co-operation of all agencies, official and non-official and of all individuals of good will and social sense who are interested in the welfare of India. There is so much work to be done and it is of such varied kind that there is scope for every one who cares to join the cavalcade of service students, teachers, men of leisure, political leaders, writers, labourers, craftsmen, professional men everybody."

Absence of Coutinual Education. Last but not the least is the problem of absence of continuation of Education. According to Kothari commission, "The very purpose of the literacy campaign will be defeated, if it does not continue in some form to keep the process of learning alive."

Provision of Continuation of Education. According to Kothari Commission, "In conditions of rapid change and advancing knowledge man must continue to learn in order to live in full." So hectic efforts should be made for the continuation of education of adults. Kothari Commission has suggested that in schools provision should be made to impart the education of such subjects which the adults want to study further, part-time teaching should be organised and institutions like Central Adult Women Welfare Council, should be setup in large number.

14

Population and Environmental Factors

Ours is a country of vast natural beauty. There are high mountains, large rivers and the fertile land, but unfortunately like other countries of the world, there is a problem of pollution and change of the environment in our cities. So, there is a great need of environmental education.

The Concept

Environmental education is an education through environment, about environment and for the environment. According to the United States Environmental Education Act, 1970 "Environmental education means the educational process dealing with man's relationship with his natural and man-made surroundings, and includes the relation of population, pollution, resource allocation and depletion, conservation, transportation, technology, and urban and rural planning to the total human environment."

According to Finnish National Commission, "Environmental education is a way of implementing the goals of environment protection. Environmental education is not a separate branch of science or subjects of study. It should be carried to the principle of life-long integrated education."

Dr. R.C. Sharma, in his book 'Environmental Education' writes, "Environmental education is education through, about and for environment. Its scope is, therefore, very wide. It begins from using environment as a medium of learning, and includes all that Kalidasa, Wordsworth and others have said in appreciation of nature and also all scientists and scholars have disclosed about our physical and social environment, and finally include all that we say and do for conserving our resources and for beautifying our surroundings including urban and country planning."

Purposes and Aims

In October, 1975 an International Workshop was organised in Belgrade, on environmental education. In the Belgrade Charter, following were declared as the goals and objectives of Environmental Education-

Aim. The chief aim of environmental education is the awakening of the World population in regard to environment and its problems.

Goals to be Achieved. The following goals were to be achieved-

Awareness. To assist the persons and social groups to have awareness about the problems of environment.

Knowledge. To assist the persons and social groups to have the complete knowledge about the environmental problems.

Attitude. To change the attitude of the persons and social groups about the environment and motivate them to protect the environment.

Skills. To develop the skills amongst the persons and social groups to solve the environmental problems.

Participation. To encourage the persons and social groups for the active participation in solving the environmental problems.

The objectives of environmental education can be divided into three categories: (A) Cognitive, (B) Affective and (C) Psychomotor.

Cognitive objectives are those objectives which are concerned with recall or recognition of the Knowledge about environmental education. They also cover the mental skills and abilities. Affective objectives cover those objectives which describe the changes in the interests with activity skills.

The following cognitive goals are to be achieved through environmental education:

1. To help in achieving the knowledge of the environment
2. To assist in achieving the knowledge of the environment of distant places.
3. To help in understanding the biotic and abiotic environment
4. To assist in understanding the co-relation at different levels of life in connection with the tropical problems.
5. To assist in understanding the evil effects of increase in population and uncontrolled use of natural resources.
6. To examine the tendencies of increasing population and explain them in the light of socio-economic development of the country.
7. To evaluate the destruction of natural and physical resources and suggest remedies to check them.
8. To search the reasons for the social tension and suggest the ways to remove it.

Following are the effective objects of environmental education-

1. To create interest in understanding the vegetational species of near and distant places.
2. To create of feeling of interest in the community and society in understanding the different environmental problems.
3. To demonstrate tolerance towards different races, religion and cultures.
4. To admire the contribution of nature.
5. To give importance to the feelings of equality, liberty, truth, justice and brotherhood.

6. To pay respect to the boundaries of different nations.
7. To give importance to the cleanliness of our environment.

Following are the psychomotor objectives of environmental education:

1. To take active part in the programmes through which air, water and noise pollution may be minimised.
2. To participate in the programmes of the cleanliness of the neighbouring places.
3. To participate in the urban and rural planning.
4. To participate in the programmes of food pollution.

The Curriculum

Wurzelbacher prepared a curriculum for environmental education in 1976 and included the following items:

1. Man and Environment,
2. Population and Urbanization,
3. Ecology,
4. Economics and Environment,
5. Urban and Regional Planning,
6. Social Resources,
7. Government Policy and Citizen,
8. Tree and Water Resources,
9. Wildlife Resources,
10. Air Pollution,
11. Out-door Recreation and Role of Citizens.

In the modern studies and researches environmental education has been given place as an interdisciplinary subject. In addition to it, it has been given a holistic form. Under it, ecological, social, and cultural problems are also studied. It is related to the real problems of life.

Technical Methods

Due to the wide scope of environmental education, its method of teaching and aids are of various types. Generally, the following methods are adopted to teach environmental education:

1. Class discussion,
2. Small Group Projects,
3. Field Trip,
4. Out-door Study,
5. Use of Exhibits, and
6. Simulation and Games.

Class Discussion. Under this system, there is a discussion on a topic or problem. The different aspects of environment are in the class room.

Small Group Projects. Small Group Projects are very useful for a wide study of the subject. Under this system the entire class is divided in small groups and a definite plan is put before every group. The particular group works on a particular project. For example, if a group is asked to work on a plane of local lake, it will discuss and study the following items-

(a) Which group of persons are dependable on the lake? (b) What is the effect of lake on the social life of the community? (c) What is the total area of the lake? (d) What type of persons and animals live inside the lake and the surrounding areas? (e) What type of plants are inside the lake and the surrounding area? (f) What type of nasty things are in the water of the lake? (g) How can the lake may be made more useful and developed?

Field Trip. Field Trip is an effective method of teaching. Field Trip is organised to study the environmental conditions of a particular place. By this method the students get the direct experience. Field Trips can be organised for community resources viz. Factory, Post Office, Bank, Local market etc.

Out-door Study. For the out-door study, there is a great need of planning and co-ordination. For the out-door trips, its aims, programmes, and field work etc. should be pre-determined. The students, through the out-door trip can study about the environment of rivers, caves and hill are as.

Use of Exhibits. The use of exhibits is very useful for environmental education. The different topics can be taught in a very interesting and simple manner through this method. An exhibition can be organised for a particular topic. The due co-operation of the students is very essential for it.

Simulation and Games. The use of simulation and games is very useful for environmental education. It develops amongst the students the independent thinking and right attitudes towards the environment.

Resources. For environmental education following resources are used

Local Resources. The environment of the students residences nasty things that pollute the water, items that pollute the air etc.

National Organizations. Telephones, Bulletins on environmental education, magazines such as 'Your Environment', Directory etc.

College Property. College play ground, college garden etc.

Printed Material. Government publications, annual reports on environment, periodicals, books, posters, charts etc.

Audio-visual Aids. Films, film-strips, individual slides, commercial T.V., education T.V., Commercial slides and radio etc.

The concept of the population education is new for the entire world. The reason for its origin and growth is the rapid increase of population. According to Dr. Vidyavati Mallaya, the total population on the entire world was 150 crores in the beginning of the twentieth century, at present it is about 450 crores and shall be about 700 crores at the end of twentieth century. Thus, it is evident that there has been rapid increase in population during the last twenty-five years.

The increase in population has posed a serious problem for the entire world because it has adverse effects on the national and international life. Increase in population not only effects the progress and prosperity of a nation but it also effects the international security and world peace. In fact, the entire human race is in danger due to the unprecedented increase in the population. Dr. Lulla & Dr. Murty are of the opinion, "The most serious problem of population explosion has plagued the world in our times."

Population Explosion in India and its Effects. The increase of population in India is much higher than other countries of the world. According to the census of 1991, it was about 68.3 crores and at present it is about 88 crores. In our country, a child is homed on every one and a half second. About 21 crore children are born in a year and the population of the children below the age-group of 15 is about 42% of the total population. Every seventh person of the world is an Indian. About 14% of the total population of the world resides in India, while we have only 2.4% of the total land of the world.

The evil effects of the increase of population in our country can be seen in our individual, social, political and economic lives. Though there has been increase in our national income, yet the standard of living is going down day by day. Crores of people are living below the poverty line and there has been rapid increase in unemployed youths. All the progress made in the field of agriculture and industry is unable to bring fruitful result due to the growing population. In a report of NCERT, it has been said, "The ever swelling numbers seem to undermine all plans of qualitative improvement"

In order to control the increasing population two steps are most essential:

1. Family Planning.

2. Population Education.

We have taken certain concrete steps for the family planning, but the desired results have not been achieved and so we need a concrete programme of population education, which may be properly implemented.

The concept of population education is still in an undeveloped stage. Some people use the words 'sex-education' and 'Family Life Education' 'Population Education'. In 1962, Prof. Walland of Columbia University used the term 'Population Education' and since then the term is widely used. However, recently Prof. Burieson has requested to use the term 'Population Awareness' for the term 'Population Education'.

Though the population education is widely popular in the advanced countries, yet it has no generally accepted meaning or definition. In the Asian Regional Workshop on Population and Family Life Education convened by UNESCO's Regional Office in September, 1970, it was said "Population education is an educational programme which provides for a study of the population situation of the family, community, nation and world; with the purpose of developing in the students rational and responsible attitudes and behaviour towards the situation."

If we analyse the above statement, we find the following three elements in it:

1. Population Education is an educational programme.
2. Population Education provides the opportunities to study the effects of increase in population on individual, family, society, nation and the world.
3. Population Education is imparted to the students to be vigilant and have right objectives towards the increase in population.

In short, we can say, "Population education views population not as a problem to be controlled, but rather as a phenomenon both social and biological to be handled." Pamphlets were issued by the Population Education Unit of Central Pedagogical Institute, Allahabad, September, 1973.

Significance and Placement

The following points may be noted in favour of population education:

1. Small family is a happy family, if the boys and girls study

the subject of population education, they shall definitely adopt family planning.

2. If Biology is an essential subject and has been selected in the curriculum for the studies, population education should be given place in the curriculum.

3. Marriage age in India is much less as compared to advanced countries. So the boys and girls should be aware of the problems of increase in population before the marriage.

4. We have adopted the concept of welfare state and it is the duty of the State to look after the health, welfare and complete development of the citizens. The State can fulfill its responsibilities only if the citizens are aware of the evil effects of the increase of population. This can be done only through population education.

5. The rapid increase of population has adverse effects on economic progress, social progress and the standard of living. It is only through population education, boys and girls may be made conversant with this fact.

From the above discussion, we come to conclusion, "No thoughtful person can ignore the importance and need of population education in the context of modem times." Dr. Lulla and Dr. Murty.

The following are the chief objectives of population education:

1. To impart the knowledge of the increase of population and its reasons to the students.

2. To make the students conversant with the evil effects of increase in population on the individual, society and on the economic, social, political and cultural life of the nation and the world.

3. To make the students conversant with the low standard of living of the people of large families and less income and thus inculcate in them the feeling of having small families in their future life.

4. To impart the knowledge of the problems of increase in population viz. spread of famines and diseases, increase in social conflicts, hurdle in peace and prosperity of the nation and others; and thus encourage them to have population control.

In the National Seminar on Population Education held at Bombay in August, 1969, it was said, "The objective of population education should be to enable the students to understand that the family size is controllable, that population limitations can facilitate the development of a higher quality of life in the nation and that a small family size can contribute materially to the quality of living for the individual family."

Difficulties and Remedies

As the scope of population education is very wide so there are many problems in the field of its education. Here we are giving a brief account of such problems and also giving some suggestions to solve them:

Problem: Shortage of Literature to Teach Population Education. There is a great shortage of literature to teach the subject at all the levels of studies. In most of our colleges, there is no literature at all. Under these circumstances, students are unable to know anything about the increase of population and the reasons for its increase, what to say anything about its evil effects. It is the reason that we are unable to propagate population education in our schools.

Solution: Availability of Suitable Literature. In order to have population education in curriculum of our schools, suitable literature should be prepared and made available to the schools. The literature should be in simple language so that the students of primary and secondary schools may study it In addition to it, population education should be included in the books of social sciences.

Problem: Lack of Knowledge of Population Education to the Teachers. Most of our teachers do not have any knowledge of population education. There are several reasons for it. The chief reason is that the books have been written on population education. Another factor is that there is no definite plan for teaching the population education. Our central Government, State Governments and Universities have no plans in this regard. Another reason is that there is no place for population education in the curricula of different schools, colleges and universities. Under these circumstances of different schools, colleges be expected to have the knowledge of population education.

Solution: To Make Arrangements for the Adequate Knowledge of Population Education for Teachers. If we expect from the teachers to impart knowledge of population education to the students, we should make hectic efforts that the teachers are well-equipped in this field of knowledge. Education department of every state should be entrusted with the task of establishing a centre of population education and the teachers be asked to study there. They should be given leave on full pay for the purpose. In the curricula of colleges and universities, population education should be included and the same be prepared by these centres.

Problem: Lack of Apparatuses on Population in the Colleges. Yet another problem of population education is the lack of apparatuses of such education in the colleges. Even no attention is paid on purchasing such apparatuses.

Solution: Provision of Apparatuses: All the authorities should keep in mind that apparatuses are most essential for the teaching of population education. Colleges must have the following things:

1. Useful films and other audio-visual aids for the teaching of population education.
2. Different types of charts, pictures and models depicting the population problem of the nation and other countries.

Problem: Lack of Research Work on Population Education. In our country, almost negligible research work has been done on the population education. There are no facilities for the same. Not only this there are many allusions about the need of population education.

Solution: Provision for Research Work. In order to acquaint the teachers and students with the effects of increasing population, adequate arrangements should be made for the research work in the field of population education. This work should be in connection with the following things-

1. How can the suitable environment be made in the colleges for population education?
2. What contribution can be made by the college managing committees and education departments for the expansion of population education?
3. What types of works can be useful for providing the thorough knowledge of population education to the teachers?
4. How can the general public be made aware of the need of population education?

Problem: Non-co-operation of Illiterate and Semi-literate Guardians for Population Education. In a study, it was found that illiterate and semi-literate guardians are against the provision of population education in the colleges. They are of the opinion that population education is family planning education only, which has nothing to do with the education of the children. It is sex-education which will spoil the character of the students. Population education is concerned with the dates which cannot be of any use for the students.

Solution: End of Non-cooperation of the Guardians. In order to satisfy the illiterate and semi-literate guardians due publicity should be given to the concept of population education through films, news-papers, lectures and other small books. Population education weeks and functions should be organised in the colleges and the guardians be invited in them in order to aquaint them with the real concept of population education.

These steps are precious and can consume a long time but if we have patience, they can prove to be very fruitful and then there will be no protests from the side of guardians and they shall definitely co-operate for making special provisions for the population education in the colleges.

15

Education for Every One

One of the chief aims of the constitution is to provide equal opportunities of education to all. How the equal opportunities be provided is the burning problem of the Modern India. Now, it is greatly felt that the backward classes of the society may improve their condition through education. Now, there is a social awakening towards education. Many scholars are working on the problem of changing the structure of education to provide equal opportunities of education for all the persons. Those who believe in the ideal of social justice, equality, and democracy must try to contribute their might for providing equal opportunities of education irrespective of caste, creed or sex.

The tendency to limit the educational opportunities is prevalent in the country since a long time. Often it is said that only those, who have the capability of receiving education should receive the education. How can those get the education who have no capabilities ? The leaders of the society never exerted full zeal and zeast to make all the people educated. However, the attitude changed in the later half of the 19th century and in the 20th century some efforts were made in the field of equal opportunities of education. After independence, in our constitution we adopted the concept of universalization of primary education. Since then, many steps have been taken in the field of providing equal opportunities to all sections of the society but still there is lot to be done in this direction.

Reasons for the Dissymmetry in Educational Opportunities:

There are many factors in the field of providing equal opportunities of education to all the persons of the society. Here, we are giving a brief account of them:

1. There are some places in our country where there are no primary, secondary schools, what to say about the institutions of higher education.
2. In the modern times, emphasis in on the development of education. But we have the unbalanced planning. There are some places where there are plenty of opportunities but there are other places where there is no such provision.
3. Another reason of the inequality in the field of education is that the major portion of our population is living below the poverty line and the children of poor families are unable to get suitable opportunities.
4. The elementary or primary education is free but at the later stages of study there is need of the huge amount and the children of poor families can not afford to have expensive education.
5. At different stages of study, there are different types of schools. The students, studying in below standard schools at lower stage of study, find it very difficult to get admission at the higher stage of study. Generally, the students studying in the rural areas have to run from pillar to post to get admission in the university.
6. The dissymmetry also arise due to the family atmosphere. The students residing in the dirty places of city or village find it very difficult to receive higher education. Their parents are illiterate and stop the studies of their wards if there are any type of hurdles.
7. The great difference between the education of boys and girls is also one of the chief causes of this dissymmetry.
8. Educational difference between the advanced classes and backward classes is also one of the potent cause of this dissymmetry.

9. There are no good arrangements for the handicapped students and so there is a great dissymmetry.

Hurdles in Equalization of Educational Opportunities

1. First, the main hurdle is that how the turn 'Equalization' be defined.
2. It is a problem before the educationists and administrators that the equal opportunities be provided to all the sections of the society.
3. In addition to social injustice, how can the intellectual and economic wastage can be stopped, is one of the burning problems.
4. Considering the needs of the student, how can their mental status be raised, is another problem.
5. Even if we provide the equal opportunities for all, it is not possible to achieve the equal results because the environment of family and schools is one of the potent factors of intellectual development of the students.
6. As it is totally impossible to ignore the environmental factor from the educational ability, so it is not good to provide the similar type of education to all the students. However, it can not be presumed that all the students living in dirty places are incapable.
7. There is no set criteria for judging the high capabilities of students,
8. The amount of the scholarships given to the students at every level is the same, whether they are living in big cities or small villages. This similarity does not appear to be just.
9. In technological institutes, the admission tests are held only in English language and so the English medium student get the advantage and thus the very spirit of equal opportunities is lost.
10. The handicapped students do not get the opportunity of

suitable educational standard due to the lack of resources and facilities.

11. Equal opportunities for women education is also a difficult task due to our pre-notions about the women education. Some parents do not allow their daughters to have higher education because they think that it is a sheer wastage. Some steps for the equalization of educational opportunities:

Certain concrete steps can be suggested for the equalization of educational opportunities. They are:

1. First of all, steps should be taken to remove the short-comings of society, community and family from the educational point of view.
2. The whole system of education should be modified in such a way that educational environment may be created in the entire nation.
3. Changes should be made in the diversive tendencies of language, place, standard of living, culture and social systems etc. so that equal opportunities may be given to all.
4. It is very necessary to make adequate changes in the system of educational evaluation so that there may be no possibility of favouritism.
5. The aims of education should be modified according to the needs of the time.
6. Equality in education should not only mean to achieve equal results but due importance be given to the efforts to raise the standard of education.
7. Unhealthy environment is the greatest hurdle in the field of the development of the child, so efforts should be made for the total environment to be more clean.
8. The evaluation of equality should be judged from the ratio of equality. So ability should be judged from the point of view of standard of living *etc.*

9. We shall have to change our attitudes towards women-education of backward classes, schedule castes and schedule tribes and handicapped persons. We shall have to remove all the hurdles and evils of the society of such persons and then only we shall be able to give the practical shape to equalization of educational opportunities.

Kothari Commission has made it clear that in India two types of inequalities are found in the field of education (a) in the education of boys and girls and (b) in the education of developed and backward classes, in older to remove these inequalities, the Commission recommended that upto the end of Fifth Five Year Plan lower Secondary Education should be made free and thereafter in the period of 10 years higher secondary and university education should be given free to the poor and meritorious students. The Commission also emphasised the need of reducing the cost of education. In the libraries of educational institutions, sufficient number of text-books should be kept and meritorious students should be granted financial help to enable them to purchase the text-books.

At the secondary education stages 15 percent students should be granted scholarships. By the year 1976, five percent of the students of post-graduate course should be granted scholarship. This percentage should be increased to 25 by the year 1986. The Commission also recommended the adoption of a system for granting educational scholarships. A system of university scholarships should also be started. 500 scholarships should be granted to the students, who should be selected to receive education in foreign countries.

Kothari Commission also suggested that within 20 years more than 10% handicapped persons should be educated. The Commission gave more emphasis on the women education and recommended for the organization at the national level to provide jobs to women. The. Commission also recommended for the expansion education amongst the scheduled tribes.

Under the educational policy of 1986, there is great provision of equalization of educational opportunities. Under the policy, there is provision of universalisation of primary education, vacationalization of secondary educational, job-oriented scientific education, and specialization of higher education. There is also provision of open university system. It is expected that with the proper implementation of this policy, our goal of equalization of educational opportunities shall be achieved.

Educating the Disadvantaged

India is a developing country but still a vast majority of the people are below standard. The number of handicapped in the country is also very great. One will find these handicapped people begging on the streets here and there. The provisions for the teaching of these people should also be made with great zeal and courage.

The handicapped people can be divided in three categories:

1. Mentally handicapped,
2. Physically handicapped, and
3. Socially handicapped.

The number of mentally retarded people in the country is very great. Physically handicapped people are also of different types: some are lepers, some are blind and some dumb and other physically handicapped. There are also people who are socially handicapped. These people are so poor that for them it is not possible to think of any type of education.

Practical Steps

During the pre-independence period, almost negligible efforts were made for the education of handicapped. There were only few organisations that used to take some steps in this direction. The government was not interested in their-education. However, after the independence, the national government came forward with the active programme of the welfare of these people. A number of schools and colleges were opened for the education of these people. Amongst the prominent are (l) National Centre for the blind, Dehradun, (2) National library, New Delhi, (3) Training Centre for the Dumb, Hyderabad, (4) School for the Blind,

Dehradun, (5) Training Centre for the Teachers for the Handicapped at Bombay and others. The education budget for the education of handicapped is increasing day by day. Indian government spent 23.06 lakhs rupees on the education of handicapped in the year 1955-56. The amount rose to Rs. 60.07 lakhs in the year 1970-71. In 1974-75 Rs 1 crore were spent for the education of handicapped. At present, the annual budget is more than three crore rupees.

The Difficulties

The government has made all out efforts for the education of handicapped but still there is a lot to be done in this direction. There are certain hurdles in this field. Many of our schemes are not completed due to the lack of funds. The allocation of funds made by the Centre and State Governments are very meagre. The number of handicapped is in lakhs but the financial allocation is not up to the mark. The number of educational Institutions for the handicapped is also not sufficient. There is great need for the increase in the number. The teachers of the school of handicapped are not fully trained. There is a great dearth of good teachers in this field. The curriculum should be village oriented, so that handicapped persons can perform certain functions in the villages. The administration of the schools of handicapped is also not up to the mark.

It is true that some things have been done for the education of handicapped but the number of handicapped is so great that still all efforts appear to be negligible. All our attempts should be made in this direction.

The vast majority of the people of India consists of those persons who are backward in all fields. The caste system of the country has done a great loss in the upliftment of people of India. There are backward classes, scheduled castes, scheduled tribes and tribal people who are educationally very backward. In article 341 and 342 of the Indian Constitution, there is a list of scheduled castes and scheduled tribes. From the educational point of view, they are far behind to those who belong to the upper class. Some efforts were made for the education of scheduled castes, scheduled tribes and tribal people in the pre-independence era. In the Macaulay's declaration of 1835, it was said that the doors of the Government colleges shall be opened only for those who belong to the higher class. However, in 1858, doors of these colleges were also opened for the people of scheduled castes and scheduled tribes. Hunter Commission in the year 1882 said that the education of the scheduled castes, scheduled tribes was totally neglected. The Commission recommended for the opening of special types of schools for these people. Hunter Commission also recommended that hectic efforts should be made for the education of tribal people. Upto the year 1921, 1922 only 6 per cent of the population of backward people were getting elementary knowledge. The percentage at the higher level was 0.1 and 0.2. In the year 1921, Mahatma Gandhi said that every effort should be made to educate the people of scheduled castes and scheduled tribes.

In 1902 the number of children of tribal people getting education in different Provinces was 4,534 in Madras, 7,667 in Bomaby, 30,302 in Bengal, 3,204 in Central Province and Barar and 16,094 in Assam. In 1936-37 the number rose to 15,603 in Madras, 29,102 in Bombay, 25,597 in Central Province Barar and 40,934 in Assam. The above data fully reveal that almost negligible efforts were made for the education of children of these people.

Scene after Independence

After the dawn of Independence, the Government greatly felt the need for the propagation of education for all the people of the country. In Article 45 of the Indian Constitution it was said that within ten years the education for all the children of the country upto the age of 14 shall be made compulsory. Article 15, 17, 19, 25 and 46 are related for the raising of social status and propagation of the education for those who were greatly neglected. Article 17 is in connection with the untouchability. Article 46 is in regard to the economic development of backward people. In article 25 it is said that the doors of religious institutions of Hindus shall be opened for all the people. In artical 29, it is said that the doors of Government and Government aided institutions shall be opened for all the people of the country

Under the Five Year Plans, provisions were made for the education of backward people and scheduled castes. In the first Five Year Plan Rs. 17 crores were spent for the education of scheduled castes. However, Rs. 53 crores were spent for the purpose under the Third Five Year Plan. Upto the year 1971 the percentage of scheduled castes receiving education was only 5. Hectic efforts were made for the education of scheduled tribes. Certain efforts were also made for the propagation of education in the tribal people of the country. The result of these efforts was that by the end of 1981,14.03 percent of the total population of scheduled castes and tribes became literate. Until now about 16 percent of their total population is literate.

As we have already said, a huge amount has been spent for the propagation of education amongst the scheduled castes, scheduled tribes and tribal people but still there is a lot to be done. There are some hurdles in this field. Among these people, there is no environment of education. Still there are thousands and thousands who do not think that is necessary for them to send their children to the schools. Those children who go to the school at primary level leave their education at the secondary level. Untouchability is a crime in our country but still it persists in one form or the other. There are still villages where the children of scheduled castes cannot receive education with the children of upper castes due to threat of upper casts. The economic condition of the people of scheduled castes, scheduled tribes and tribal people is also very poor and so they do not understand the need of education. Under these circumstances, a huge amount spent for the education is wasted: It is true that the Central Government as well as the State Governments of different provinces are making hectic efforts in this direction but the money allocated for the purpose is utilized somewhere else. The Government has also made provision for the scholarship for the students of scheduled castes and scheduled tribes. They are given free education up to the University level, but there are very few who utilise this opportunity.

As we have already said that with a view to remove these hurdles an environment should be created amongst the people of these castes and tribes and they should realise that education is a must for their development. The Government endeavours are not enough. More and more social agencies should come forward for this great task.

The Case of Drop-outs

A large percentage of children between the age group of 6 to 11 years in our country are not sent to school due to their domestic circumstances. There is also a large percentage of such children who are sent to school but they drop-out before completing their primary education. Because of the unprecedented growth in population in our country, the number of such students is increasing day-by-day. These illiterate children are curse for our democratic set-up. For such students a scheme of non-formal education has been started. In order to understand this scheme, it will be essential to know the difference between formal, informal and non-formal education.

Regular Education

In formal education, there is a prescribed curriculum. There are prescribed text-books and pre-fixed time-table and set rules for admission and examination. The duration of the session is also pre-fixed. Due to these rules and regulations the convenience is seldom taken account. The teacher does not have any liberty to make any change in the already prescribed rules and routines. The children have to sit in a group under a fixed time-table and they are taught something according to the prescribed curriculum. Thus, the formal education is not so much for children and it is for the facility of teachers and administration. In this type of education, children are taught experiences of others in order to give them a basis for their happy future life. Generally, the education given from the primary stage to the University level is called formal education.

Distance Education

Unlike formal education there are no set roles and regulations in informal education. Every children picks it up in natural and social environments. In his natural environment consisting of trees, plants, birds, animals, hub, mountains, forest, gardens, summer, winter and rainy seasons, a child happens to learn many things on his own. Similarly in a social environment which includes family, neighbourhood, Markets, plays, television, radio, cinema, railway station etc. the child happens to learn many things himself. There are no prefixed aims in learning. In fact, a person is motivated by his needs in learning many things consciously and unconsciously and expands his experiences. Chance and incidentalness play the vital role in this type of education. However, this type of education and learning is not less important than formal type of education and learning. It is the reason that all the great educators of modern times have emphasized the necessity of enriching the natural and social environment of the child to the utmost extant so that he may learn many things by himself.

Non-formal education is also free from the traditions of rules and regulations but there are goals to be realized through it. In this type of education, certain curriculum and procedures of evaluation have to be followed, but for following them, there is no fixed place and time duration. The procedures for this type of education are also quite flexible. In this type of education, the convenience of students is given more importance and convenience of teachers and administration is given secondary consideration. Thus, non-formal type of education is entirely organised according to the needs and convenience of students. Consequently, a child may receive this type of education while busy in his home, duty or while doing some thing for earning his bread. Some times non-formal education functions as competition to primary education in the sense that it teaches those things to non-school going children which they might not have learnt if they had attended the schools. However, it is to be noted that non-formal education is in education which may replace primary education. It is only complementary to it for those children who are deprived of the facility of going to primary schools, because of their adverse home circumstance. It is also for those children who have dropped out of primary schools before receiving in full It is also to be kept in mind that non-formal education is altogether different from adult education.

The purpose of adult education is to make adults learn within a stipulated period of time and then to educate them into the basic elements of life in general. In adult education, the life occupation is accepted as the basis of the education. In this education an adult acquires knowledge in formal manner, and non-formal education after acquiring some seasonable literacy programmes are organised for developing experience where knowledge and literacy is made practical and purposeful as the programmes are based on the real life. In non-formal education, literacy alone is not the chief goal. In fact, the entire education is so organised as to make closely related the personal mode of life and also the occupation relating to some industry or craft within the easy reach of children. Due to this close relationship, even after acquiring adulthood the individual shall remain not only literate but also remember his acquired knowledge and experience.

It is not very difficult to draw and outline of the curriculum for non-formal education. The basis of organization of the curriculum is the local needs, industries and crafts suitable for the boys and girls concerned. The rural environment is different from the urban one and so the curriculum of rural children shall be different from the other children. The needs of boys are different from the girls. We shall have to take into account the varying needs of the boys and girls for framing their curriculum. The interest, capacities and age of children too should be kept in view. Agriculture and rural industries are accepted as the basis of curriculum organization of rural children. Urban industries, mills, factories and other kinds of livelihood are the basis of curriculum organization for urban children.

For the organization of curriculum, the help of experienced workers, farmers, teachers and others is also taken. The co-operation of the voluntary organizations of the neighbourhood should also be sought for procuring the necessary help at times. The materials, such as lanterns and baskets and Jugs etc. may be lent to the village people at the time of their special social functions. This will create a feeling of brotherhood in them and the people shall consider the centre as their home.

Good Aspects

As we have already stated that the boys and girls coming the centre should be grouped in sections according to their age and capacity. They should be educated of the basis of following motivations:

1. Intellectual, 2. Political, 3. Religious, 4. Social, and 5. Economic.

1. Under the intellectual motivation, children should be prompted to learn on the basis of their interests. They should at least pick-up the preliminary knowledge of those subjects which are taught to children of primary schools.

2. Under the political motivation, the boys and girls should be taught the rights and duties of citizenship. They should be given the elementary knowledge of working of Village Block, Panchayat, District Board, Municipal Board, State and Central Government. Newspapers, radio talks and Television programmes should be made available for the purpose.

3. Under the religious motivation, children should be encouraged to have the feeling of religious tolerance. Equality of all religions should be the basic ideal before them.

4. Under the social motivations, attempt should be made to wipe out the distinction of caste, colour and creed from the minds of Children. Children of Scheduled castes and Scheduled tribes should not be discriminated and all out efforts should be made for their upliftment. The spirit of equality and brotherhood should be infused amongst the children.

5. Under the economic motivation, the children should be made to learn that education is for their economic development. It will brighten their future and increase their working efficiency and help in raising the standard of their life.

For making the above motivations as the basis for educating children, it is essential to enlist the co-operation of able teachers, conveners and supervisor, along with acquiring reading materials. The non-formal education in India is at a very preliminary experimental stage, in some states different kinds of work has been done in this direction while it has yet to be started in most of the states.

16
Private Education

Education is a life long process. Formal education has contributed a lot in the expansion of primary, secondary and university education but due to its rigidity, it is not able to meet all the educational needs of the modern scientific and technological era. So a need for such an educational system was felt which may be flexible and within the approach of everybody. The result was the distance education. Distance education is the coordinated form of formal and non-formal education and it has good points of both of them. Some scholars have termed it as Open Education and others as Correspondence Education. However, the term Distance Education is more appropriate.

The Concept

Distance education is in fact a form of Open Education. It is a device by which people residing in remote regions receive education according to their interests and aptitudes. In this form of education, teacher has little importance. The education is imparted through information, correspondence, radio and television. It is true that in this form of education teacher and taught are not before each-other and teacher does not directly observe the activities of students but students are benefited by the planning and direction. It is a from of education in which teacher does not take the responsibility of oral teaching but becomes instrumental in imparting knowledge to those who want to get it at the place of their own choice.

Thus, in distance education teacher and taught remain apart. They have no or very little contact. It is the education which is planned by an educational institution or organization. Generally, we do not need any class room or school for teaching but in the teaching of practical skills we have to use them. Radio, Television, Video-cassettes and film strips are used for teaching. Basically, distance education is learning centres education which derives facilities to students to receive education at place of their choice.

In modern times all the developed and many under developed countries have adopted the system of distance education and this system has drawn the attention of most of all education lovers. In India equipments for providing education are inadequate and because of the rising population, the number of illiterate person is increasing day by day. It has not been possible for us to meet the educational needs of all those who desire to receive education. The utility of distance education has so much recognized these days that 60 countries have jointly established on International Council of Distance Education. The traditional education can benefit only for job. If a student is admitted in some school or college he shall have remain there till he finishes the prescribed course successfully. During this period, a number of teachers teach him at a particular place and according to a fixed time-table. Under this traditional system, the poor are deprived of the facilities of higher education because in existing system, higher education is quite expensive. A large number of persons reside in rural areas and it is very difficult for them to receive higher education.

This is an age of democracy. In a democratic set up it is very necessary to give benefit to all. If many people can not go to schools, colleges and universities, we shall have to take education to their very door steps. If all can not get education and traditional centres of education, we shall have to device ways and means for taking education to them. And under these circumstances, chances of distance education are greatly needed.

The present system of education was started at the time when there were very few persons to receive education and for them the oral system of teaching was considered as quite suitable. In present times, the techniques of imparting education have been so much refined that it has become quite easy to provide education to all. The progress has enabled people of any social and economic status to receive education without difficulty. If people receive education through these techniques they not only become more enlightened, but the entire nation shall be benefited. The method of distance education is of democratic outlook and it is a new method for providing education to all.

The utility of distance education is from the following point of view:

(1) As we have already said that the demand of education is creasing day by day and it is not possible to meet this demand through formal education and so distance education is greatly needed.

(2) Education is a long-life process. We can get formal education for only few years, but distance education can be received throughout the life.

(3) In present times the education is not confined to a class of people. The principle of education for all has been excepted and so expansion of distance education is essential. In our country a large number of girls, handicapped persons and children of poor families are devoid of formal education. So it was felt to device a system of education by which people can get education at their home and so need of distance education was greatly felt.

(4) In order to take the advantage of modern technology, distance education is essential. Due to the development of technology radio, television, video-cassettes and computer are not only the source of recreation but they can also be of great use for increasing our knowledge.

(5) Quite a large number of persons after completing their formal education go for a job or any other employment and leave their studies. Distance education helps a lot in increasing their skill and ability.

(6) Distance education is greatly needed for the equalization

of educational opportunities so that lower class of the society can get the opportunity of education through it.

(7) It is a matter of great shame that still about 48% of our population is illiterate. We have adopted many programmes for the removal of illiteracy and the programme of distance education is one of them. Distance education has been greatly instrumental in our adult literacy mission.

(8) Distance education is essential for the help of formal education. In modern times, it is very difficult to get admission in the institutes of higher education and so we have to take the help of distance education.

Courses by Correspondence

The beginning of distance education is from the correspondence system. By introducing many modifications in the correspondence system, the path towards distance education has been made smoother. It has been possible due to development of educational technology. One of the chief disadvantages of correspondence system was the total absence of the teacher in it. However, in distance education the students get at times, the benefit of the presence of teachers and it has made distance education more acceptable. Some regional or local centres are opened were students get the advantage of consulting some teachers. The chief purpose of distance education is to make higher education available to those who have been deprived of it because of their adverse circumstances. Under the distance education system students residing any where in the country can receive higher education. In our country first the correspondence courses were started but now the distance education is day by day taking the job of correspondence course. Indira Gandhi Open University has doing a commendable job for educating those who could not get higher education due to the one reason or the other. Other Open Universities and regional centres of Indira Gandhi Open University are contributing a lot in this direction.

Good Aspects

As we have already said that in distance education, there is no provision of face to face class-room teaching sometimes through contact programmes some arrangements are made for classroom lectures for two or three weeks. In place of classroom teaching correspondence lessons are sent to students. In addition to these lessons, some supplementary material is also provided. A team of experts prepares these materials according to the needs. The lessons are generally good and the students are able to grasp them. The nature of the lesson is as such that the students can not acquire so much knowledge by consulting one or two books on the subjects.

In addition to correspondence lessons, radio, television, video cassette, tapes are used. Attempts are also made to make distance education more useful through broadcasting information, library facility, mobile teaching squad etc.

Bad Aspects

Some people have criticized the working of open universities through distance education on the ground that it will lead to deterioration of academic standards. These persons are of the view that a student who receives the university degree through courses based on distance education can not be equal in competency in knowledge to the students who have earned University degree by studying according to the traditional method in classroom situation under the guidance of teachers and help of good books. In reply to this criticism, the supporters of Open University system say that the lessons of the Open University are prepared by a panel of expert teachers and they are of the nature that one can not get the same knowledge through a lecture of a teacher or reading by one or two books.

Some critics of the distance education and open universities are of the opinion that the lessons and reading materials of distance education are nothing but just a disconnected assemblage of fragments of certain books and so students are seldom able to grasp to them. However, lessons and reading material supplied by Indra Gandni Open University ,have shut the mouths of these criticise. The material supplied by the university is of very high standard. Still there is no denying that fact that open universities can not fully replace the traditional universities. There are some subjects which can be taught only, traditional universities for research work too open universities can not match the traditional universities.

The distance educations is criticised that in distance education use of radio, television, video and cassettes, tapes is most essential and in a country like India where there is so much power shortage and regular failure of electricity, teaching through these method is nothing but a fools paradise. For this criticism one can say that we can solve the problem if the programmes are broadcasted several times. In due course of time we may be able to solve our problems of power shortage in electricity failure and then this criticism shall have no weight.

Education in Continuance

Education is the around development of a person. It is a life long process. Education is for refinement and enlightenment. It is a continuous process. No one becomes educated by nearly receiving some literacy. An educated person is one who can utilise his education for solving his different problems and who can benefit others by the same. It is the education which develops one's intellectual and cultural horizon.

In India, people are generally not so keen to obtain knowledge as people are in developed nations. Many people in our country take admissions in Schools, Colleges and Universities but drop-out in the middle of the session without completing the prescribed course of studies. Some do so due to their adverse circumstances and some due to their bad companies. Thus, there is a large number of persons who are not able to complete their formal education. However, their desire to acquire further knowledge is not killed after some times they may like to continue their education. For them, continuing education is a boon. Under these circumstances, it is the duty of the government and social leaders to provide facilities of continuing education to drop-outs, farmers, labourers and half educated individuals.

Along with Career

Persons engage in agriculture, industries, sciences and different services are all contributing in the national development in one form or the other. All the people employed in service or business have the great importance in the field of development of the nation. All these persons on the basis of their varying experiences learn many things automatically. But in addition to their particular skills and experiences they need to acquire some such knowledge which may enable them to become enlightened. This knowledge may be in political field, economic field or such other fields. It is only through the continuing education that this knowledge may be imparted to them.

Any person, engaged in any job may have many such interests which are not directly related to his job. These interest gradually fade away when he does not get opportunity to develop them further. On the other hand, if he gets opportunity to develop them, he may sharpen his interest to such an extent that he may be able to produce some striking things in the area of his interest. If a person is provided with the facility to use his leisure in workshop of his interest, he may contribute a lot to the society. It is only through continuing education one may utilize his leisure in a creative manner. On the other hand, if he has nothing to do during his leisure time he will waste it in reading some cheap literature, deteriorating to his character and personality. Thus, continuing education is helpful in checking his deterioration and to put him on right path of further progress.

Persons engaged in one or the other industries drift away from the latest developments taking place in the world in other areas than their own due to their environment in their jobs. For them too continuing education is essential. Persons engaged in health services, family welfare enterprises and other types of social services can also be benefited by continuing education. They can be imparted knowledge about the latest development with the help of books or public lectures. Provisions should be made for continuing education for Gram Sewaks, Block Development Officers, Doctors, Lawyers and Engineers and others busy in their specialized areas. For these persons libraries and study centres should be opened where they may get the opportunity to increase their knowledge. Cinema, Radio, T.V. and other audio-visual aids also play the vital role in the field of continuing education.

Continuing education should be planned for literate and illiterate farmers and labourers of rural areas and urban areas. Through the continuing education we can make our citizens engaged in services and business more enlightened, cultured and progressive.

Movement for Literacy

As we have already said that continuing education is not only helpful for those who are engaged in some jobs or business but it also helps the illiterates and semi-literates to achieve knowledge and contribute their might in the development of the nation. After the achievement of independence, our government have started many schemes for spreading literacy among to illiterate persons. Throughout the country, thousands of centres for adult and social education have been opened and crores of rupees have been spent for the purpose in different Five Year Plans. A large number of libraries have been opened for the semi- literate person. Radio and T.V. are also contributing their might for the purpose. A large number of programmes are relayed for the education of these persons. Many primary schools run the classes of adult and social education in the evening.

In accordance with the directives of National Policy on Education, 1986 (NPE) and the implementation strategies envisaged in the Programme Action, the Government has formulated a comprehensive programme known as National Literacy Mission in the field of adult education. The objectives of National Literacy Mission are to impart functional literacy to 800 lakh illiterate persons in 15-36 age group, 300 lakh by 1990 and an additional 500 lakh by 1995. At present, there are 513 projects in operation in various states and union territories.

Voluntary agencies have been playing an important role in the Adult Education Programme. There are at present 382 voluntary agencies working in the field. In addition 40 Shramik Vidyapeeths and 16 state resource centres are functioning in different states to cater to worker's education and to provide technical resource support to the programme.

Launched in 1986, the Mass Programme of Functional Literacy

covered over 4.20 lakh learners. During 1987 a still ambitious programme has been adopted involving both students and teachers of schools and colleges with inputs for research studies on the success of the programme. The programme has been designed keeping in view the needs and language of learners.

Inspite of the great efforts, we have not been able to achieve our targets. Investigations have revealed that illiterates and semi-literate adults have special interests in such subjects as, (1) ancient history, (2) basic religious matters, (3) the diseases which generally attack animals and destroy agriculture and gardening, (4) the fundamentals of economics, (5) short but healthy novels and interesting stories, (6) folk stories, (7) folk songs, (8) psychology of adults, (9) fundamentals of philosophy, (10) first aid, (11) prevention of ordinary diseases, (12) matters regarding health and sanitation. (13) psychology of child behaviour, (14) information about bringing up young children. (15) music, (16) liking, habits of people of other lands, (17) modern international and national events, (18) the modern history of the country and (19) modern scientific achievements. This list of subjects reveal that an adult wants to understand many things about life. It is through continuing adult education we may be able to satisfy his lust for knowledge.

In our country' hectic endeavours have been made for adult education but very little work has been done for those adults who had to leave primary school studies prematurely. In a report of UNESCO about 60% children of Asian countries happen to abandon their primary education before successfully competing it. In our country no adequate facilities are available to retain literacy. Of course, there are some books for their continuing education but they too are not made available to all the persons. These books are not very useful. The result is that there is quite a large number of persons, especially women, who are keen for their education but they have no opportunities. It is the duty of the government and social workers to come forward for their continuing education. The government and the educational agencies should not only publish the good books for their continuing education but also made them available to needy persons.

17
Unity Factor

There are some tendencies at work in our country which are hindering our national integration. Different languages, states, classes and castes, political parties, tendency of ignoring national interest for personal ones, regionalism, poverty and different communities are some such elements which are challenging our national unity. We have adopted a democratic system of government. Hence, diversities prevailing in the country have to be recognised. It is not necessary that individual differences often enrich our national life. But these diversities should not take such a shape as to endanger our national security and unity. Today, the diversities widespread in the country have threatened our national security. Some humiliating incidents have happened in our country in the name of language and regionalism. Boundary disputes between two states, quarrel between two states for a particular city, and communal riots and fighting in some places, are blots on the good name of our country. This shows that we are not following the right course. Some people demand a separate state on the basis of regions. Today, the unprincipled behaviour of some political parties and their internal groupism are likely to strangulate the nation. Most of the political parties seem to be affected by personality cult instead of following some principles. The division of Congress and other parties is not so much a quarrel of principles as it is show of personalities or for personal interest by dancing at the tune of some individuals. All these conditions are against the development of a healthy democratic system. Therefore, national integration has become a problem and is one of the main problems of our education. Hence, we shall try to find out its solutions.

Unity at Political Level

Today, there are some persons of confused mind in our country who doubt the political unity of the country. It is true that several kings ruled over this country and there had been many independent kingdoms from time to time. But at the same time, it is to be noted that a current has always been flowing throughout the country which kept the country united. Our places of pilgrimage are not centralised within a particular region. They are spread throughout the country, Rameshwaram, Dwarika, Jagannathpuri and Badrinath are the glaring examples. It was a wonderful wisdom of our religious leaders that they established places of pilgrimage in the four corners of the country in order that people from one corner may go to the other and may visit the whole country, may know each other and consider themselves of this vast land with a feeling of oneness. Since the beginning of Indian Civilization and culture, our countrymen have been anxious to go on pilgrimage and they have been visiting different places of pilgrimage. People from-north to south, south to north, east to west and west to east, have been going from one part of the country to the other. Thus there has been cultural exchange since older days and people have been considering themselves as citizens of one country.

Different rivers of our country have been considered sacred and adorable. Such rivers do not belong to one region alone. Krishna, Kaveri and Godavari of the South, Sindhu of West, Ganga, Yamuna, Sarayu and Gomti of North and Brahmputra of east have been considered holy and worth worship. Similarly, mountains of different regions in the country have been considered sacred. Different cities of the country have been recognised as places of pilgrimage and centres of cultures. Thus, it is clear that our great men have always tried to unite the country with a cultural thread and they have always been successful in their efforts.

This feeling of cultural unity inspired our religious leaders and social reformers to inculcate the feeling of common citizenship in our countrymen. It is because of this feeling that whenever our great leaders have raised their voice on any issue, the whole country has followed them. It was because of this that all the groups in the country fought the struggle for freedom under the banner of Indian National Congress, forgetting their religion, caste or community and consequently won independence. The unity shown by the people for winning freedom was not artificial, but something natural. In fact, that was the voice of country's conscience. Gandhiji's 'Dandi March' and 'Quit India Movement' had shaken the country so much that even the British Empire had begun to doubt its permanency. Many such examples and incidents may be cited to prove when on incident in one corner of the country moved the whole nation. This is a glaring example of our unshakable national unity. Chinese invasion in 1962 and Indo-Pak war of 1965 had united the whole country and it was evidenced that same feeling was running the views of the whole nation: The period of Ashoka the Great and the Great Emperor Akbar gave us a glimpse of this kind of unity. The rebellion of 1857 supports our feeling of oneness. Needless to say that we should make our political and national unity durable and should not encourage deceptive forces.

Sentimental Union

Emotional unity of our countrymen is essential for our national integration. So long as our countrymen do not consider themselves as one and do not realize that first and foremost they are citizen of this country and their personal, sectarian, social and religious interests are secondary, there can be no national integration. They must be made to feel that from historical, geographical point of view, India has always been one country and one nation and will always remain so. They should be convinced that ours is a culture which every person should be proud of. In foreign country whenever is a talk of Indian culture before any Indian living abroad, he is over-joyed and feels a natural pride.

When we see bay of Bengal, Kumari Antreep of Indian Ocean in the South, Gulf of Kutch in the west and Himalayas in the north, an emotional current runs within us and this current fills us with reverence to India. The same feeling is created when we stand on the banks of Ganga, Yamuna, Sindhu, Krishna, Kaveri, Godavari or Brahmaputra. Whenever we remember our sacred rivers, our heart is filled with joy and then we think of these saints and great men who created new chapters of our culture from time to time and tried to unite us. Our rivers and mountains are not only geographical units, but different constituents of our culture have been produced in their vicinity. Our Indian culture has been created by the thinkers, living close to the jungles, valleys and rivers, so our culture does not have that artificiality which is found in industrial cultures. We have to make this emotional unity stronger. Education is a powerful means for the fulfillment of this aim. The poets and authors of our country should praise our mountains, rivers and oceans in such a way that attracted by praise the people are lost in them. We should attract the attention of our people to this through education. By doing so all will be emotionally integrated and will rise above their personal interests for good of the country.

A United Society

In our country different groups based on community, religion, caste, poverty and wealth are found. These groups remain indifferent to each other and there is lack of national unity. They are wanting the feeling of brotherhood. There is influence of caste in some religion, sectarian feeling in the other and some particular religion in another. In fact, the situation is very pitiable. For national integration, it is necessary that people of different classes and communities are brought to each other and feeling of unity is infused in them.

For this, some collective programmes should be arranged and people of all classes, communities and different religions should be invited. Every community should be made to feel that the interest of their community lies in the interest of the country which is the first and foremost than anything else. So, no class or community can make progress by ignoring the interest of the nation. Needless to say that we have to forego communalism, religionism and regionalism for social unity. This does not, however, mean that we should have no love for our community, religion or region and should forsake them. It only means that we should first think of the country and after that of anything. We have to inculcate the feeling of 'Nation first, anything afterwards'. It was only due to this feeling that people coming from different countries of Europe were able to establish a nation in America. Similarly, there are followers of several languages, regions and religions in Russia. But these elements never proved a hioderance for the unity of the country because the people there kept national good over all. Religionism, casteism, regionalism and linguism have been encouraged by some of the political parties in our country and these parties have acted against national unity. All of us know very well that at the time of elections different political parties plead for religion, class, caste and region and want to secure votes on the basis of these slogans. A candidate is selected from that caste or religion which dominates a particular area. Such an action is just a misuse of caste for political interest and it creates conditions for national disintegration. All such policies will have to be changed for the sake of national Integration.

Beyond Baniers

Some people are of the opinion that for national integration, inter-caste and inter-state marriages should be encouraged. This means that people should marry in to other castes and religions, forgetting their own caste and religion. Similarly, persons of different regions north, south, east and west should not hesitate in natural marriages. The children born of such marriages will be above caste, religion and regionalism. They will consider themselves Indians first and anything else afterwards. In support of this argument, people cite the example of U.S.A. and Japan. The Spanish, German, French and British people who settled in America after migrating from different countries of Europe, accepted inter-caste marriages. The off-spring of these people consider themselves an American first and take pride in calling themselves as such. Similarly, in Japan also followers of different religions are found in one family and their off-spring call themselves Japanese first and not of this or that religion or caste. Thus, national and integration in America and Japan has been very much encouraged. In our country, this process should be adopted voluntarily and anyone who is desirous of intercaste marriage should be encouraged and should be given special social recognition. But we should bear it in mind that in the context of social situation in our country, it will not be wise to arouse a countrywide current for intercaste marriages. But whenever such examples are found, due importance should be given to them, because such step is a good means for national integration.

Economy, a Factor for Unity

The economic inequalities pervading the country are weakening her. Some have a wealth of lakhs and crores and some are dying for want of two square-meals in a day. These inequalities will have to be removed for the sake of national integration and so that no specific class or community remains backward. For this, it is necessary that minorities and backward persons are given special help. They should be given special facilities of education, houses and government services. If the backward classes are satisfied and feel comfortable, they will contribute to the national integration.

Language for the Nation

The question of national language has become very important for us. According to the Constitution, Hindi in the Devnagri Script has been accepted as state language and in 1965 Hindi was to occupy the place of national language of the country. But in 1965 when this place was accorded to Hindi, riots broke out in South and in Calcutta and these are, in fact, a blot on the nation. Although majority of people in different regions of the country are prepared to accept Hindi as national language but they were forced to follow so slow policy regarding Hindi due to riots and disturbances in January and February of 1965.

If we want to encourage national integration, we should not be in a haste for Hindi. So long as people of non-Hindi speaking areas do not agree to accept 'Hindi', the clause of the Constitution regarding Hindi should be kept in abeyance. We should prepare the non-Hindi People for accepting Hindi with national love. Although it is time that we can not continue a foreign language as link language for ever. Our general Indian public cannot learn English. Some say we shall have to accept some Indian language. This does not mean that knowledge of English is not useful for us.

In order to take benefit from international culture and knowledge, the knowledge of English is very necessary. So the subject of English should not only be available in our schools, colleges and universities but it should be compulsory at degree stage. Inspite of all this we have to adopt our own language, and so far that language is Hindi. So long as the related clauses of the Constitution are not changed, we should strive for the acceptance of Hindi as a national language in such a way that one day the whole country may be prepared to accept it gladly. But as long as non-Hindi people do not show their willingness to accept it, Hindi should not be imposed on them as it will be against national integration. Therefore, we should remember that our national language Hindi is helpful in national integration rather than an obstruction. Evidently, we have to work in this direction cautiously, affectionately, sympathetically and with wise entreaty.

Role of Education

We have indicated in previous pages that in education is a powerful means for national integration. Through education we can inspire the future citizens for it. So the aim of national integration is to be kept supreme over all while organising the different components of education. In framing the curriculum, the class-room teaching, in educational centres, cultural activities, in the organisation of co-curricular activities, in the management of schools, in the various stage of education (schools, colleges or universities), in the appointment of teachers, in the distribution of educational facilities, in the composition of text-books we should follow such policies as will encourage national integration rather helping the tendencies of class, community, religion etc.

In the existing situation of the country and the international context, the need for unity should be emphasized more. We have to be careful that no disruptive forces flourish against national integration, if we follow the suggestions given in previous pages, we shall be successful in maintaining national unity.

The spirit of a country is inherent in its culture. The chief function of education has always been to transmit the culture of the country to future generations. Different countries have different cultures. Hence, different countries try to transmit their cultures to the children and youth of country through their specific systems of education. After the British rule becoming well established in our country in the nineteenth century, the education system was shaped according to the British deals. Hence the education system always remained aloof from the Indian background, but after the achievement of freedom in 1947, the problem of removing the education system from this serious defect has become very important for us. Now we want to Indianise our education. In this chapter, we will discuss this problem.

Indianisation: the Concept

Different persons have given different views regarding the meaning of Indianisation. The meaning of Indianisation was considered to be the following of Indian methods in place of British methods in the Indian national life. This was a narrow meaning of Indianisation. According to the wider meaning of Indianisation, it is to include the foreign elements in the Indian Public life that it is made richer while maintaining its national and good points of our culture, characteristics. This meaning also includes the inculcation of the feeling of Social and National responsibility in the public life of the country. It is to be remembered that we have to overcome the tendency of Hindunisation, purported by some narrow-minded persons in our effort for Indianisation. In fact, we have to keep Muslims, Christians and other countrymen with us in the sequence of indianisation, otherwise Indianisation will be meaningless.

Indianisation does not mean making it governmental. Its aim is the development of the feeling of proper social and national responsibility in the people. National feeling should not be interpreted in the political context alone. The national feeling goes further by including political sincerity in it attachment to the country, feeling of pride for our cultural heritage, respect for national language, national flag, great men of the nation, national anthem and national beliefs are all included in it. Those foreigners who come upto our expectations in these various contests, can also be considered fully mixed up in this national feeling. For example, Smt. Annie Besant and Mr. Stocks, though they were not born in India, will always remain a part of our national life since they proved true to our expectations. Contrary to this many persons who were born in India, can never come in the purview of our definition of Indianisation, if they have declared themselves deadly against our country. The national feeling of a person is his inner inclination his religion, caste, language or political party have very little influence on it. By Indianisation we mean this favourable inner inclination of an Indian though he may belong to any religion, language or political faith.

The Indianisation of education means that education has got to be geared to the needs and aspirations of the country. For this adjustment we have to continue to move with the ever changing nature of Indian culture. To make education capable of fulfilling the demand of the country and to make it according to the means and functions needed at a particular time, will be called Indianisation of Indian education.

After the winning of freedom in 1947, new needs and aspirations have arised in the Indian public life. Consequently, the unsuitability of education continuing since the British times disturbed our minds. So, the rulers of the country made several efforts to bring the needed changes in the educational system of the country. In these efforts generally the following three main characteristics may be noticed:

Efforts of Reinclusion of the Basic Elements of Ancient Education. The establishment of D.A.V. Colleges and some Gurukuls on the basis on the views of Swami Dayanand is a symbol of such an effort. Some educational centres established by Ram Krishna Mission and Shantiniketan established by Ravindra Nath Tagore are other examples of such an effort.

Efforts of Making the Education of the Country Modern. Education policy framers and the rulers of our country have realised it well that education can be capable of preparing worthy citizens according to the present day needs only when modern western knowledge and science are adequately included in our education.

Basic Education. The educational system initiated by Mahatma

Gandhi was a praiseworthy effort of inculcating self-reliance, constructive skill and practical knowledge in our students. Being dis-satisfied with the then prevailing education, Mahatma Gandhi advised to implement this scheme. It was a revolutionary step for a change in the very base of our education system i.e. at the stage of primary education. This revolutionary step had the following main points:-

(1) The child will be the centre of education.

(2) He will learn while working.

(3) The work alone by the child during the process of learning will be productive.

(4) Some craft will be the pivot of education.

(5) Children will imbibe the feeling of dignity of manual labour.

(6) The medium of education shall be the mother tongue.

(7) The various subjects will be taught by co-relating them with the selected craft.

(8) The teachers and student will do their work based on the ideals of truth and non-violence.

(9) The teachers and students, both will work for social upliftment.

Evidently, the above ideals were placed before us to provide a strong base for education and prepare worthy citizens. But basic education did not succeed according to its ideals because of several reasons, although it was accepted as a national policy of education for primary level. We have mentioned the causes for the failure of basic education in a separate chapter earlier. However, it is true that basic education has not been able to achieve its proposed objectives so far, but it must be admitted that basic education has been a revolutionary effort in the direction of Indianisation.

University Commission of 1948-49, Secondary Education Commission of 1952-53 and Acharya Narendra Deo Committees of 1939, 1952-53 the universitv and Secondary Education

Commissions established by the Indian Government and Acharya Narendra Deo Committees appointed by the Government of U.P. , have made efforts of Indianisation and modernisation of University and Secondary education in their specific contexts. It is not necessary for him at the recommendations of these Commissions here, because they have already been discussed under separate chapters earlier.

This Commission appointed by the Indian Government is yet another revolutionary effort for the Indianisation of education. We nave already discussed some of the main recommendations of this Commission in a separate chapter. It is not necessary to repeat them here again. However, the essence of these recommendations is briefly given below, as it fits in with the needs of Indianisation of our education.

(1) The development of the social, moral, and spiritual beliefs of Indians should be made possible through education.

(2) The development of democratic ideals should be done through education.

(3) Increase in production is possible only through education.

(4) Modernisation of the country can be done through education alone.

(5) Education should help in the development of social and national integration.

Policy for Education

In July 1968, our Government announced National Education Policy on the basis of the recommendations of Kothari Commission. This declaration is a symbol of our efforts of Indianisation. The following are some of the main elements of this declaration:

(1) To bring education close to public life.

(2) To make efforts for the qualitative improvement at all the stages of education.

For bringing education close to the public life; the following programmes should be adopted.

(a) To develop new moral and social beliefs.

(b) To make special attention to science and industry at every stage of education as far as possible.

In order to achieve the above objects, the Indian Government has decided to work according to the following principles in the field of education.

Increase in the Salary and Allowances of Teachers. In this regard, the government has decided that it will continue to strive to achieve the above objectives. It must be remembered that the State Government are trying to improve the status of the teachers through all possible means with the help and aspiration of the Central Government and University Grants Commission. A glowing example of this effort are the new scales of pay of the teachers at various levels, implemented by the U. P Government and some other states in the country.

Encouragement of All Indian Languages. In order to improve the culture, literature and philosophy and public life, the government has decided to develop all Indian languages, the national language and culture. Along with it, for expansion of knowledge, it has stressed the need of encouraging the study of English and some other international languages.

National Service and Work Experience. The aim of national service and work experience is to be achieved according to the capacity of the students at every stage of education.

Equality of Education Opportunity. Equal opportunities of education are to be provided to the children of various regions, such as, hill areas, sea beach and barren lands and to backward and disabled children, children of tribal areas and gifted children.

Science Education and Research. In order to make the country prosperous, science education should be emphasised and new Research should be conducted in this fixed programme.

Development of Talent. Talent (meritorious persons) in the country should be discovered and developed.

Education in Agriculture and Industry. Special attention should be paid to the development of agriculture and different industries in order to make the country self-sufficient.

Preparation of Books. Various original books on science and knowledge should be prepared and the gifted authors should be rewarded for the work.

Reforms in the Defective Examination System. For the proper evaluation of students achievement, the examination system should be reformed.

Necessary Changes in Secondary Education. Secondary Education should be extended to those areas where it has not been provided so far. Facilities for technical and vocational education should be available at the secondary stage.

University Education:

(i) Technical and vocational educational should be extended to the University stage.

(ii) Laboratories, libraries and other necessary material-aid should be arranged for this stage.

(iii) New Universities should be established cautiously.

(iv) Improvements in Research, Training and Postgraduate curriculum should be brought about.

(v) Some model research centres should be established.

(vi) Short-term education and correspondence education plan should be started.

(vii) Literacy and adult education should be extended.

(viii) Proper attention should be paid on the educational structure. This structure should be uniform for the whole country.

(ix) Necessary resources be developed for the games and sports of students.

(x) Secondary Education up to 10 years, higher secondary education for two years and Graduate education for three years, that is, the pattern of 10+2+3 should be implemented throughout the country.

In fact, our leaders in the sphere of education have no interest as to how to Indianise education. However, whatever has been discussed in the different pages of this chapter, there can be no doubt, in fact, that our national government is looking towards Indianisation.

Language Issue

Language problem has been prevalent in our country in one form or the other since ancient periods. Earlier Sanskrit was the main language of our country but at that time there too was a conflict between Sanskrit, Prakrit and Pali. In the Muslim period, Arabic and the Persian were the official languages but Urdu and Hindi were also adopted. In 1835, Lord Macauley gave great emphasis to the English language and since then all out efforts were made to make English the medium of instruction. During the British period, medium of instruction was English. After independence the question was that which language should be adopted as the medium of instruction. Language problem can be seen in two forms: (1) Problem of the medium of the teaching; and (2) Problem of study of different languages at different stages.

Instruction Medium

As we have already said that in Ancient India, Sanskrit was the medium of instructions. Later on Pali and Prakrit took place of Sanskrit During the middle ages, Arabic and Persian were the medium of instruction. During the reign of Akbar, Hindi and Urdu were also given great importance. After the arrival of Britishers in India, there was a visit change in the educational policy. In 1935 Lord Macauley emphasised that English should be the medium of instruction and it remained the medium of instruction for more than hundred years.

After the independence, controversy of the medium of instruction arose. Different scholars put forward the different views regarding medium of instruction. Some of the scholars were of the opinion that English should remain the medium of teaching while others were in favour of state language Hindi. Some pleaded for the regional languages. Radhakrishnan Commission recommended that Indian Languages should be the medium of instruction in place of English. Mudaliar Commission recommended that up to the Secondary stage, Mother tongue or the regional language should be the medium of instruction, the Commission was of the view that English should be replaced by Hindi and it should be compulsory in all universities. In 1955 the languages Commission also recommended that Hindi should be the medium of instruction, and university examination should be held in Hindi. Kothari commission was of the view that the regional languages should be the medium of instruction up to the primary and secondary stage. Even at the higher stage of study, regional languages should be the medium of instruction. English should be replaced by Hindi.

From the above discussion, we come to the conclusion that the problem of medium of instruction is very tedious. The only solution of the problem is that English should be replaced by the regional languages and State language Hindi. Hindi should be compulsory in all the universities of the country.

Languages as Subjects

In Ancient India there was no such problem. Sanskrit was the main language which was studied from one corner of the country to other corner of the country. In addition to Sanskrit, Prakrit, and Pali were also studied. During the Muslim period the study of Arabic and Persian was compulsory. In addition, Urdu and Hindi were also studied. During British period, three stages of education became clear Primary, secondary and higher. At all stages of study, study of English was compulsory. In addition, Urdu and Hindi were also studied. Facilities for the study of Hindi, Urdu and regional languages were also provided. Up to the secondary stage and higher stage of study, English was compulsory. In the Constitution of independent India, it was provided that English shall be replaced by Hindi during 15 Years. Radhakrishnan Commission was of the opinion that at secondary stages and University stage, study of three languages should be compulsory. (1) Mother tongue, (2) State language, (3) Hindi in almost all the institutions of the country. Mudaliar Commission recommended that Hindi should be integral part of the curriculum of all the universities. English should be replaced by Hindi Kothari Commission recommended that study of three languages:

(1) Mother tongue (regional language), (2) State language, Hindi and (3) One of the Indian or European languages. The Commission also recommended that the book of science and technology should be written in regional languages. In institutions of All India level, English should remain the medium of instruction, but by and by it should be replaced by Hindi. Hindi should be studied at all the stages, but it should not be thrust upon all the persons.

From the above discussion, it is evident that different Commissions have put-forth different views regarding the study of different languages, in our opinion mother tongue should be compulsory at primary and secondary stage of study. In addition to it, the State language should also find place in the curriculum. At higher stages of study too, Hindi should be compulsory. All out efforts should be made that the latest books of science and technology are written in Hindi Language and by and by English should be replaced by the State language Hindi. The development of regional languages is also very necessary. It is hoped that in a short span of time we should be in the position that all good books are available in State language Hindi and the regional languages.

18

Moral Aspects

The development of morality is an important aspect for the formation of good character. Today, there is deterioration of morality in society. The moral aspect has been neglected not only at the social level but at the national level also. In the educational programmes only moral development has been neglected.

Major Objectives

In the modern age, the aim of education is alround development of personality. In the present education system, provision has not been made for intellectual education by giving importance to intellectual development. Thus to successful life, important human qualities such as sympathy, co-operation, mercy, compassion, love, truth, sincerity etc., have been ignored. The development of such human qualities along with intellectual development should be the aim of moral education.

Significance of Character

Character is very important in life. "Nothing is lost when wealth is lost, something is lost when health is lost but everything is lost when character is lost. "Thus character is the most important aspect of personality.

Character is related to morality. The definition of man of character is very wide. Generally, only that man is a man of character whose feelings are human and are directed towards the good and happiness of others. Such a personality can be developed by moral education. For the formation of character of future citizens, moral education should be given from their childhood. The method of moral education has to be different from that of intellectual education. It cannot be given only through lectures. Children by nature like to imitate. So for moral education, it is necessary that the teachers are of good characters.

Role of Religion

The ideal of character formation is kept in the background of all religions. Religion is specially important in moral education from this point of view. All the religion teach us to adopt truth, non-violence, compassion, and pity. But today, religion has taken the form of groupism and communalism which is harmful for character development. No religion prevailing today can be called human religion. In the present circumstances, moral education can only be related to human religion. So in the absence of suitable conditions, the teachers should adopt a religion which is based on the principles of humanity and this alone should be made the basis and medium of moral education.

Importance of Behaviour

Good behaviour is a significant part and powerful medium of moral education. The practical aspect of the teaching of good manners is very gradual. It begins with the first stage of the development of life. Being imitative by nature the children can learn many things of good manners in their family. The parents can make their children cultured by paying attention to their behaviour and by telling them many other things about it gradually. Thus, children can become familiar with the methods and techniques of dealing properly with other people. So the parents and guardians should be fully cultured. Good manners can form background of moral education but for this teachers should be well mannered in order that they may be ideals and worth imitating for children.

Attention is paid to the student's age, intelligence capacity and mental level while determining educational programmes. Similarly, for moral education also programmes should be designed to suit the students of different levels.

Primary Stage. At primary stage, due attention should be paid to the interest of students. The educational programmes should be sufficiently interesting. For this, poems, stories and songs etc., may be very suitable. Considering the understanding level at the primary level, the curriculum should be brief and teaching methods should be easy. Education in obedience to parents, keeping of love and sympathy amongst brother's can be given through quotations from Ramayan. Story of Eklavya from the Mahabharat will teach lessons of devotedness and faith in the teacher. Moral education can easily be given by selecting stories from ancient Indian books like Vedas, Puranas and Panchatantra etc., Shravan, Prahlad, Dhruv and Harish Chandra in ancient Indian religious books and such other characters in medieval works may be guiding examples for moral education.

The children may be made familiar with the different religions and societies of today in order to develop an international understanding.

Secondary Stage. At the secondary stage, the mental level of students becomes so much mature that more concrete programmes for character formation may be started. In order to make the youth successful in future life, the programmes at this stage should be of various kinds.

At the secondary stage, students should be given opportunities to work for the welfare of man and society and efforts should be made to inculcate in them ethical virtues. For the formation of character, illustrations and stories may be cited according to need. But care should be taken to safeguard the personal feelings of the students, as up to this age sentiments and discretion develops in them.

College and Higher Stage. At the college and higher stage, the students prepare themselves for future life. So at this stage, the programme of moral education should be wide. A man of character, rising above the consideration of nation, community, class, religion and group, etc. is full of human sentiments. He considers the entire world as his home and others as members of his family. At this stage, the teacher holds an important position for moral education and he may place his character as mirror from which the students will imbibe in their ideals.

The problem of religious education is one of the most burning problems of the country. There have been divergent views of scholars about the religious education. Some are of the opinion that religious education should be included in the curriculum while others feel that in a secular democracy, religious, education is not essential. Even western scholars have different opinion. Ryburn is of the opinion that for the alround development of the student, religious education is most essential. Ross says that religious education should be included in the curriculum. He writes, "It is through religions that the feet of youth can be set on the road to the absolute values, truth, beauty and goodness". It is only through religious education that the feelings of universal brotherhood can be developed amongst the masses. An eminent Indian philosopher Dr. Radhakrishnan has written, 'The troubles in the whole world including India are due to the fact that education has become a mere intellectual exercise and not the acquisition of moral and spiritual values." The moral and spiritual values can be achieved only through the religious education. We are also of the opinion that some kind of religious education is essential in our country.

The Nature. Now, the question arises that in a secular democracy like India what should be the nature of religious education. Since ancient times religious education has been the part and parcel of the curriculum of education in our country. In ancient days the basis of education was the religion and the ultimate goal of education was to acquire 'Moksha'. In medieval times also, religious education was imparted. Mosques were the centres of education in which the religious education was imparted. It is only during the British period that the importance of religious education was not felt. In free India also there is in fact, no provision for the religious education but as we have already said that for the alround development of child and removing the chaos prevailing in the Indian society religious education should be included in the curriculum. India is a country in which believers of different religions live together. Under these circumstances, the education should not be according to the beliefs of one or the other religion but the basic principles of all the religions should be taught. In fact, our religious education should be a moral or ethical education. There is no need to teach the deep principles of Hindu or Muslim religion but those principles must be taught which are concerned with the development of character.

Our religious education should not only be theoretical but it should be practical. The teacher should put up the examples of moral values before the students. The students should be taught in such a way that religious education may develop in them the feeling of nationalism and internationalism. Those who are against the religious education say that religious education is impractical and unpsychological. It develops hatred among the people . But they are wrong. If we go deeply into the matter we find that all these evils develop only when we are narrow-minded. When we only talk of one religion or the other, one sect of the other, the feeling of communalism develop. Our submission is that religious education is in fact the moral education. The students should be taught in such a way that feelings of communalism may not develop. Ethical values should be encouraged in our teaching. Good points of all the religions, which are for the development of our character, fellow-feeling of nationalism should be taught to the students. The aim of our education should be the universal brotherhood. Only then the real purpose will be served and we shall be able to achieve our goal of human welfare.

Discipline, a Must

In our educational system the indiscipline is common. After independence, we have hardly been successful in minimising the gravity of this problem in our educational institutions. The Secondary Education Commission has observed, "No amount of improvement and reconstruction in education will bear much fruit if the schools themselves undermine the indiscipline." Prof. Humayan Kabir is of the opinion, "Failure to take effective steps at this stage can so aggravate the problem that may shake the very foundation of national life." A number of factors are responsible for the growing indiscipline in our educational institutions. The mistake lies partly with the present social, economic and political conditions, partly with the conditions of our homes and partly with the party politics in our institutions. Professor Humayan Kabir in his small treatise 'Student Indiscipline' has diagnosed the following four causes of indiscipline :

1. The loss of leadership by teachers.

2. Growth of economic difficulties.

3. Defects in the existing system of education.

4. General loss of idealism.

Here, we will deal with all of them and also discuss the opinion of eminent educationists in this regard:

Loss of Leadership by Teachers: The teachers of today are not the Gunus of the olden days. Their prestige has gone down. They are not better than the labourers in the eyes of students. They are the spiritual parents of olden days. There are numerous reasons which act as handicaps in teacher's attempt to act as the leader of students and society. Sweeping criticism of the present system of education, inadequate salaries, and the consequent frustration, entry of such persons in the profession who are the teachers by compulsion and not by choice are the reasons for this state of affairs. Some other factors responsible for this are the control of the politicians over the educational institutions and the acceptance of tuition by the teachers on almost commercial basis and the strained relations between the authorities and the teachers, etc. The Secondary Education Commission has observed, "Discipline among students can only be promoted if there is discipline among the staff both within the school and in organizations connected with the teaching profession."

Growth of Economic Difficulties. Education in India is absolutely unprofitable. Problem of unemployment is the greatest problem that we are facing. Our education system does not ensure any betterment of financial condition. The present day education does not enable youths to earn their livelihood. Have a look upon the records of employment exchanges of India and you will be shocked to know that educated class is starving. When such is the condition, how can the indiscipline be removed from the educational institutions. A young man studying in university knows that it will be difficult for him to get a job, even if he passes bis B.A. or M.A. His mind is always worried and tense. This creates feeling of insecurity in him which leads to indiscipline. In educational institutions, the gap between the poor and the rich students is too wide. This leads to discontentment with the existing order and gradually the students become indisciplined.

Defects in the Existing System. Our existing system of education is quite defective. It is purely indifferent to the development of character among pupils. Our young men are mostly, at present, ill-equipped youth, filled with a robust optimism in the beginning of their educational career. The present system of education does not create the thirst for knowledge, the zeal to work hard and ambition to be high in wisdom. Our examination system is also defective. According to Francis W. Parker, "The fundamental reason the children do not act is because they do not have the conditions of right action. Maulana Azad had said, "I am convinced that if the young are at tune restless and turbulent, it is not due to any intrinsic defect in them. The restlessness is largely due to the fact that they do not have enough channels for the expression of their youthful urges."

Most of the educational institutions, running on the commercial lines, fail to establish spiritual and moral links between the teachers and the students. This creates indiscipline. The money-minded authorities do not care for the welfare of the children, there is no provision for personal contact between the students and teachers, as the classes are being kept overcrowded. Untrained and unqualified teachers are appointed on lesser salaries. Too much talk of self discipline has also done some harm. There is no check on the students. This loud talk reveals that there are no rules for them. They are the cruel kings of their society and can do whatever they like.

General Loss of Idealism. The standard of worality is falling day by day in every walk of life. Idealism, morality goodness, truth and beauty are merely on paper and not in actual practice. The alround deterioration of ideals, virtues and morality is a potent cause for growing indiscipline amongst our students.

The youth festival held at Delhi analyzed the following causes of indiscipline:

(a) Economic difficulties, (b) Bad home atmosphere; (c) Faulty system of education; (d) Unemployment among educated youths; (e) Corrupt social influences; (f) Over-crowded classes and larger enrolments; (g) Politics; (h) Lack of proper attention to problems of students.

Political Interference

Active politics is one of the important causes of indiscipline. Mahatma Gandhi was of the opinion that politics and religion are synonymous, indicating the same truth. But now-a-days-politics has nothing to do with religion. It is prevalent in its most corrupt form and our students are the victim of this dirty politics which has resulted in indiscipline in every walk of life. A Commission under the chairmanship of Mr. Harish Chandra, former judge of the Allahabad High Court, was set up. The Commission recommended, "Political parties should not carry their politics and rivalries into the campus of educational institutions and should avoid uncalled for interference with their working. There should, however, be no objection to students establishing clubs of their own where they may discuss and debate the ideologies, thoughts and principles of the various political parties in the country from academic standpoint. "

Late Maulana Azad also remarked, "A student must have knowledge of political movements, but should acquire that knowldege as a student. This is not a stage of plunging into politics and there can be no greater disservice to the country than to allow the students to be swept away by political passions. The growing unrest and indiscipline among students is not the result of certain errors from the side of students but is also a responsibility of those who have not been able to channelise their energies in the right direction. "

In Nut-shell. In a nut-shell, we can say that there are several factors of indiscipline in schools. They are personal, social, political, educational and psychological.

Personal Factors. (a) Physical and mental deformity, (b) intellectual inferiority or superiority, (c)stonny age of adolescence and (d) bad habits.

Social Factors. (a) disturbed state of society, (b) bad home environment, (c) lack of parent's education and (d) evils of society.

Political Factors. (a) mistaken belief of Swaraj or Freedom, (b) bad influence of political parties and (c) mistaken concept of democracy and secularism.

Educational Causes. (a) no proper aim of education, (b) frequent changes in curriculum, (c) organisational shortcomings, (d) lack of moral education, (c) lack of healthy and attractive school surrounding, (f) dearth of zealous teachers and (g) lack rof ight type of co-curricular activities in schools.

The main psychological causes of indiscipline in schools are:

(a) repression of student's instincts, (b) weakness of parents and teachers and (c) unpsychological handling of pupils.

Indiscipline is of two kinds, viz. (i) Group indiscipline, (ii) Individual Indiscipline. It is difficult to deal with group indiscipline; some of the typical acts of group indiscipline are; (a) Strikes and gang-behaviour, (b) Aggressive fighting and quarrelling; (c) Rowdyism. Individual Indiscipline is comparatively easier one to tackle. Some of the acts of individual indiscipline are: (a) Truance and late coming (b) Cheating and telling a lie; (c) Stealing; (d) Scabbing.

It is essential to point out various internal causes of tussle between the students and the authorities. They are :

(a) Demand for removal of a teacher on the grounds of inefficiency from the point of view of the students.

(b) Retention of the teacher whom management wants to transfer or retire.

(c) Refusal of the authorities to permit some students to appear in the examination, due to the shortage of attendance or unsatisfactory work.

(d) Demand for any type of holiday.

(e) Demand for the change of the dates of the examination or stiffness of the examination papers.

(f) Demand for the establishment of students union.

(g) Demand for the remission of fine or fines and enhancement of funds.

The common forms of indiscipline prevalent in the schools are: (i) Disrespect for authorities and college rules and regulations, (ii) Disrespect for teachers, i.e. disobedience, (iii) Late coming, (iv) Not doing home work, (v) Unrully behaviour in the class, i. e. making noise, (vi) Damaging and spoiling the college property, (vii) Writing indecent and abusive Language upon the walls and other parts of the college building, (viii) Making uncalled for remarks for the fair sex, (ix) Forming gangs and organising strikes, (x) Using unfair means in the examination, (xi) Delay in paying the fees, (xii) Dishonest dealing, *i.e.* stealing, (xiii) Aggressive behaviour, i.e. bullying, teasing, beating, etc.

The remedies of school indiscipline may be classified under two heads, viz.; (a) positive, (b) Negative.

Positive Remedies. Under positive checks, we may have the following remedies: (a) Pupil self-Government, (b) Restoration of the lost leadership to the students, (c) Improvement in the economic lot of the students, (d) Parent-Teacher relationship, (e) Reform in the system of education, (f) School environment- tradition, law and regulation, (g) Material conditions of work, (h) Corporate life of the school, (i) Games and co-curricular activities, (j) Revival of the sense of values, (k) Rewards, (1) Control over external influences.

Negative Checks. Under negative type of checks, following measures are generally adopted in the institutions in order to maintain discipline, law and order, 1. Corporal punishment, 2. Extra work given as a punishment, 3. Fine 4. Work other than class work given as punishment, 5. Isolation, 6. Moral punishment, 7. Suspension and expulsion.

Steps Desirable. So far as possible only positive types of checks should be enforced. Negative types of checks should be rarely used, when there is no alternative . Negative checks do not change the feeling of the students while positive checks are capable of that. By negative checks, the students get frustrated. They do not commit the acts of indiscipline before the teachers but in the absence of a teacher they become most indisciplined. Our aim is to achieve self discipline and positive types of checks will be helpful in our task. Self disciplined students are the real builders of the nation and are the real guards of democracy and this kind of discipline can only be achieved by positive type of checks.

There are many reasons for this decline in the standard of our education. Following are some of the main causes which are responsible for the decline of standard of education in India.

The development of education in India is taking place rapidly. The number of students receiving education is constantly increasing and it is likely to increase more in the near future. Although the number of students is rapidly increasing yet it has not been possible to provide them necessary facilities. The number of able teachers is also not increasing with the same proportion.

Suggestions. In order to solve the above mentioned problem Kothari Commission has recommended that selective system of admissions should be adopted in the universities. The number of students in the educational institutions should be determined keeping in view the facilities available in the institutions concerned and the number of teachers. The university should prescribe necessary qualification for admission and the best students should be selected from among those desiring to seek admission in the universities. The new and modern methods should be adopted while selecting the students. Until these methods are fully developed, the percentage of marks secured by the students in pre-university examination should be made the basis of their admission. Each university should establish a Board of University Admission. In order to help the students to select different subjects of higher education, the University Grants Commission should establish Central Testing Organisation.

Another reason for the low standard of education in our institutions is that the students do not have the same faculties which are provided to the students of the universities in other countries of the world. The libraries of universities are not properly equipped and are not able to make available all the necessary books to the students. Due to the lack of books the students are not able to study properly. The environment and the conditions in which our universities are imparting education are likely to lower the standard of education. In many degree colleges, there is not even proper seating arrangements for the students. There are thousands of such degree colleges, which do not possess even playgrounds. In such conditions, the lowering of the standard of education is quite natural.

Suggestions. A high committee should be appointed for providing necessary facilities to the students. The Government of India and the State Governments have been making every possible endeavour to provide grants in order to remove the difficulties of the students and equip properly the libraries etc. But it may be made clear here that only the Government's efforts alone will not solve this problem. The non-Government institutions should also come forward and make as much contribution as possible in this field. It is the sacred duty of the rich class of the society to spend as much as possible to raise the standard of higher education. In progressive countries life America, non-government institutions contribute a lot in the field of higher education. The rich class and the non-government institutions of India should also emulate the example of America.

Teachers' Plight

The conditions of the teachers teaching at the university stage is also not up to the mark. It is true that new U.G.C. scales are quite charming but to some of the states teachers are not paid according to them. The accomodation facilities are also not proper and most of the teachers teachings at the higher stage live outside the university or college campus.

Suggestions. All the states should immediately implement the U.G.C. scales. In addition, the teachers should be given proper places for living and studying. It is the duty of the Government to see that university teachers are very highly paid so that brilliant students may like to choose teaching profession instead of other services.

Another reason for the low standard of education is that the teachers have been burdened with too much work. The conditions of working of the teachers are such that they are not able to perform the teaching work properly. At the university stage where prominence is given to the research work, it is completely improper to burden them with too much work.

Suggestions. In order to remove the above-mentioned defects, it is necessary to reduce the hours of working of the teachers. Besides this, they should be encouraged to devote their utmost time in the research work. Each teacher should be given one year leave with salary within a period of 5 years of service for increasing his knowledge and for travelling to foreign countries. They should also be provided with concessional tickets. They should have complete freedom in performing the teaching functions. Only teaching work should be taken from them. It is very bad practice to burden the teachers with administrative and other works of educational institutions. The suggestions made by Kothari Commission in respect of the promotion of the teachers, improvement in the condition of their service and work etc. are very important and should be implemented with immediate effect.

A Great Difference

Another reason for the decline in the standard of higher education is that there is a wide gulf between the teachers and the students. While in western countries the students and the teachers work together like a family and perform some type of functions in their interest. In India, it appears that the interests of the students and teachers are separate from each other.

Suggestions. In order to establish close contact between the teachers and the students, it is necessary to adopt tutorial system. Besidesreducing the number of students in each class, at different hours 4 or 5 students should meet a teacher and hold discussions with him. Debates and discussions should be organised. These debates and discussions help to establish close relations between the teachers and the students. They are able to increase their knowledge with the help of the teachers.

Defective examination system is also one of the chief causes leading to the decline in the standard of university education. It was pointed out by Radha Krishnan Commission that only one suggestion is made to reform university education, it would be in respect of present examination system. Too much importance is given to the essay type of examinations. Consequently, the students think that they will achieve success by studying some selective questions and so they do not devote their full heart and soul into the studies throughout the year. Most of the students study only selected questions and hence the standard of education is constantly declining. Besides this, the number of pass marks is so low that they secure them very easily.

Suggestions. To reform the present examination system, it is necessary to give less prominence to the essay-type examination and give emphasis on internal assessment or evaluation. In place of essay-type examination, objective tests would be more useful. So far students securing 60 per cent; 45 per cent or 48 per cent and 33 per cent marks are awarded first, second and third divisions respectively. The above mentioned percentage of marks should be increased to 70, 55 and 40 respectively.

Party-Politics. The prevalence of cheap party-politics is yet another cause which is responsible for the decline in the standard of education in Indian universities. Different political guides endeavour to make their influence in the universities. In every province, there are some particular persons who are ever eager to establish their control over universities. Consequently, because of party politics such teachers are appointed who are not properly suitable for teaching work. The groupism of the teachers also lowers the standard of teaching. The teachers remain busy in group party-politics and they do not get sufficient time to throw themselves heart and soul into the teaching work.

Suggestions. The need for keeping the college and universities away from party-politics need not be over-emphasised. All the political parties and scholars should consider this problem seriously. We should think that the future of our country depends upon the progress of higher education. If the standard of higher education goes on constantly declining, we cannot make progress in any field. A conference should be organised for keeping the universities away from party-politics. There should be free discussion in this conference over this problem. Thereafter, a date should be fixed, on which the suggestions should be submitted in this connection. Government should implement the suggestions of the said Committee. As far as possible the politicians should not be appointed in the universities. The Vice-Chancellors should be appointed from among the prominent educationists of the country and they should keep themselves away from party politics and the influence of prominent politicians.

Last but not the least, the growing indiscipline among the students is also one of the chief causes responsible for the decline in the standards of higher education. This indiscipline can be of many types and there are many causes for it. The prominent among these causes are the social and economic difficulties; growing unemployment; non-availability of educational facilities, group party politics; lack of interesting subjects in the curriculum etc.

Suggestions. Kothari Commission has suggested that not only the teachers but also the students, parents, guardians; society, Government and political parties should work together to solve this problem. Such type of programmes should be organised in colleges and universities as may keep the students busy in constructive work and keep them away from party politics. Every possible endeavour should be made to solve the problem of unemployment. Unless and until the problem of indiscipline is satisfactorily solved in the colleges and universities, it would be wishful thinking to hope for an improvement in the standard of our higher education.

It is clear from the above discussions, that there are many reasons which are responsible for the decline in the standard of higher education. It is not only necessary but also expedient to check the decline in the standard of teaching and every possible effort should be made to improve the existing standard of higher education. If we intend to come at par with other advanced countries of the world, it should be our sacred task to work sincerely to raise the standard of higher education.

19 Negative Aspects

The development of education gives birth to several types of problems. With the development of Indian education, problems of Indian Education also increased. Some of the problems are as old as the modern education system itself. We will briefly discuss the chief problems of Indian Education:

Education without Purpose

The aim of education which was in the pre-independence period cannot continue to be accepted in the independent India. It is a matter of great regret that there is no definite aim before the Indian students. Innumerable young men and women are receiving education in schools and colleges without having any definite aim before them. They have no goal or aim in their life. Most of the young students consider the getting of jobs as the ultimate aim of their education.

It has to be admitted that we have not been able to change aims of our education in accordance with the changing situation and circumstances of the country. Kothari Commission has remarked in very clear words that the most important reform in the education is to change it or to make endeavour so that it may be related to the life of the people, their needs and aspirations and, thus, we will have to develop education as a powerful weapon for bringing about social, economic and cultural changes, which are necessary for the achievement of national objectives. According to this aim, the development of education be made in such a way so that it may lead to social and national unity, tendencies of modernisation may be made mobile and social, and moral values may be established.

In short, we may say that modern education should aim at fulfilment of the needs of the citizens and develop the feeling of universal brotherhood among them. Thus, under the present political, economic and social changes the aim of education should not remain bound to the old route of the period of British regime. Structural changes are needed in the present system of education.

Curriculum, not Perfect

Another chief problem of Indian education is defective and unbalanced curriculum. The curriculum which is prescribed for the study of the students emphasises only bookish knowledge. The relation of curriculum has not been established with life and consequently many young persons who have received higher education are facing the problem of unemployment.

The Secondary Education Commission has pointed out the following defects of the curriculum:

(a) The present curriculum is very narrow.

(b) It is bookish and theoretical.

(c) It includes more subjects than are required and many of them are useless and unnecessary.

(d) Emphasis is not given on teaching the boys practical subjects and other types of activities, which may help development of the versatile personality of the child.

(e) The curriculum does not fulfil the different needs and interests of the students.

(f) The curriculum lacks technical and professional subjects.

The Kothari Commission has also dealt with in detail the defects of the curriculum. The Commission has pointed out that in the background of the important efforts that are being made in the foreign countries in the development of curriculum, it appears that the basis of the curriculum in India is very narrow and out of date. The Curriculum emphasises bookish knowledge and cramming. There is insufficient provision for practical activities and experience and there is prominence of external and internal examinations. Besides since adequate importance is not given to the development of skills, proper aptitude, tendencies and values, the curriculum is not complete to keep pace with the lives of the people. Keeping in view these things, the Commission has recommended that there is urgent necessity of improving the curriculum, raising its standard and for reforming it.

Teaching Methods: Old and New

Another serious problem of our education is that teaching methods have not been changed in accordance with the change of tune and circumstances. Even today the education is not child-centered in India whereas in other countries, endeavour has been made to make it as much child-centered as possible. While other countries of the world have been adopting new methods of teaching, even today we are adopting the conventional and out-of-date teaching methods. The conventional and out-of-date methods are very much detrimental for the education of our country and hence new teaching methods, keeping in view the needs and circumstances of the present times, should be adopted with immediate effect

Examination System: the Weaker Side

The problem of examination system in India is as serious as the problem of curriculum and the methods of teaching. The aim of our education has become only to pass examination.

Mostly, only one examination is held in a year, with the result, that the student are not able to acquire proper and real knowledge. The number of the examiners is so large that no harmony can be established in their decisions. It depends upon the mood, individual ability, knowledge of the subject and environment to award marks to the examinees. Mostly, essay type of examinations are organised, which are completely unpsychological.

The different Committees and Commissions, which have been appointed to suggest ways and means to reform education, have pointed out the seriousness of the problem of defective examination system. The University Education Commission has remarked that although the seriousness and complication of this problem has been increasing with great speed, constructive steps have not been taken to reform it. The Mudaliar and Kothari Commissions also have pointed out the seriousness of this problem. It is, therefore, necessary that all-out efforts should be made to solve this problem as expeditiously as possible.

Stagnation and Wastage

India is an underdeveloped and poor country and the percentage of literacy is very low. Keeping this situation in view, it is very unfortunate that the problem of wastage and stagnation has been existing in the field of education for a very long time. Because of the defective administration, defective environment, defective curriculum and defective examination system, lakhs of students fail every year. Kothari Commission has expressed the view that the rate of wastage is from 1/3 to 1/2 in class 1. The problem of wastage and stagnation exists at all stages of education. There are some students, who leave education in the middle and there is a large number of students, who fail every year in the examinations.

Management and Control

The problem of control and management of education is also one of the chief problems in India. Mostly, the education up to primary and junior high school is organised by the local district board and municipalities. Some schools are directly under the control of the State Government, whereas some institutions are under the control of private managements. Some institutions are also under the control of religious institutions. Likewise, secondary schools are also under the control of local boards, private and religious institutions. There are also Government schools. Most of the schools are non-government and they are managed by the management committees of the schools concerned. Generally, the members of the managing committees are such as make the institutions serve their personal interests.

It is a matter of great regret that some members of the

management committees are so influential that even the higher officials of the State Education Department hesitate to take any action against them. The Education Board of the State are not able to function properly because of groupism and party politics. It is a matter of great regret that groupism, favouritism, corruption etc. are rampant in primary as well as secondary schools. Teachers of secondary schools are also the victims of anger of the members of the management committees. Most of the managers of non-Government schools are not competent and fit to shoulder the grave responsibility of education. Caste feeling, individual rivalry, jealousy, groupism and corruption are rampant in the management committees of the non-Government schools. The poor teachers of these schools become the victims of these difficulties.

Most of the universities in India are under the control of State Governments. Only 5 Universities are under the control of Central Government. In the universities also, the control and administration are very loose. The problem of control in the affiliated colleges of the universities has become so serious that its solution seems to be very difficult. Many colleges are run by private and religious institutions and they include all those defects which exist in the field of secondary education. There are very few institutions at present which are run with the feeling of public welfare. Most of the teaching institutions have become the means of earning money and their managers consider it their aim to realise utmost money from the Government and the people.

It is important to note here that the condition of the Government schools and colleges is far better than the non-Government institutions. Kothari Commission has made important suggestions in regard to the management, administration and control of education at different stages. If the suggestions of the Kothari Commission are properly implemented, the problem of control, management and administration of education at different stages can be solved.

Discipline, not in Force

Indiscipline is increasing day by day among the Indian students. It is such a serious problem that it has attracted our attention and anxiety of all the scholars and educationists of the country. This problem is absent at the primary stage. By the time the students enter the secondary stage, they become adolescent. They tend to flout the established rules. Their indiscipline takes the collective form of Individuality, the student continues the old tradition of discipline, but when he is swept off by the mounting tides of collective tendency, he becomes a prey of indiscipline. There are many causes for the prevalence of indiscipline among the students. The prominent among such causes are (a) defective examination system; (b) defective economic system; (c) impracticable curriculum; and (d) wastage and stagnation. According to Kothari Commission, the modern, social and economic system are, to a great extent, responsible for the indiscipline among the students. The Commission has also pointed out that the chief cause of indiscipline among the students is the interference of the politicians in the schools, colleges and universities.

The Commission has seriously analysed the causes of unrest among students. Explaining its causes, the commission observes that "there is a variety of causes which have brought about these ugly expressions of uncivilised behaviour *e.g.*, the uncertain future facing educated youngmen leading to a sense of frustration which breeds irresponsibility, mechanical and unsatisfactory nature of many curricular programmes, the totally inadequate facilities for teaching and learning in the large bulk of institutions; the poor student-teacher contact, the inefficiency and lack of knowledge on the part of many teachers and their failure to interest themselves in student's problems; the absence of imagination and tact combined with firmness on the part of heads of institutions; the prevalence of what has come to be known as teacher's politics....... The attempt by political parties to interfere in their work, and by no means the least, the impact of the conditions of public life in the country, the falling standards of discipline among the adults and a weakening of their civic consciousness and integrity."

In order to solve the problem of indiscipline, it is necessary to remove the above mentioned causes. It can be suggested that the number of students in classes should be reduced, the curriculum should be made useful and practical; examination system should be reformed, aimlessness of education should be ended, sports, games and cultural programmes should be organised, well-trained teachers should be appointed and they should be kept away from party politics. If we really wish to improve the education in the country; we shall have to uproot the causes of indiscipline.

The Education Commission has classified the remedies for student indiscipline into two categories viz. removal of education deficiencies that contribute it and setting up of a consultative and administrative machinery to prevent the occurrence of indiscipline.

The remedies of the first group are regarded as the core of the problem. In fact, "the incentives to positive discipline have to come from the opportunities that the institution presents and the intellectual and social demands it makes on the students". As regards second remedy, it has been suggested that polarisation between teachers, students and administration should be avoided. Joint councils of students and teachers should be appointed. All this should create a spirit of comradeship between the teachers and the students. If this "spirit could be created, many of the problems of discipline which are disastrous to our academic life at present will become easier to solve and, will be hoped, disappear in course of time."

Practical Problems

It is very difficult and complicated problem in India as to which language (national language Hindi, international language English or regional languages) should be the medium of education. Since the beginning of 19th century, the medium of instruction has remained a controversial issue. Different Scholars and Commissions have given different views in this regard. In 1956, the State Organisation Commission defined the frontiers of all states. This gave rise to the controversy of language issue. In 1957, the official language commission suggested that Hindi should be developed as the obvious linguistic medium of instruction and ruled out English as the language of India's mass medium. The Radhakrishnan Commission also recommended that the medium of instruction should be any Indian language except Sanskrit. In

1966, Kothari Commission recommended that the regional language should not only be made the medium of instructions at the primary and secondary stages but they should also be made the medium of education at the university stage. Hence, Hindi should be developed as a link language and the use of English should also be continued. The language policy of Kothari Commission was severely criticised and many scholars even remarked that it was only a conspiracy to continue the use of English in India.

At present in different states, education is imparted through the medium of regional languages at the primary and secondary stages. At the higher stages also, endeavours are being made to make the regional languages as the medium of education. But the influence of English has yet not declined at this stage and English language continues to be the medium of education in different universities. Thus, the problem of language still remains a problem and it is very essential that this problem should be solved in the earliest possible time and the language controversy should be at rest forever.

Another chief problem of education in India is the problem of education of women. The Constitution of India has enshrined in the principle of equality of men and women. However, we find that women of India still flag behind in many respects. In 1932, as compared to 100 boys, only 55 girls were receiving education at the primary stage. At the secondary stage, this number was only 26. Thereafter, the education of women has greatly expanded but still the percentage of women is very low. The main cause of this narrow view-point "is the failure to understand the importance of education. It is really a matter of great satisfaction that our Government is conscious of its responsibility towards the education of women and is taking every possible step to encourage the education of women." The Kothari Commission has also emphasized that for some time priority should be given to the education of women in our educational system and only then the problem of education of women can be solved.

It was pointed out earlier that the number of illiterates is far greater in India than the number of literates. At present, the population of India has swelled near about 90 crores. About 70 per cent of the total population is illiterate. There has been no appreciable increase in the percentage of literacy.

The efforts that have been made by the Government in regard to education of adults have not met with much success. Proper curriculum and proper teaching method should be adopted for the education of the adult and able sufficient teachers should be appointed to make the scheme of adult education a success. The Kothari Commission has made some very important suggestions to achieve these goals. The prominent among such suggestions are the establishment of 'Adult Education Department in Universities', proper provision of libraries and the establishment of Social Welfare Councils. It may be admitted that we cannot achieve the goal determined by the Kothari Commission so soon. But we can certainly act according to the suggestions of the Commission so as to solve the problem of adult education in India, so that the problem of illiteracy may be solved in India in near future.

Industrialisation is progressing with great speed in India. Consequently, the number of weak persons is constantly increasing. The education of these workers also pose serious problems before as. Although Government has been emphasizing on the education of the workers is the programmes of the expansion of adult education yet sufficient success has not so far been achieved in this field.

Along with the problem of education of the workers, the problem of the education of the disabled persons is also very serious. There are mainly two types of disabled persons (a) mentally retarded persons, and (b) physically disabled persons. Mentally retarded children are those, whose I.Q. is below 35. At present about 33% of "school going children are mentally retarded to varying degrees. According to Kothari Commission the number of disabled children in India was 25 lacs out of which 14 to 18 lacs were said to be mentally retarded children.

With the expansion of civilisation, mental diseases are also increasing. Poverty, bad company, lack of opportunities to education, cruel and apathetic behaviour of the parents, family quarrels, etc. are the causes of mental diseases. There are also lacs of physically disabled children in India. The Government have made many efforts for the education of disabled persons, but so far sufficient arrangement has not been made for the education of all types of disabled persons.

With the rapid development of industrialisation in India, the problem of technical and professional education is also becoming complicated. No special provision was made for the professional and technical education before independence.

Great efforts have been made in this direction after the achievement of independence. Despite tremendous increase in the number of schools and the students, there is still shortage of skilled craftsmen and trained persons in the field of different professions. It is true that many engineers and overseers are facing the problem of unemployment but in other professions there is still shortage of skilled and trained persons.

System as a Whole

Last but not the least problem that we have before us, is that our educational system is not in accordance with the political, social and economic conditions of the time. In the modern period, India has adopted a democratic set up and hence education should also be completely democratic. In the economic field, importance has been given to the socialist programme and hence, our education system should also aim to inculcate the feeling of socialism in the citizens. Because of the social changes, the feelings of caste distinction and untouchability have greatly reduced but still these evils exist in the society. Our educational system should be organised in such a way as may be able to root out completely these evils from our society. Education plays an important role in establishing harmony with the vast changing world and hence our education should be able to adopt itself in accordance with the rapid changes that are taking place in different fields in the world. If we are able to solve only this problem and make our educational system in accordance with the changing circumstances, the rest of the problems will automatically be solved.

Conclusion. It is obvious from the above discussion that in the modern period, there are many problems in the field of Indian education. These problems are so serious that they cannot be solved within a very short period. They require constant study and research and sincere efforts for their solution. However, it may be remarked that our progress depends upon the solution of these problems and the sooner we solve these problems the better it will be. If we are able to solve these problems within a short span of period, India will find her place among the progressive and developed nations of the world.

Fiscal Aspects

The problem of finance is probably the greatest obstacle in the expansion of Indian Education. Although different types of schemes are formulated for the expansion of education but it is not possible to implement them properly because the Government is not able to provide necessary finance for them.

Various Stages of Education and Educational Finance: In all the provinces in India, primary education has been made free and hence the complete responsibility of the primary education is on the local Government. The responsibility of secondary education is also on the State Government and it is the duty of the Government to make necessary provision of finance for it. The Central Government is to a great extent, responsible for higher education. In order to give financial help to the universities, the Central Government has established an institution known as University Grants Commission.

It is true that most of the burden of the primary and secondary education is shouldered by the State Governments but the Central Government also gives financial aid to the State Governments in this field and local institutions such as Municipalities, Corporations, District Board, Gram Panchayats etc., also share some of the responsibility of primary education. Thus, we see that the Central Government not only gives utmost help in the field of university education but it also grants financial help to the State Governments in the field of primary and secondary education.

In view of the provision of free primary education, the whole responsibility of collecting money for the same has come on governments. The State Governments grant financial help for the pre-primary education also. At both these stages two types of institutions are working. Most of the schools are run by Municipalities, Corporations, District Boards, Panchayats, etc. There are also schools which are run by non-government institutions and local bodies. Provision of free primary education has been made in the Non-Government schools also. Besides these schools there are also such schools which receive no financial help from the Government and carry on their work only by the fee received from the Students.

At the secondary stage also, there are three types of schools. Some schools are run by the State Governments and the responsibility of their finance is wholly on State Governments. Some schools are run by local bodies, such as Municipalities, Corporations, etc. The responsibility of finance of these institutions is both on the local institutions and the State Governments. The Central Government also gives some financial assistance to the State Governments in this respect. The number of Non-Government schools is much at the secondary stage. These schools receive financial help in the form of grant-in-aid from the State Governments.

20
The Stalemate

The Concept

At different stages there different term of education. Any student who receives education at any stage is expected to complete his education within that prescribed period. In practice, we find that many students who join the schools or colleges very enthusiastically, leave education after some time. Such type of students do not complete the study of their curriculum and consequently the time, money and energy spent on such students proves to be mere wastage. It is rightly remarked:

"The most popular use of the word 'Wastage' in education means, the wastage of time, effort and money after those students who do not successfully complete the course of study undertaken by them."

While clarifying the meaning of the word 'Wastage' Hartog Committee remarked the following:

"By wastage we mean premature withdrawal of children from schools at any stage before completion of the primary Courses."

The Definition

As stated earlier there is a definite term for the education of curriculum at every stage. The students at every stage of education are excepted to pass the examination after studying their whole curriculum but it has been found in general practice that many students are not able to pass the examination in one class or in more than one class within the prescribed period. In other words we may say that they do not pass every year in that class. Thus, they stagnate in the same class whereas their other colleagues pass that class and study in the next class. This process has been called the process of stagnation. Thus, by stagnation we mean the stay of students in a particular class for more than one year. According to the Report of the Hartog Committee:

"By stagnation we mean the retention of a child in a lower class for the period of more than one year".

At Lower Level

It was the Hartog Committee that for the first time pointed out the 'Wastage' and 'Stagnation' taking place in Primary Education.

The meaning and definition of the word 'Wastage' and 'Stagnation' given by the Hartog Committee have already been mentioned earlier. It was pointed out by the Hartog Committee, "Primary Education is ineffective, unless it atleast produces literacy ."On the average, no child who has not completed primary course of at least 4 years will not become permanently literate. The Hartog Committee also devoted its attention, to the wastage and stagnation that was taking place in the secondary education. As in the case of primary education, the wastage and stagnation were eating the vitals of the secondary education also.

A Committee of the educationalists set-up in the year 1983 was of the opinion that out of 100 students taking admission in class 1 only 41 reach up to class V and 26 up to class VI. The average percentage of H.S. and equivalent examinations in different years was 45.8

Wastage and Stagnation in University Education. The problems of wastage and stagnation exist probably in a greater degree at the stage of University Education. In this connection, the University Education Commission has remarked that great wastage of public money is taking place every year but what is still more regrettable is the fact that there is the indifference towards the serious loss of public money as there is for the wastage of time, money and energy of the students and their parents or guardians and their ambition and aspiration. Dr. Kamath and Dr. Deshmukh in their paper on the wastage at university level wrote that even in an eminent collage, Furgusson College, Poona, it is prevalent. In this college, out of 408 students admitted in the faculty of arts, 193 left the studies without completing their courses. In the faculty of Science out of 1423 students 594 left the studies without completing their course.

The Roots

Faulty Administration. Our educational system cannot said to be completely free from any defects. There are very few schools which can claim to be successful in making the mental, physical and moral development of the child. In most of the classes and colleges, the standard of teaching is low, there is lack of trained teachers, lack of educational implements or aims is a special feature and there is a great lack of educational buildings built in healthy environment. In such conditions, neither the students are able to throw themselves heart and soul into the scared task of acquiring and learning of Knowledge nor the teachers are able to do their teaching work with complete enthusiasm and skill. Secondly, both the teacher as well as the students are burdened with the task of receiving education and imparting education respectively, just pass their time.

Reform in Administration. In order to solve the problem of 'Wastage' and 'Stagnation' the teaching standard of the educational institutions should be raised; teachers should be trained, necessary educational implements should be provided, educational buildings should be built in healthy environment; schools and colleges should be made more attractive and proper provision should be made for the entertainment and sports and games of the students.

Vicious Environment. Ordinarily the students have to pass their time in vicious environment in schools as well as out side the schools. In each class there are a number of such boys whose habits and behaviour, method of conversation, etc. are deplorable. Such type of students never sincerely aim to pass their classes every year and other students by coming in contact with them start ignoring their studies.

The environment outside the schools and colleges, specially in the cities, has become very vicious. Obscene songs played on loudspeakers, exciting advertisements of films, dirty processions, films, etc., are proving great obstacles in the study of the students. If these conditions persist, it will not be astonishing if the problems of wastage and stagnation assume even more serious form and nature in a near future.

Improvement in Environment. It is necessary to change and improve the environment in which the students pass their times in the schools and outside the schools. It can be done only with the joint efforts of the Government, the people and the teachers, it is the sacred duty of the Government to inculcate qualities of social reform, sanitation, health and co-operation, etc. in the parents and guardians of the students and should make provision for general health entertainment and adult education. The government should by law ban the playing on of obscene songs on loudspeakers, the exhibition of exiting advertisement of the films and the boys and girls up to the age of 18 years should be prohibited to enter the cinema houses. Dirty films and advertisement on television should be stopped. So for as teachers are concerned they should perform their duties by building a healthy environment in the schools.

Ineffective Method of Teaching. The teaching methods which are prevalent in most of the educational institutions do not make the desired effects upon the students. Incompetent and untrained teachers, lack of proper aims and implements of teaching, lack of space, excessive number of students in classes etc. are some of the main defects of the present educational system. Because of the existence of these defects in the present teaching methods, the method of teaching has become at present dull and consequently the prevalent teaching methods fail to create a desire in the students towards their lessons.

Psychological Methods of Teaching. In order to solve satisfactorily the problem of 'Wastage' and 'Stagnation' at different stages of education, it is necessary that new and psychological methods of teaching should be adopted. Trained teachers, necessary implements of education, good educational buildings built unhealthy environment, etc. are necessary for improving the prevalent teaching methods.

Defective Curriculum. Yet another cause of 'Wastage' and 'Stagnation' in education is the prevalence of defective curriculum. The present curriculum is rigid and one-track and it includes a large number of subjects. The children of the cities as well as of the village have to study the same curricuIum, no matter whether their interest is towards it or not. Besides this, no endeavour has been made to make the curriculum interesting by including some handicrafts or other such subjects.

Reform in Curriculum. In order to solve the problem of 'Wastage and Stagnation' reform in curriculum has become necessary and expedient. Any curriculum cannot be regarded as appropriate and suitable for an indefinite period. It is necessary to change it in accordance with needs and circumstances on the basis of experience and experiments. Consequently, the curriculum of the schools should be modified and if necessary completely reorganised keeping in view the local environment and needs. Separate curricula should be prepared for the students of the rural and urban areas and subjects should be by keeping in mind the interest and needs of the boys and girls. Utmost endeavour should be made to make the curriculum simple, interesting and practical. It should also include some handicrafts which should fulfil the local needs.

Defective Examination System. Another cause which is responsible for 'Wastage' and 'Stagnation' in education is the defective examination system. Nearly 50 per cent of the students fail in different examinations every year. This large number of failure of students is because of the defective examination system.

Change in Examination System. The present system of examinations is full of many defects and it should be changed and reorganised as soon as possible. The students should be awarded marks on the basis of works done by them in classes throughout the whole year and not on the basis of annual examination only. According to R.V. Panuekar, "Schools are established in order that children may be taught, not that they may be foiled." This statement must be given serious consideration and efforts should be made to make the necessary provision so that the wastage caused by the large number of failure of students every year may be minimized as much as possible.

Pupil's Health. It has been observed for several years the physical conditions of the students has been deteriorating. It is because of the lack of edible things, lack of nourishing food and because of the increase of different diseases. Because of being weak and ill, majority of Indian students are not able to devote themselves properly to their studies and consequently they are not able to complete their course within the prescribed period.

Improvement in Pupil's Health. The Government should pay special attention towards the improvement in the health of the students. It is the responsibility of the Government to make proper provision of health and nourishing diet for all the students. In all the progressive countries, food or other type of provision is made for the nourishing diet for the students. Our Government should also give special attention to solve this problem.

Illiteracy of Guardians. A survey made in the: state of Maharashtra revealed that "Wastage and Stagnation' is comparatively more in of the children of backward class. The main cause of this is that guardians of the children are illiterate. Being them selveses illiterate, they fail to understand the cultural and social importance of the education to their children. Consequently, even if they admit their children in some schools, they take them out of those schools sometime because from their point of view the time thus proves to be a wastage. What is true of the guardians of these backward classes, is attitude of most of the Indian people because the majority of our population continues to be illiterate.

Eduction of Guardians. The guardians of children will understand the importance of education of their children only when they themselves are educated. In order to educate the illiterate guardians night schools, adult schools and part-time schools should be established in a large number.

Financial Handicaps. The financial handicaps are also

responsible for 'Wastage' and 'Stagnation'. It is true that 60 percent of the wastage caused in primary education is because of the financial handicaps. The financial condition of the Indian people is so miserable that when provision has been made for free education of their children they find themselves unable to meet other expenses connected with the education. Besides, they have always before them the question as to whether they should send their children to schools or to a place, where they may earn something to contribute to their major income.

So far as the education of girls is concerned, they are taken out of the school only after providing the knowledge of alphabets, etc. It is because of the fact that girls do not get in return any financial help from the education of the girls.

Increase in Individual Income and Control on Prices. In order to check the 'Wastage' and 'Stagnation' in education, it is necessary to improve the financial condition of the guardians. Our Government is very conscious of this gross situation and have been making every possible endeavour to improve the financial conditions of their people. The country is moving rapidly on the path of industrialisation and every possible effort is being made to increase the production of food grains and other agricultural commodities. The efforts that have been made so for to improve the financial condition of the people, have resulted in the increase in per capita income of the Indian people.

Undoubtedly, the increase, in per capita income may solve much of the financial difficulties of the people but yet another serious thing which needs proper consideration is the Question as whether this increase will be sufficient keeping in view the constant soaring of prices of essential commodities. There has been much increase in the paces of our commodities. The experience of last few years clearly indicates that the economic conditions of the middle and lower classes have deteriorated. Unless these problems are satisfactorily solved, it would be futile to hope that the problems of 'Stagnation and Wastage' in education will be solved in the near future.

Social Evils. Yet another cause which is responsible for 'Wastage' and Stagnation' in education is prevalence of many social evil in Indian society. Co-education of girls and boy is still looked with suspicion. Consequently, if at one place there is no separate provision for the education of girls then they remain deprived of education and in case they are fortunate to get admission in some schools, then they are forced on account of certain circumstances to leave education after a few years because of the prevalence of social evils of early marriages. Many girls and boys leave their studies at a premature age. This and many other social evils are responsible to a great extent for the prevalent 'Wastage and Stagnation', that is taking place in the field of education at different stage.

Suggestions. The evil cannot be remedied by taking certain concrete steps. In our society the roots of feelings of opposition to co-education, early marriages have gone so deep that unless they are rooted out completely, it is not possible to check the 'Wastage and Stagnation' in education in the near future.

There can be only two ways to solve the prevalent feelings and view-points. Either the society should be completely changed through revolution or the defects of the society should be removed slowly and gradually. The second way seems to be more poetical and proper but its responsibility lies upon the shoulders of young men and women of the country. If they throw themselves heart and soul into this work, they can develop a new consciousness among the people and they can form a new era of science and technology in the country.

Faulty Examination System

Clara M. Brown defines evaluations in a very clear form when he says, "Evaluation is essential in the never ending cycle of formulating goals, measuring progress towards them and determining of the new goals which emerge as a result of new warning. Evaluation involves measurement which means objective quantitative evidence. But it is broader than measurement and implies that considerations have been given to certain values, standards and that interpretation of the evidence has been made in the light of the particular situation."

The term 'Evaluation' is a new term and includes examination of academic and of non-academic nature in its broader sense.

Wringstone says, "Evaluation is relatively new concept of measurement that is implied in conventional tests and examinations. " The term 'Examination' is used for only the academic subjects, while evaluation covers all the changes that take place in development of a man's personality and measures the qualities of an individual in every walk of life.

The Significance

Examination is an important factor of our educational system. In fact, life is an examination. If you enjoy it in its full sense, you get through and if you do not, you fail. Examinations are in existence since times immemorial. So the persons like Sir Michael Sadler are of the opinion- "To close down, examinations would be to give the signal for educational saturation. "It is the only method by which you can test the knowledge of a student in the college. The examinations in institutions serve the following purposes:

1. Examinations stimulate teaching and learning.
2. The examination provide opportunity for the teachers to know their defects and improve their teachings.
3. Examinations facilitate the problem of uniformity of standards. In the absence of an examination system, there will be no uniformity in the standards of the various institutions, which is essential in a democratic country.
4. Examination is the best device which is used for measuring the efficiency of the institution.
5. Examination is the only method by which the aptitude of the student can be judged. The examination determines not only the contents of education but also the methods of teaching, in fact the entire approach to education. They have so pervaded the entire atmosphere of school life that they have become the main motivating force for all efforts on the part of pupil as well as teacher.

Defects of the Present System. The deficiencies, inadequacies and harmful consequences of the existing system of public examinations are well-known. They are known to be capricious, invalid, unreliable and inadequate, that they impart instruction to its detriment by making the syllabus narrow. Killing initiative in the teacher and encouraging cramming in the students at the examination time and in neglect of the work during the second year; and that they tend to have an adverse effect on discipline. In the opinion of Wardha Committee, "As a measure of the work of individual pupils or the schools, by a consensus of expert opinion, examinations are neither valid nor complete. They are inadequate and unreliable, capricious and arbitrary. "W. H. Ryburn, while criticising the present system of examination, has remarked, "It goes without saying that examinations are the enemies of creative work, at least as they are usually conducted."

Some of the main defects of our examinations are given below :

Lack of Definite Aim. Examination system at present is very haphazard in its approach. It lacks definite aim. It fails to tackle various problems of students.

Not the Real Tests of Student's Knowledge. Our examinations do not test the real knowledge of the students. They only measure the partial knowledge of the students. The present system of examination encourages 'Pick and Choose' approach. It sets premium on speculation and guessing.

In this respect, the Zakir Hussain Report on Basic Education (1938) has accurately stated facts-

"The system of examinations prevailing in our country has proved a curse to education. A bad system of education has, if anything, been made worse according to examinations a place out of all proportion to their utility. As a measure of the work of the individual pupils of the schools by consensus of expert opinion, examinations are neither valid nor complete. They are inadequate and unreliable and arbitrary. We should take care to guard against their painful influence."

Lowering Education Standard. The present examination system is the main cause of the lowering of the standards of education.

The one-sided approach of the examinations signifies memory but does not ensure the extension of rational and creative powers of the students. According to Thomson, the examination is, "A presumptuous attempt to gauge the depth of human ignorance."

Cultivation of Fatalistic Ideas. Due to present system of examination, the students have become perfect fatalists. The creativity of the students has been replaced by positivity. The students do not study properly and try to get through by reading notes, solved papers, etc.

Not Valid Means. The intrinsic merits of the examinees can not be judged with the present examination system. The present system does not consider the subject-matter or mastery over the subject. In descriptive papers, too much emphasis is laid on hand-writing and expression. Certain other factors such as logical reasons, the complete knowledge of the subject are ignored. The present system only touches the surface and not the depth.

Emotional Strain and Mental Tension. "Examinations cause emotional disturbance to the examinees and therefore, they are not real incentive to learning." *-H.G. Stead*

Pressure Upon the Teachers. Teachers have to work a lot for examining the answer books. Answer books cannot be examined properly by a teacher.

Lowers Moral Standards. Most of the students are robbed of honesty, sincerity and purity due to these examinations.

Ignorance the Qualities of Character. Examinations fail to provide any method to test the originality, initiative, truthfulness, honesty and sociability. Examination is the sole aim and cramming is the sole method.

Division System. The division system creates a feeling of superiority and of inferiority. Education Commission has suggested the following remedies for the same:-

1. "The number of external examination should be reduced and the element of subjectivity in the essay type test should be minimized by introducing objective tests and also changing the type of questions."

2. "In order to find out the pupil's all round progress and to determine his future, a proper system of school records should be maintained for every pupil indicating the work done by him from time to time."

3. "In the final assessment of the pupils, due credit should be given to the internal tests and the school records of the pupils."

4. "There should be only one public examination at the completion of the Secondary School Course."

5. "The system of symbolic rather than numerical marking should be adopted for evaluating and grading the working of the pupils in external and internal examinations."

6. "The certificates awarded should also make indication of the marks scored by the students in his school tests."

7. "The system of compartmental examination should be introduced at the final public examination. "

Besides these, there are certain more suggestions which are placed here;-

Monthly Tests. More importance should be given to monthly tests to test the progress of students.

Decentralisation. To ensure reliability, validity and uniformity in exminations, standardizing the system of marking is essential.

Proper Selection of Subject. The students are compelled to take certain subjects as there is no provision in the curriculum to get rid of them. Students should be asked to study the subjects of their own choice and interest

Oral Tests. In addition to written tests, oral tests should also be introduced for every student. The qualities, like alertness, intelligence, special interests, mental outlook can be better judged by viva-voce tests than written tests.

Proper Selection of Examiners. Only those persons should be made examiners who have control over themselves.

The Objective Type

Keeping in view the defects of essay type examination, objective type of examination was devised in the 20th century. It is also, therefore, called New Type Examination. The main merit of this type of examination is that it enables the real evaluation of the knowledge acquired by the students. .

Objective Examination are of the following two types:

Standardized Objective Test. In this type of test, different questions are very carefully constructed. Those questions which are suitable and valuable, are selected and kept in standardized groups. These are constructed by experts.

Teacher-made Objective Test. These tests are constructed by the teacher himself. These tests can be used at special occasions in special form.

(i) The questions set in objective or new type examination are small and clear.

(ii) About 100-150 questions which are based on the whole subjects are constructed in it.

(iii) The answer to the questions is either 'Yes' or 'No', and therefore, there is no need to write long essays.

(iv) Every Examiner has a list of questions so that it is easier for him to examine the answers.

(v) Since this type of examination does not require long essays in answers, the question of impressing the examiner through language, style and good writing does not arise.

(vi) It is convenient for the student to answer the questions because answers are very-short,

(vii) In this system, it is very easy and convenient for the teacher to construct questions after little practice.

(viii) The evaluation of these tests is objective. Therefore, the question of the discontentment of the students does not at all arise.

(ix) This system easily distinguishes of low and sharp intelligence so that the teacher is able to make separate arrangement of teaching for the boys of low intelligence.

(x) This system is very suitable from economic point of view because it costs far less than the traditional examination.

In New-Type Examination, about 35 types of questions are constructed. However, Five types of questions are prominent, they are:-

Completion Type of Question. In this type of questions, some sentences are given in which some blank space is left for some words. The student have to fill-up the blank space with suitable words. For example, the Ramayan was written by..... Now the students will write Tulsidas and thus the sentence will be completed.

Yes-No or True-false Type Question. In such type of questions, the answer is yes or no, true or false. For example a question is given "Ram had killed Kans". The students will be required to write 'No' or 'False' and give correct answer.

Examination Test. In this type of examination the students are asked to write the names of things, places and persons in right order. For example, if the names of some prominent leaders like Morarji Desai, Dr. Rajendra Prasad, Jawaharlal Nehru, Govind Ballabh Pant, Vinoba Bhave are written in a question, the student will be required to write their names according to their importance. The order in which the student will write the names of the leaders will indicate his ability.

Reasoning Test. This is devised for the test of reasoning ability of the student. For example, if a student is asked, "Rita is the name of one of the two sisters, what can be the name of the other sister?" And if the student has some reasoning ability, he can say that the name of the other sister can be 'Gita'.

Simple Recall Test. In such type of questions, the ability of recalling the memory of the students is tested. For example, if a question is asked as to who discovered America, the student will write Columbus to give the correct answer.

Indian Education Commission

The IEC has made the following recommendations regarding the reform in the system of 'examination (1) The new approach to evaluation will attempt to improve the written examination so that it becomes a valid and reliable measure of educational achievement and to devise teachniqes for measuring those important aspects of the student's growth that can not be measured by written examinations.

Evaluation of the Primary Stage. Evaluation at this stage should help pupils to improve their achievement in the basic skills and develop right habits and attitudes.

It would be desirable to treat classes I to IV as unguided to enable children to advance at their own-pace. Where toil is not feasible, class I to IV may be treated as one block divided into two groups-one for slow and the other for fast learners. Teachers should be appropriately trained for the graded system.

Evaluation at the Higher Primary Stage. In addition to written examination, weightage should be given at this stage to oral tests as a part of internal assessment. Diagnostic testing should be through simple teacher are made tests. Cumulative record cards are important in indicating pupil's growth and development but should be very simple and should be introduced in a phased manner.

External Examination. Although the first national standard of attainment is to be stage, it is not considered necessary or desirable to prescribe a rigid and uniform level of attainment through a compulsory external examination. However, for the proper maintenance of standards periodic surveys of the level of achievement of primary schools should be conducted by district school authorities through refined tests, prepared by State Evaluation Units.

Common Internal Examination. The district educational authority may arrange for a common examination at the end of the primary stage for schools in the district, using standardised and refined tests. This examination will have greater validity and reliability than the school examination and will prove the inter-school comparability or levels of performance.

The certificate at the end of the primary course should be given by the school and should be accompanied by the cumulative record card and the statement of result of the common examination if any.

In addition to the common examination, special tests may be held at the end of the primary course for the award of scholarships or certificate of merit and for the purpose of identifying talent.

Improvement in External Examinations. External examinations should be improved by raising the technical competence of paper setters, orienting question papers to objectives other than acquisition of knowledge, improving the nature of questions, adopting scientific scoring procedure, and mechanising the scoring of scripts and processing of results.

Certificates by the Board and Schools. The certificate issued by the State Board of School Education on the basis of the results of the external examination should give the candidate's performance in different subjects for which he has appeared and there should be no remark to the effect that he has passed or failed in the whole examinations. The candidate should be permitted to appear again if he so desires for the entire examination or for separate subjects in order to improve his performance.

The student should receive a certificate also from the school, giving the record of his internal assessment, as contained in his cumulative record card and this should be attached to that given by the Board.

Establishment of Experiment Schools. A few selected schools should be given the right of assessing their students themselves and holding their own final examinations at the end of class X which will be regarded as equivalent to the external examination of the State Board of School Education. The State Board of School Education will issue the Certificates to the successful candidates of these schools on the recommendations of the Schools. A Committee set up by the State Board of School Education should develop carefully worked-out criteria for the selection of such schools. The schools should be permitted to frame their own text-books and conduct their educational activities without external restrictions.

Methods of Internal Assessment. Internal assessment by schools should be comprehensive and should evaluate all aspects of student growth including those not measured by the external examination. It should be descriptive as well as qualified. Written examination conducted by schools should be unproved and teachers trained appropriately. The internal assessment should be shown separately from the external examination marks.

Higher Secondary Examination. In the period of transition higher secondary students will have to appear for two successive external examinations at the end of classes X and XI within one year, where however, the courses in classes X to XI are integrated, the examination at the end of class X need not be insisted upon.

Additional Reading

Bhaskara Rao, Digumarti (1994). *Scientific Aptitude,* New Delhi: Ashish Publishing House. ISBN 81-7024-658-X.

Bhaskara Rao, Digumarti (1995). *Animal Kingdom.* New Delhi: Discovery Publishing House. ISBN 81-7141-274-2.

Bhaskara Rao, Digumarti (1995). *Batracology.* New Delhi: Discovery Publishing House. ISBN 81-7141-279-3.

Bhaskara Rao, Digumarti (1997), *Scientific Attitude.* New Delhi: Discovery Publishing House. ISBN 81-7141-308-0.

Bhaskara Rao, Digumarti (1996). *Scientific Attitude vis-à-vis Scientific Aptitude.* New Delhi: Discovery Publishing House. ISBN 81-7141-308-0.

Bhaskara Rao, Digumarti, Editor (1996). *Encyclopaedia of Education for All,* 5 Volumes. New Delhi: APH Publishing Corporation. ISBN 81-7024-759-4 (set).

Vol. I *Education for All: The World Conference.* ISBN 81-7024-760-8.

Vol. II *Education for All: The EPA-9 Summit.* ISBN 81-7024-761-6.

Vol. III *Education for All: Quality Education for All.* ISBN 81-7024-762-6.

Vol. IV *Education for All: Planning and Monitoring.* ISBN 81-7024-763-4.

Vol. V *Education for All: The Indian Scenario.* ISBN 81-7024-764-0.

Bhaskara Rao, Digumarti, Editor (1996). *Global Perceptions on Peace Education,* 3 Volumes. New Delhi: Discovery Publishing House. ISBN 81-7141-319-6.

Bhaskara Rao, Digumarti, Editor (1996). *National Policy on Education*. 2 Volumes. New Delhi: Anmol Publications Pvt. Ltd. ISBN 81-7488-323-1.

Bhaskara Rao, Digumarti, Editor (1997). *Care the Child*, 2 Volumes. New Delhi: Discovery Publishing House. ISBN 81-7141-394-3.

Bhaskara Rao, Digumarti, Editor (1997). *Education for the 21st Century*. New Delhi: Discovery Publishing House. ISBN 81-7141-389-7.

Bhaskara Rao, Digumarti, Editor (1997). *Reflections on Scientific Attitude*. New Delhi: Discovery Publishing House, ISBN 81-7141-319-6.

Bhaskara Rao, Digumarti, Editor (1997). *Success Story of a Primary Education Project*. New Delhi: APH Publishing Corporation. ISBN 81-7024-850-7.

Bhaskara Rao, Digumarti, Editor (1997). *World Food Summit*. New Delhi: Discovery Publishing House. ISBN 81-7141-386-2.

Bhaskara Rao, Digumarti, Editor (1998). *Adolescence Education*. New Delhi: Discovery Publishing House. ISBN 81-7141-432-X.

Bhaskara Rao, Digumarti, Editor (1998). *Community and School Nutrition Education*. New Delhi: Discovery Publishing House. ISBN 81-7141-435-4.

Bhaskara Rao, Digumarti, Editor (1998). *District Primary Education Programme*. New Delhi: Discovery Publishing House. ISBN 81-7141-396-X.

Bhaskara Rao, Digumarti, Editor (1998). *Earth Summit*, 2 Volumes. New Delhi: Discovery Publishing House. ISBN 81-7141-435-4.

Bhaskara Rao, Digumarti, Editor (1998). *National Policy on Education: Towards an Enlightened and Humane Society*, New Delhi: Discovery Publishing House. ISBN 81-7141-426-5.

Bhaskara Rao, Digumarti, Editor (1998). *Reforming School Education*. New Delhi: Discovery Publishing House. ISBN 81-7141-403-6.

Bhaskara Rao, Digumarti, Editor (1998). *Teacher Education in India*. New Delhi: Discovery Publishing House. ISBN 81-7141-406-0.

Bhaskara Rao, Digumarti, Editor (1998). *World Summit for Social Development*. New Delhi: Discovery Publishing House. ISBN 81-7141-420-6.

Bhaskara Rao, Digumarti, Editor (2000). *Education for All: Achieving the Goal*, 3 Volumes, New Delhi: APH Publishing Corporation. ISBN 81-7648-152-1.

Vol. I *The Global Consensus*. ISBN 81-7648-155-6.

Vol. II *Mid-Decade Review Reports of Regional Seminars*. ISBN 81-7648-154-8.

Vol. III *Issues and Trends*. ISBN 81-7648-155-6.

Bhaskara Rao, Digumarti, Editor (2000), *International Encyclopaedia of AIDS*, 11 Volumes in 13 Parts. New Delhi: Discovery Publishing House. ISBN 81-7141-6 (Set).

Vol. 1 *Introduction to HIV/AIDS*. ISBN 81-7141-523-7.

Vol. 2 *HIV/AIDS—Issues and Challenges*, 2 Parts. ISBN 81-7141-524-5.

Vol. 3 *HIV/AIDS—Socio Economic Realities*. ISBN 81-7141-524-3.

Vol. 4 *HIV/AIDS—Law Ethics and Human Rights*, 2 Parts. ISBN 81-7141-526-1.

Vol. 5 *AIDS and NGOs*. ISBN 81-7141-527-X.

Vol. 6 *AIDS and Home Care*. ISBN 81-7141-528-8.

Vol. 7 *STD Case Management*. ISBN 81-7141-529-6.

Vol. 8 *HIV/AIDS Prevention and Care—Teaching Modules for Nurses and Midwives*. ISBN 81-7141-530-X.

Vol. 9 *HIV Prevention Education for Education for Educational Institutions*. ISBN 81-7141-531-8.

Vol. 10 *Instructional Modules for AIDS Education*. ISBN 81-7141-532-6.

Vol. 11 *School Health Education to Prevent AIDS and STD—A Package for Curriculum Planners*. ISBN 81-7141-5338-4.

Bhaskara Rao, Digumarti, Editor (2000). *International Encyclopaedia of Science and Technology Education*, 11 Volumes. New Delhi: Discovery Publishing House. ISBN 81-7141-548-2 (Set).

Vol. 1 *Science and Technology Education*. ISBN 81-7141-568-7.

Vol. 2 *Science Education in Developing Countries*. ISBN 81-7141-570-9.

Vol. 3 *Organisational Structure of Science*. ISBN 81-7141-570-9.

Vol. 4 *Science Education in Asia and the Pacific*. ISBN 81-7141-571-7.

Vol. 5 *Science and Technology Education for All*. ISBN 81-7141-572-5.

Vol. 6 *Values, Ethics, Talent and Girls in Science and Technology Education*. ISBN 81-7141-573-3.

Vol. 7 *Popularization of Science and Technology Education*. ISBN 81-7141-574-1.

Vol. 8 *Science, Power and Society*. ISBN 81-7141-575-X.

Vol. 9 *Information Technology*. ISBN 81-7141-576-8.

Vol. 10 *Teacher Training in Science and Technology Education*. ISBN 81-7141-577-6.

Vol. 11 *Teacher Training in Science and Technology: A Curriculum Framework*. ISBN 81-7141-578-4.

Bhaskara Rao, Digumarti, Editor (2001). *Distance Education in Different Countries*. New Delhi: APH Publishing Corporation. ISBN 81-7648-229-3.

Bhaskara Rao, Digumarti, Editor (2001). *Decentralised Management of Education (Management of Education in Panchayati Raj and Municipal Bodies)*. New Delhi: Discovery Publishing House. ISBN 81-7141-617-9.

Bhaskara Rao, Digumarti, Editor (2001). *Electrochemistry for Environmental Protection*. New Delhi: Discovery Publishing House. ISBN 81-7141-619-5.

Bhaskara Rao, Digumarti, Editor (2001). *Global Educational Studies*. New Delhi: Discovery Publishing House. ISBN 81-7141-616-0.

Bhaskara Rao, Digumarti, Editor (2001). *Global Synthesis of Educational Assessment*. New Delhi: Discovery Publishing House. ISBN 81-7141-613-6.

Bhaskara Rao, Digumarti, Editor (2000). *International Encyclopaedia of Human Rights*. 7 Volumes in 13 Parts. New Delhi: Discovery Publishing House. (Royal Size). ISBN 81-7141-567-9 (Set).

Vol. 1 *International Instruments of Human Rights*, 2 Parts. ISBN 81-7141-595-4.

Vol. 2 *Regional Instruments of Human Rights*. ISBN 81-7141-604-7.

Vol. 3 *Human Rights and the United Nations*, 2 Parts. ISBN 81-7141-605-5.

Vol. 4 *Fact Files of Human Rights*, 3 Parts. ISBN 81-7141-605-3.

Vol. 5 *Study Stories of Human Rights*, 3 Parts. ISBN 81-7141-607-3.

Vol. 6 *International Meetings on Human Rights*, 2 Parts. ISBN 81-7141-608-X.

Vol. 7 *Professional Training in Human Rights*. ISBN 81-7141-609-8.

Bhaskara Rao, Digumarti, Editor (2001). *Jomtein Decade of Education*. New Delhi: Discovery Publishing House. ISBN 81-7141-618-7.

Bhaskara Rao, Digumarti, Editor (2001). *Nuclear Materials: Issues and Concerns*, 2 Volumes. New Delhi: Discovery Publishing House. ISBN 81-7141-611-X.

Bhaskara Rao, Digumarti, Editor (2001). *World Conference on Education for All*. New Delhi: APH Publishing Corporation. ISBN 81-7141-274-9.

Bhaskara Rao, Digumarti, Editor (2001). *World Conference on Higher Education*, New Delhi: Discovery Publishing House. ISBN 81-7141-610-1.

Bhaskara Rao, Digumarti, Editor (2001). *World Conference on Science*. New Delhi: Discovery Publishing House. ISBN 81-7141-612-8.

Bhaskara Rao, Digumarti, Editor (2003). *Inspiring Experience in Teacher Education*. New Delhi: Discovery Publishing House. ISBN 81-7141-656-X.

Bhaskara Rao, Digumarti, Editor (2003). *International Studies in Education*, 3 Volumes, New Delhi: Discovery Publishing House. ISBN 81-7141-647-0.

Bhaskara Rao, Digumarti, Editor (2003). *Military Conversion: Impact on Science and Technology,* New Delhi: Discovery Publishing House. ISBN 81-7141-578-4.

Bhaskara Rao, Digumarti, Editor (2003). *United Nations Millennium Summit*. New Delhi: Discovery Publishing House. ISBN 81-7141-632-2.

Bhaskara Rao, Digumarti, Editor (2003). *World Assembly on Aging*. New Delhi: Discovery Publishing House. ISBN 81-7141-637-3.

Bhaskara Rao, Digumarti, Editor (2004). *World Conference on Human Rights*. New Delhi: Discovery Publishing House. ISBN 81-7141-661-6.

Bhaskara Rao, Digumarti, Editor (2003). *World Education Forum*. New Delhi: Discovery Publishing House. ISBN 81-7141-639-X.

Bhaskara Rao, Digumarti, Editor (2004). *Education Employment and Human Resource Development*. New Delhi: Discovery Publishing House. ISBN 81-7141-681-0.

Bhaskara Rao, Digumarti, Editor (2004). *Successfully Schooling*. New Delhi: Discovery Publishing House. ISBN 81-7141-677-2.

Bhaskara Rao, Digumarti, Editor (2004). *European Education and Teachers*. New Delhi: Discovery Publishing House. ISBN 81-7141-702-7.

Bhaskara Rao, Digumarti, Editor (2004). *Teachers in a Changing World*. New Delhi: Discovery Publishing House. ISBN 81-7141-694-2.

Bhaskara Rao, Digumarti, Editor (2004). *Learning to Live Together*, 4 Volumes. New Delhi: Discovery Publishing House.

Vol. 1 *International Conference on Learning to Live Together.*

Vol. 2 *Globalisation and Living Together.*

Vol. 3 *Curriculum for Learning to Live Together.*

Vol. 4 *Science Education for the Contemporary Society.*

Bhaskara Rao, Digumarti (2004). *International Guidelines on Open and Distance Education,* New Delhi: Discovery Publishing House.

Bhaskara Rao, Digumarti, Editor (2004). *Adult Learning in the 21st Century*. New Delhi: Discovery Publishing House.

Bhaskara Rao, Digumarti, Editor (2004). *Educational Practices: Research and Recommendations*. New Delhi: Discovery Publishing House.

Bhaskara Rao, Digumarti, Editor (2004). *Chernobyl: Never Again*. New Delhi: APH Publishing Corporation.

Bhaskara Rao, Digumarti, Editor (2004). *Virology and Immunology*. New Delhi: APH Publishing Corporation.

Bhaskara Rao, Digumarti, C.A.P. Swami and B.S.V. Dutt (1997). *Self-Evaluation in Student Teaching*. New Delhi: Discovery Publishing House. ISBN 81-7141-374-9.

Bhaskara Rao, Digumarti and B.S.V. Dutt, Editors (2003). *Education: Programmes and Policies*. New Delhi: APH Publishing Corporation. ISBN 81-7648-470-9.

Bhaskara Rao, Digumarti and D. Naresh Kumar (2004). *School Teacher Effectiveness*. New Delhi: Discovery Publishing House.

Bhaskara Rao, Digumarti and D. Sridhar (2002). *Job Satisfaction of School Teachers*. New Delhi: Discovery Publishing House. ISBN 81-7141-652-7.

Bhaskara Rao, Digumarti and Digumarti Pushpa Latha (1994). *Achievement in Biology*. New Delhi: Discovery Publishing House. ISBN 81-7141-264-5.

Bhaskara Rao, Digumarti, C. Sridevi and K. Vijaya (1995). *Achievement in Social Studies*. New Delhi: Discovery Publishing House. ISBN 81-7141-281-5.

Bhaskara Rao, Digumarti and Digumarti Pushpa Latha (1995). *Achievement in English*. New Delhi: Discovery Publishing House. ISBN 81-7141-283-1.

Bhaskara Rao, Digumarti and Digumarti Pushpa Latha (1994). *Achievement in Science*. New Delhi: Discovery Publishing House. ISBN 81-7141-280-70.

Bhaskara Rao, Digumarti and Digumarti Pushpa Latha (1995). *Achievement in Mathematics*. New Delhi: Discovery Publishing House. ISBN 81-7141-278-5.

Bhaskara Rao, Digumarti and Digumarti Pushpa Latha, Editors (1998). *International Encyclopaedia of Women*. 5 Volumes. New Delhi: Discovery Publishing House. ISBN 81-7141-410-9.

Vol. 1 *Status of World's Women*. ISBN 81-7141-494-X.

Vol. 2 *Women, Education and Empowerment*. ISBN 81-7141-498-1.

Vol. 3 *Women Challenges and Advancement*. ISBN 81-7141-497-4.

Vol. 4 *Women and Family Health*. ISBN 81-7141-497-4.

Vol. 5 *Women and International Action*. ISBN 81-7141-498-2.

Bhaskara Rao, Digumarti, Digumarti Pushpa Latha and Digumarti Harshitha, Editors (2001). *Biological Warfare*. New Delhi: Discovery Publishing House. ISBN 81-7141-597-0.

Bhaskara Rao, Digumarti, Digumarti Pushpa Latha and Digumarti Harshitha, Editors (2001). *Women as Educators*. New Delhi: Discovery Publishing House. ISBN 81-7141-602-0.

Bhaskara Rao, Digumarti and Digumarti Harshitha, Editors (2001). *Education in India*. New Delhi: APH Publishing Corporation. ISBN 81-7141-207-2.

Bhaskara Rao, Digumarti, Digumarti Pushpa Latha and Digumarti Harshitha, Editors (2001). *Assessing Learning Achievement*. New Delhi: Discovery Publishing House. ISBN 81-7141-601-2.

Bhaskara Rao, Digumarti, Digumarti Pushpa Latha and Digumarti Harshitha, Editors (2001). *Energy Security*. New Delhi: Discovery Publishing House. ISBN 81-7141-598-9.

Bhaskara Rao, Digumarti, Digumarti Harshitha and K.R.S.S. Rao, Editors (1999). *Advanced Biotechnology*. New Delhi: Discovery Publishing House. ISBN 81-7141-516-4.

Bhaskara Rao, Digumarti and K.R.S. Sambhasiva Rao, Editors (1996). *Current Trends in Indian Education*. New Delhi: Discovery Publishing House. ISBN 81-7141-311-0.

Bhaskara Rao, Digumarti and K. Vijaya (1995). *A Text Book of Evaluation*. Ambala Cantt: The Associated Publishers.

Bhaskara Rao, Digumarti and N.V.M. Mohana Rao (2002). *Problems of Mentally Handicapped Children*. New Delhi: Discovery Publishing House. ISBN 81-7141-645-4.

Bhaskara Rao, Digumarti and S. Chandra Mohan (2002). *Sports Management*. New Delhi: APH Publishing Corporation. ISBN 81-7648-467-9.

Bhaskara Rao, Digumarti and Sk. Johni Basha (2004). *Teachers' Population Education Awareness*. New Delhi: APH Publishing Corporation.

Bhaskara Rao, Digumarti, V.V. Rao, V.V. Lakshmi and V.V. Krishna, Editors (1999). *Status and Advancement of Women*. New Delhi: APH Publishing Corporation. ISBN 81-7648-169-6.

Babu, P.C., Author and Digumarti Bhaskara Rao, Editor (2004). *Flowers of Wisdom*. New Delhi: Discovery Publishing House. ISBN 81-7141-695-0.

Bhagya Lakshmi, Lingineni, Author and Digumarti Bhaskara Rao, Editor (2000). *Reading and Comprehension*. New Delhi: Discovery Publishing House. ISBN 81-7141-543-1.

Bhuvaneswara Lakshmi, Gadde, Author and Digumarti Bhaskara Rao, Editor (2000). *Attitude Towards Science*. New Delhi: Discovery Publishing House. ISBN 81-7141-541-6.

Devraj, T.A.S., Author and Digumarti Bhaskara Rao, Editor (1997). *Trace Analysis of Uranium and Thorium*. New Delhi: Discovery Publishing House. ISBN 81-7141-375-7.

Durga Rani, K., Author and Digumarti Bhaskara Rao, Editor (2000). *Educational Aspirations and Scientific Attitudes*. New Delhi: Discovery Publishing House. ISBN 81-7141-555-55.

Dutt, B.S.V. and Digumarti Bhaskara Rao (2001). *Empowering Primary Teachers*. New Delhi: Discovery Publishing House. ISBN 81-7141-615.2.

Ediger, Marlow and Digumarti Bhaskara Rao (1996). *Science Curriculum*. New Delhi: Discovery Publishing House. ISBN 81-7141-321-8.

Ediger, Marlow and Digumarti Bhaskara Rao (2000). *Teaching Mathematics Successfully*. New Delhi: Discovery Publishing House. ISBN 81-7141-552-0.

Ediger, Marlow and Digumarti Bhaskara Rao (2001). *Teaching Science Successfully*. New Delhi: Discovery Publishing House. ISBN 81-7141-600-4.

Ediger, Marlow and Digumarti Bhaskara Rao (2001). *Teaching Social Studies Successfully*. New Delhi: Discovery Publishing House. ISBN 81-7141-596-2.

Ediger, Marlow and Digumarti Bhaskara Rao (2002). *Philosophy and Curriculum*. New Delhi: Discovery Publishing House. ISBN 81-7141-631-4.

Ediger, Marlow and Digumarti Bhaskara Rao (2002). *Improving School Administration*. New Delhi: Discovery Publishing House. ISBN 81-7141-633-0.

Ediger, Marlow and Digumarti Bhaskara Rao (2002). *Elementary Curriculum*. New Delhi: Discovery Publishing House. ISBN 81-7141-658-6.

Ediger, Marlow and Digumarti Bhaskara Rao (2003). *Language Arts Curriculum*. New Delhi: Discovery Publishing House. ISBN 81-7141-657-8.

Ediger, Marlow and Digumarti Bhaskara Rao (2004). *Teaching Language Arts Successfully*. New Delhi: Discovery Publishing House. ISBN 81-7141-678-0.

Ediger, Marlow and Digumarti Bhaskara Rao (2004). *Teaching Mathematics in Elementary Schools*. New Delhi: Discovery Publishing House. ISBN 81-7141-687-X.

Ediger, Marlow and Digumarti Bhaskara Rao (2004). *Teaching Science in Elementary Schools*. New Delhi: Discovery Publishing House. ISBN 81-7141-709-4.

Ediger, Marlow and Digumarti Bhaskara Rao (2004). *School Curriculum and Administration*. New Delhi: Discovery Publishing House. ISBN 81-7141-709-4.

Ediger, Marlow and Digumarti Bhaskara Rao (2004). *Modern Elementary School*. New Delhi: Discovery Publishing House.

Ediger, Marlow and Digumarti Bhaskara Rao (2004): *Relevancy in Elementary Curriculum*. New Delhi: Discovery Publishing House. ISBN 81-7141-751-5.

Ediger, Marlow and Digumarti Bhaskara Rao, (2004). *Teaching Social Studies in Elementary Schools*. New Delhi: Discovery Publishing House.

Ediger Marlow, B.S.V. Dutt and Digumarti Bhaskara Rao (2004). *Teaching English Successfully*. New Delhi: Discovery Publishing House. ISBN 81-7141-707-8.

Harshitha, Digumarti and Digumarti Bhaskara Rao, Editors (2004). *Educational Innovations*. New Delhi: Discovery Publishing House.

Indira Devi, Author and J. Prasanth Kumar and Digumarti Bhaskara Rao, Editors (2004). *Values in Language Text Books*. New Delhi: Discovery Publishing House.

Jayasree, Kandi, Author and Digumarti Bhaskara Rao, Editor (1999). *Correlates of Socialisation*. New Delhi: Discovery Publishing House. ISBN 81-7141-517-2.

John Babu, Chikati, Author and T.J.R. Prasad, G.M. Madhukar and Digumarti Bhaskara Rao, Editors (1996). *Problem Solving in Mathematics*. New Delhi: APH Publishing Corporation. ISBN 81-7648-273-0.

Lalitha, T., Author and K.S. Prabhakaram, D.S.N. Sastry and Digumarti Bhaskara Rao, Editors (2004). *Educational Philosophic Beliefs*. New Delhi: Discovery Publishing House. ISBN 81-7141-765-5.

Madhu Bala, Jampala, Author and Digumarti Bhaskara Rao, Editor (2004). *Adjustment Problems of Hearing Impaired*. New Delhi: Discovery Publishing House.

Marja, Talvi and Digumarti Bhaskara Rao, Editors (1996). *Educational Leadership and Social Changes*. New Delhi: Discovery Publishing House. ISBN 81-7141-320-X.

Nirmala Jyothi, M., Author and Digumarti Bhaskara Rao, Editor (2003). *Non-detention Systems in School Education*. New Delhi: Discovery Publishing House. ISBN 81-7141-654-3.

Prabhakaram, K.S., Author and Digumarti Bhaskara Rao, Editor (1998). *Concept Attainment Model in Mathematics Teaching*. New Delhi: Discovery Publishing House. ISBN 81-7141-424-9.

Prasanth Kumar, J., Author and Digumarti Bhaskara Rao, Editor (1998). *Effectiveness of Distance Education System*. New Delhi: Discovery Publishing House. ISBN 81-7141-437-0.

Prasanth Kumar, J., Author and G. Sundara Rao and Digumarti Bhaskara Rao, Editors (2000). *Open University Student Support Services*. New Delhi: Discovery Publishing House. ISBN 81-7141-550-4.

Ramatulasamma, K., Author and Digumarti Bhaskara Rao, Editor (2002). *Job Satisfaction of Teacher Educators*, New Delhi: Discovery Publishing House. ISBN 81-7141-655-1.

Rama Krishnaiah, D., Author and Digumarti Bhaskara Rao, Editor (1998). *Job Satisfaction of College Teachers*, New Delhi: Discovery Publishing House. ISBN 81-7141-438-9.

Rama Kumar Ratnam, M., Author and Digumarti Bhaskara Rao, Editor (1998). *Dukka: Suffering in Early Buddhism*. New Delhi: Discovery Publishing House. ISBN 81-7141-653-5.

Rathaiah, Lavu and Digumarti Bhaskara Rao, Editors (1996). *International Innovations in Education*. New Delhi: Discovery Publishing House. ISBN 81-7141-359-5.

Ramesh, Ganta and Digumarti Bhaskara Rao, Editors (1998). *Environmental Education: Problems and Prospects*. New Delhi: Discovery Publishing House. ISBN 81-7141-423-0.

Rathaiah, Lavu and Digumarti Bhaskara Rao (1997). *Achievement Correlates*. New Delhi: Discovery Publishing House. ISBN 81-7141-385-4.

Reddy, Sudhakar Y., Author, and Digumarti Bhaskara Rao, Editor (2003). *Creativity in Adolescents*. New Delhi: Discovery Publishing House. ISBN 81-7141-659-4.

Reddy, M.S., Author and Digumarti Bhaskara Rao, Editor (2004). *Creativity in College Students*. New Delhi: Discovery Publishing House. ISBN 81-7141-697-7.

Radramamba, B., Author and Digumarti Bhaskara Rao, Editor (2003). *Problems of Teaching*. New Delhi: APH Publishing Corporation. ISBN 81-7648-462-8.

Sanjeeva Rao, P.C., Author and Digumarti Bhaskara Rao, Editor (1996). *A Text Book of Geology*. New Delhi: Discovery Publishing House. ISBN 81-7141-313-7.

Satya Narayana V., Author and Digumarti Bhaskara Rao, Editor (2001). *Physical Education, Social Attitudes and Leadership Qualities*. New Delhi: Discovery Publishing House. ISBN 81-7141-593-8.

Srinivasulu Reddy, M., and K.R.S. Sambasiva Rao, Authors and Digumarti Bhaskara Rao, Editor (1999). *A Text Book of Aquaculture*. New Delhi: Discovery Publishing House. ISBN 81-7141-482-6.

Srinivasa Rao, Mandalapu, Author and Digumarti Bhaskara Rao, Editor (2004). *Achievement Motivation and Achievement in Mathematics*. New Delhi: Discovery Publishing House. ISBN 81-7141-674-8.

Vanaja, M. Author and Digumarti Bhaskara Rao, Editor (1999). *Inquiry Training Model*. New Delhi: Discovery Publishing House. ISBN 81-7141-515-6.

Vanaja. M. and N. Sneha Latha, Authors and Digumarti Bhaskara Rao, Editor (2004). *Student Shyness*. New Delhi: APH Publishing Corporation.

Valeri V. Koustiouk, Author and Digumarti Bhaskara Rao, Editor (2002). *A Text Book of Cryogenics*. New Delhi: Discovery Publishing House. ISBN 81-7141-642-X.

Valeri V. Koustiouk, Author and Digumarti Bhaskara Rao, Editor (2004). *Refrigeration and Environment*. New Delhi: APH Publishing Corporation.

Veena Kumari, Balusu and Digumarti Bhaskara Rao (1996). *Operation Black Board*. New Delhi: Ashish Publishing Corporation. ISBN 81-7024-711-X.

Veena Kumari, Balusu, Author and Digumarti Bhaskara Rao, Editor (2000). *Psycho-Social Correlates of Achievement*, New Delhi: Discovery Publishing House. ISBN 81-7141-547-4.

Vanaja, M., Author and Digumarti Bhaskara Rao, Editor (1999). *Inquiry Training Model*. New Delhi: Discovery Publishing House. ISBN 81-7141-515-6.

Venkata Rao, P. and Digumarti Bhaskara Rao (1989). *A Text Book of Zoology—Junior Intermediate*. Guntur: Vignan Publishers.

Venkata Rao, P. and Digumarti Bhaskara Rao (1989). *A Text Book of Zoology—Senior Intermediate*. Guntur: Vignan Publishers.

Venugopala Rao, K., Author and Digumarti Bhaskara Rao, Editor (2000). *Teacher Morale in Secondary Schools*. New Delhi: Discovery Publishing House. ISBN 81-7141-551-2.

Vidya, C., Author and Digumarti Bhaskara Rao. Editor (1996). *A Text Book of Nutrition*. New Delhi: Discovery Publishing House. ISBN 81-7141-309-9.

Vidya Bharathi, D., Author and Digumarti Bhaskara Rao, Editor (2000). *Educational Philosophies of Swami Vivekananda and John Dewey*. New Delhi: APH Publishing Corporation. ISBN 81-7648-309-9.

Books in Telugu Language

Bhaskara Rao, Digumarti (1986). *Dhrushya Sravana Bodhanapakaranalu* (Audio Visual Teaching Aids). Guntur: Nagarjuna Publishers.

Bhaskara Rao, Digumarti (1993). *Jeevasashtra Bodhana* (Teaching of Biology). Guntur: Nagarjuna Publishers.

Bhaskara Rao, Digumarti (1995). *Vignanasasthra Bodhana* (Teaching of Science) Guntur: Nagarjuna Publishers.

Bhaskara Rao, Digumarti (1997). *Vidya Manovignana Seshtram* (Educational Psychology). Guntur: Creative Press.

Bhaskara Rao, Digumarti (1998). *DSC Study Material*. Guntur: Nagarjuna Publishers.

Bhaskara Rao, Digumarti (1998). *Upadhyayudu Vidya*. (Teacher and Education). Guntur: Nagarjuna Publishers.

Bhaskara Rao, Digumarti (1998). *Vidya Drukpadalu* (Prespectives of Education). Guntur: Nagarjuna Publishers.

Bhaskara Rao, Digumarti (1999). *EdCET Teaching Aptitude*. Guntur: Nagarjuna Publishers.

Bhaskara Rao, Digumarti (2001). *Bharata Samajamulo Upadyayudu Vidya* (Teacher and Education in Emerging Indian Society). Guntur: Nagarjuna Publishers.

Bhaskara Rao, Digumarti (2001). *Bhoutika Sastra Bodhana Paddathulu* (Methods of Teaching Physical Science). Guntur: Nagarjuna Publishers.

Bhaskara Rao, Digumarti (2001). *Jeeva Sastra Bodhana Padhathulu* (Methods of Teaching Biology). Guntur: Nagarjuna Publishers.

Bhaskara Rao, Digumarti (2001). *Vidya Manovignana Sastram* (Educational Psychology). Guntur: Nagarjuna Publishers.

Bhaskara Rao, Digumarti (2003). *Patsala Yajamanyam/Paripalana* (School Management and Administration). Guntur: Nagarjuna Publishers.

Bhaskara Rao, Digumarti (2004). *Vidya Sanketika Sastram mariyu Computer Vidya* (Educational Technology and Computer Education). Guntur: Nagarjuna Publishers.